Persian Authorship and Canonicity in Late Mughal Delhi

Writing in the eighteenth century, the Persian-language littérateurs of late Mughal Delhi were aware that they could no longer take for granted the relations of Persian with Islamic imperial power, relations that had enabled Persian literary life to flourish in India since the tenth century CE.

Persian Authorship and Canonicity in Late Mughal Delhi situates the diverse textual projects of ʻAbd al-Qādir "Bīdil" and his students within the context of politically threatened but poetically prestigious Delhi, exploring the writers' use of the Perso-Arabic and Hindavī literary canons to fashion their authorship. Breaking with the tendency to categorize and characterize Persian literature according to the dynasty in power, this book argues for the indirectness and complexity of the relations between poetics and politics. Among its original contributions is an interpretation of Bīdil's Sufi adaptation of a Braj-Avadhi tale of utopian Hindu kingship, a novel hypothesis on the historicism of Sirāj al-Din ʻAlī Khān "Ārzū"'s oeuvre and a study of how Bindrāban Dās "Khvushgū" entwined the contrasting models of authorship in Bīdil and Ārzū to formulate his voice as a Sufi historian of the Persian poetic tradition.

As the first book-length work in English on ʻAbd al-Qādir "Bīdil" and his circle of Persian literati, this is a valuable resource for students and scholars of both South Asian and Iranian studies, as well as Persian literature and Sufism.

Prashant Keshavmurthy is Assistant Professor of Persian-Iranian Studies in the Institute of Islamic Studies, McGill University. His research interests include late Mughal political discourses, Safavid-Mughal commentarial practices, Persian-Urdu poetics, Persian translations of Indic language works and Islamic autobiographical discourses.

Iranian Studies
Edited by:
Homa Katouzian
University of Oxford
and
Mohamad Tavakoli
University of Toronto

Since 1967 the International Society for Iranian Studies (ISIS) has been a leading learned society for the advancement of new approaches in the study of Iranian society, history, culture, and literature. The new ISIS Iranian Studies series published by Routledge will provide a venue for the publication of original and innovative scholarly works in all areas of Iranian and Persianate Studies.

1 **Journalism in Iran**
From mission to profession
Hossein Shahidi

2 **Sadeq Hedayat**
His work and his wondrous world
Edited by Homa Katouzian

3 **Iran in the 21st Century**
Politics, economics and conflict
Edited by Homa Katouzian and Hossein Shahidi

4 **Media, Culture and Society in Iran**
Living with globalization and the Islamic State
Edited by Mehdi Semati

5 **Modern Persian Literature in Afghanistan**
Anomalous visions of history and form
Wali Ahmadi

6 **The Politics of Iranian Cinema**
Film and society in the Islamic Republic
Saeed Zeydabadi-Nejad

7 **Continuity in Iranian Identity**
Resilience of a cultural heritage
Fereshteh Davaran

8 **New Perspectives on Safavid Iran**
Empire and society
Edited by Colin P. Mitchell

9 **Islamic Tolerance**
Amīr Khusraw and pluralism
Alyssa Gabbay

10 **City of Knowledge in Twentieth Century Iran**
Shiraz, history and poetry
Setrag Manoukian

11 **Domestic Violence in Iran**
Women, marriage and Islam
Zahra Tizro

12 **Gnostic Apocalypse and Islam**
Qur'an, exegesis, messianism, and the literary origins of the Babi religion
Todd Lawson

13 **Social Movements in Iran**
Environmentalism and civil society
Simin Fadaee

14 **Iranian–Russian Encounters**
Empires and revolutions since 1800
Edited by Stephanie Cronin

15 **Iran**
Politics, history and literature
Homa Katouzian

16 **Domesticity and Consumer Culture in Iran**
Interior Revolutions of the Modern Era
Pamela Karimi

17 **The Development of the Babi/Baha'i Communities**
Exploring Baron Rosen's Archives
Youli Ioannesyan

18 **Culture and Cultural Politics Under Reza Shah**
The Pahlavi State, New Bourgeoisie and the Creation of a Modern Society in Iran
Bianca Devos and Christoph Werner

19 **Recasting Iranian Modernity**
International Relations and Social Change
Kamran Matin

20 **The *Sīh-rōzag* in Zoroastrianism**
A Textual and Historico-Religious Analysis
Enrico G. Raffaelli

21 **Literary Subterfuge and Contemporary Persian Fiction**
Who writes Iran?
Mohammad Mehdi Khorrami

22 **Nomads in Postrevolutionary Iran**
The Qashqa'i in an era of change
Lois Beck

23 **Persian Language, Literature and Culture**
New leaves, fresh looks
Edited by Kamran Talattof

24 **The Daēva Cult in the Gāthās**
An ideological archaeology of Zoroastrianism
Amir Ahmadi

25 **The Revolutionary Guards in Iranian Politics**
Elites and shifting relations
Bayram Sinkaya

26 **Kirman and the Qajar Empire**
Local dimensions of modernity in Iran, 1794–1914
James M. Gustafson

27 **The Thousand and One Borders of Iran**
Travel and identity
Fariba Adelkhah

28 **Iranian Culture**
Representation and identity
Nasrin Rahimieh

29 **The Historiography of Persian Architecture**
Edited by Mohammad Gharipour

30 **Iran and Russian Imperialism**
The ideal anarchists, 1800–1914
Moritz Deutschmann

31 **Iranian Music and Popular Entertainment**
From *Motrebi* to *Losanjelesi* and beyond
G.J. Breyley and Sasan Fatemi

32 **Gender and Dance in Iran**
Biopolitics on the twentieth-century stage
Ida Meftahi

33 **Persian Authorship and Canonicity in Late Mughal Delhi**
Building an ark
Prashant Keshavmurthy

Persian Authorship and Canonicity in Late Mughal Delhi

Building an ark

Prashant Keshavmurthy

Routledge
Taylor & Francis Group
LONDON AND NEW YORK

First published 2016
by Routledge
2 Park Square, Milton Park, Abingdon, Oxon OX14 4RN

and by Routledge
711 Third Avenue, New York, NY 10017

Routledge is an imprint of the Taylor & Francis Group, an informa business

British Library Cataloguing-in-Publication Data
A catalogue record for this book is available from the British Library

Library of Congress Cataloging-in-Publication Data
Names: Keshavmurthy, Prashant, author.
Title: Persian authorship and canonicity in late Mughal Delhi : building an Ark / Prashant Keshavmurthy.
Description: Milton Park, Abingdon, Oxon ; New York : Routledge, 2016. | Series: Iranian studies
Identifiers: LCCN 2015034027 | ISBN 9781138185982 (hardback)
Subjects: LCSH: Persian literature–India–History and criticism. | Authors, Persian–India. | Mogul Empire–History–18th century. | South Asian literature–History and criticism. | Bīdil, ʻAbd al-Qādir, 1644 or 1645–1720 or 1721–Criticism and interpretation.
Classification: LCC PK6427.6.I5 K37 2016 | DDC 891/.550995456–dc23
LC record available at http://lccn.loc.gov/2015034027

ISBN: 978-1-138-18598-2 (hbk)
ISBN: 978-1-315-64408-0 (ebk)

Typeset in Times New Roman
by Wearset Ltd, Boldon, Tyne and Wear

For Padmini Keshavamurthy, T.K. Keshavamurthy and Kiran Keshavamurthy

Contents

Acknowledgments x

Introduction: political frailty and poetic power in late Mughal Delhi 1

1 Bīdil's portrait: ekphrasis as ascetic self-transformation 15

2 Bīdil's *tarjī'-band*: the author's kenotic chorus 61

3 A Hindu allegory of the Islamic philosopher-king: the tale of Madan and Kāmdī in Bīdil's *masnavī 'Irfān* 90

4 The local universality of poetic pleasure: Sirāj al-Dīn 'Alī Khān "Ārzū" and the speaking subject 127

5 Khvushgū's dream of Ḥāfiẓ: building an ark with Ārzū and Bīdil 151

Index 175

Acknowledgments

Although written over the last three years, this book has had a longer genesis in conversations extending over decades, conversations that have transformed me from who I was at their beginning. Among the teachers, friends and colleagues I should like to thank are Bubla Basu, Pramod Menon, Sheila Menon, Salim Yusufji, Meera Sagar, Sunil Dua, Giti Chandra, Ashish Roy, Udaya Kumar, Meghant Sudan, Nikhil Govind, Arvind Thomas, Shamsur Rahman Faruqi, Jyotirmaya Sharma, Shireen Ahmed, Frances Pritchett, Muzaffar Alam, Paul Losensky, Sonia Ahsan, Nauman Naqvi, Rebecca Gould, Milind Wakankar, Dorothea von Mücke, Ayesha Irani, Rajiv Chakravarti, Arthur Dudney, Sajjad Rizvi, Kevin Schwartz, Azarmi-Dukht Safavi, Navina Najat Haidar, Mana Kia, Sonam Kachru, Hajnalka Kovacs, Arijit Sen, Sandeep Banerjee, Elisabetta Benigni, Gijs Kruijtzer, Maritta Schleyer, Luzi Yang, Julie Billaud, Margrit Pernau, Lisa Marchi, Yuthika Sharma, Mudasir Mufti, Leila El-Murr, Fabrizio Speziale, Sunil Sharma, Irina Dumitrescu, Owen Cornwall, Abhishek Kaicker, Farbod Honarpishe, Franklin Lewis, Thomas de Bruijn, Imre Bangha, Robert Wisnovsky, Pouneh Shabani-Jadidi, Reza Pourjavady, Ali Nadeem, Lara Khattab, Ajay Rao, Maria Subtelny and Mohamad Tavakoli-Targhi. Much of this book's shape and substance bears the traces of Satyanarayana Hegde's maverick erudition, generosity and exemplary kindness. I am grateful to Jane Mikkelson who disentangled my dreadlocked prose with resolutely literary focus, wide learning and tutelary editorship. To Hossein Kamaly's generosity and knowledge, I owe my first experience of reading pre-modern Persian in a group. I am indebted to my brother Kiran for having indulged me in conversations whose written results form part of this book. For what faults there are in it, I alone am responsible.

I acknowledge the permissions of *Philological Encounters* (Brill, 2016) which is about to publish a shorter version of Chapter 1 titled "Bīdil's Portrait: Asceticism and Autobiography"; of Brill Publishers which is about to publish a version of Chapter 5 titled "Khvushgū's Dream of Ḥāfiẓ: Building an Ark with Ārzū and Bīdil" in an edited volume; and of SAGE Publications India Pvt Ltd whose *Indian Economic and Social History Review* (Vol. 50, No. 1, 2013) carried a shorter version of Chapter 4.

Finally, I thank Zukunftsphilologie at the Freie Universität, Berlin, for the post-doctoral fellowship that gave me the gift of time and conversations.

kamāl-i ham-nishīn dar man a̱sar kard
vagar nah man hamān khākam kih hastam

Introduction

Political frailty and poetic power in late Mughal Delhi

Authors who know themselves to be living at the end of an old textual tradition that knows itself to be old find themselves in a strangely enabling and disabling condition at once. The past presents itself to them as a cumulative heritage of models and interpretations, having gained rather than lost in material and complexity over time. But the sense of inhabiting the end of such a tradition makes the remembrance of the past an exercise in anxiety. The Persian-language littérateurs of late Mughal Delhi of the eighteenth century inhabited a condition resembling this one. They composed poetry and prose that, in its densely allusive mastery of an approximately eight-centuries-old Persian literary tradition, called and played on the reader's familiarity with that tradition. But they also knew that they could no longer take for granted Persian's relations with Islamic imperial power, relations that had enabled its flourishing literary life in India since the tenth century CE.

The three literati studied in this book belonged to this community and knew and read each other. Yet, each constitutes a distinct instance of how a Persian-language littérateur responded to the eclipse of Mughal political authority by adapting the literary canons of Persian (and other languages) to fashion himself as an author. The Sufi poet 'Abd al-Qādir Khān, pen-named "Bīdil" (1644–1720), invoked the canons of Persian-Arabic and Avadhi to fashion himself for his readership in Delhi's threatened ruling elites as a historically transcendent Sufi exemplum of self-governance.[1] The philologist and poet Sirāj al-Dīn 'Alī Khān "Ārzū" (1687–1756), tutored in his poetry by Bīdil, adapted already authoritative Arabic-language philology in Persian to defend the temporal locality of his teacher and students' *ghazal* style. In contrast to Bīdil, who justified the difficulties of his style by claiming to have circled around the backs of his poetic predecessors to a primordial and divine source of creativity, Ārzū argued that every authoritative poetic style had been local to its age. Bindrāban Dās "Khvushgū" (1667/78–1757), tutored in his poetry and history-writing by both Bīdil and Ārzū, creatively combined his two main teachers' disparate literary-historical temporalities, canonicities, methods and genres to fashion himself as a biographer-historian of the Persian poetic past. His textual persona was historicist on Ārzū's model even as it invoked Bīdil's ahistoricist or time-cancelling and ascetically achieved Sufi intimacy with the divine.

It is a result of, rather than in spite of, the fact that the world which these literati inhabited came to an end that they bear a larger significance for the heritage of Persian in contemporary India, Central Asia and Iran. As Paul Losensky has shown, our contemporary sense of the "classical" Persian literary canon is indebted to the projects of literary synthesizing and systematizing undertaken by the Timurids in Herat of the second half of the fifteenth century.[2] It was they who patronized a culture of anthologization, editorialization and textual recuperation of the Persian poetic past that set in place our still dominant sense of a classical Persian canon.[3] Beginning their imperial careers in India as their Timurid cousins in Herat were ending theirs, the Mughals inherited this sense of an already coherent and editorially available Persian literary past. This sense enabled the particular form taken by the most prestigious if embattled of Safavid-Mughal poetic styles, namely *tāzah-gūyī*, literally "Speaking the New" or "Speaking the Fresh" but understood in practice to involve speaking old poetic themes anew.[4] I therefore translate it non-literally as "Speaking Anew." This style derived its name from its predominant trait of playing on the reader's awareness of the aforementioned classical canon to evoke new topoi, new logics of intertextual relation and new metaphors and syntax.

And yet, late Mughal practitioners of such historically informed poetic novelty knew they were among the last Persian-language literati in India. It lies outside the scope of this Introduction to speak at length of the causes and features of the long death of Persian in India. It should suffice to observe that Bīdil, Ārzū, Khvushgū and their colleagues lived in the midst of Urdu's first major North Indian elevation into a literary language; that the Mughal court's power to arbitrate literary standards and community had come to be displaced onto subimperial polities that patronized Persian as only one of two or three literary languages; that the gradual displacement of Persian by Urdu, Braj and other languages as a choice of language for poetic composition was accompanied by the explosion of Persian-language lexicography, commentary and biographical writing; that all three thinkers under focus in this book actively chose to write in Persian because they identified themselves with the Mughal state; and that this choice allowed them to assume a pedagogical oversight of nascent Urdu literary practice. Placing them thus at this conjuncture of historical trajectories lets us appreciate their manifold long-term significance.

Urdu literature's sense of its "classical" canon developed under the gaze of Delhi's late Mughal Persian-language literati. Mīr Taqī "Mīr" (1722–1810), canonized as one of Urdu's two greatest classical poets, was Ārzū's estranged step-nephew and arguably his greatest literary legatee. Dictionaries of Persian-language idioms authored by Ārzū's students, Tek Chand "Bahār" and Ānand Rām "Mukhliṣ," came to be cited as authorities by 'Alī Akbar Dehkhudā, Iran's famous nationalist lexicographer in the early twentieth century. Asadullāh Khān "Ghālib" (1797–1869), who ranked alongside Mīr in the classical Urdu canon, modeled his early *ghazal* style on Bīdil. Both also composed entire *dīvān*s or collections of poetry in Persian while Mīr's Persian-language autobiography may well have used Bīdil's as one of its models. Though Bīdil himself was forgotten in India with the fading use of Persian there, he came to be canonized as a national poet in Afghanistan during the first half of the twentieth century. In Soviet Central Asia during the same period, his poetry was defended and upheld as exemplary of "progressive" Soviet poetics. Though – or perhaps because – he was discredited for his stylistic complexities by the Neo-Classical "Literary Return" (*bāzgasht-i adabī*) movement of early nineteenth-century Iran, he has since become a model for Iranian poetic modernism and the topic of a currently copious sub-field of Persian-language literary scholarship in Iran, Afghanistan and Tajikistan.[5] Khvushgū's three-volume *tazkirah*, or biographical dictionary of Persian-language poets from all periods of the language's history, was exemplary in its encyclopedic scope of Safavid-Mughal *tazkirah*s. It remains one of our most valuable contemporaneous windows on the literary life of eighteenth-century Delhi. By as-yet unknown routes, its second volume traveled to early Qājār Iran where the master-trope by which it likened itself to Noah's Ark so appealed to literati who had witnessed the fall of the Safavids that it was they who first edited the version we possess today. If Bīdil, Ārzū, Khvushgū and their circles had such long-lasting literary, political and historical legacies, it is because of the aesthetic and conceptual complexity of their writings. I have only adumbrated this complexity in these introductory pages. The chapters to follow will extend these adumbrations through close readings.

This book aims to intervene in three disciplines: Mughal historiography, religious studies and literary studies. Muzaffar Alam and Sanjay Subrahmanyam open their *Writing the Mughal World: Studies on Culture and Politics*, published in 2012, with a critical survey of "what exactly the Mughals represented" in over a century and a half of historical scholarship.[6] They begin this survey with a brief discussion of the "revolution" in Persian history-writing brought about by fifteenth-century Iranian Timurid and Central Asian historians. This revolution was paradigmatic for subsequent history-writing sponsored by the Mughals from the sixteenth to the eighteenth century. The reason for Alam and Subrahmanyam's focus on Persian history-writing lies in the British colonial identification, beginning in the nineteenth century, of the discourse of history as the principle formulation of understandings of state. Whether in order to rule India in imitation of the Mughals or to later rule it by claiming an enlightened repudiation of the Mughal example, the British turned to Persian language history-writing authored by literati in Mughal circles to understand the Mughal state. This exclusive identification of history with visions of statehood came to be shared by Muslim Reformists writing in Urdu in the second half of the nineteenth century. It was also shared by a group of Marxist historians associated with Aligarh Muslim University and writing between the 1930s and the present. For this latter group the Mughal state, understood as no more than a fiscal mechanism for agrarian revenue extraction, was the only legitimate subject of history-writing. For each of these groups to understand the discourse of history has been to understand the state that forms the proper subject of that discourse. This premise undergirding these otherwise politically divergent bodies of scholarship is recognizably a legacy of European positivism. Alam and Subrahmanyam's introduction to their volume concludes with a list explicating the seven "new trends and themes of the changed Mughal historiography." Reading this list makes it apparent that breaking with the legacy of positivism has meant granting primary rather than tertiary attention to the question of how political power was *represented.* The primary importance now granted to this question has arisen from the recognition that literary, artistic, architectural and performative representations of political power were also constitutive of such power. Representations of power are worthy of the historian's attention because of the power of representations.

And yet, an unremarked on politico-philosophical heritage connects the positivist identification of history-writing and the state that underlies the "vulgar Marxism" of the Aligarh School's historiography with "the cultural turn" noted above. This begins to become apparent when we recall Marx's well-known philosophical debts to Hegel and recall that it is Hegel who gave modern political philosophy the concept of the collective subject. However we may assess Hegel and his legacy today, we cannot avoid acknowledging that it is the Hegelian moment in modern political philosophy that inaugurates a concern with human subject-formation. When Alam and Subrahmanyam observe a renewed attention to what I have characterized above as the power of representations they are, implicitly or explicitly, observing an attention to subject-formation. This is also the genealogy of the salience in the contemporary humanities of the work of the political philosopher and historian Michel Foucault who, towards the end of his life, described his career as a particular extension of the modern European philosophical concern with the subject.[7] Rather than a pre-given immaterial substance, the subject is, in Foucault's works, the fulcrum of certain institutionally embedded practices. It is in the context of modern institutions like the clinic and the prison that Foucault understands the discourses and practices of modern subjectivity to have taken shape. Though vastly influential in the study of post-colonial modernities, Hegelian and Foucauldian attention to modes of subject-formation have had little salience in the study of the pre-colonial Indo-Islamic world.

Among the principle institutional sites for discourses and practices of the human subject in the Indo-Islamic world were the royal court and Sufi hospice. The literati whose work forms the focus of this book were centrally concerned with the discourses and practices of the human subject. However, because of the crisis of political authority I have described above as besetting eighteenth-century Delhi, they were only tenuously related to the Mughal courts. Instead, it was in their own domestic or semi-domestic settings that they held court. Taking such settings into account, this monograph studies interrelated formulations of what Foucault called the "hermeneutics of the subject." In doing so, it extends the inquiries into the various Mughal entanglements of aesthetics with politics that Alam and Subrahmanyam remark on.

This is the point at which to remark on how this book intervenes in scholarship on Indian Sufism by offering case studies of Sufism's intricate entwinement with political power. The works of Nile Green have been the most conspicuous of the recent scholarly attempts to thus set Indian Sufism within its political contexts. However, they avoid closely reading any one Sufi text.[8] This avoidance seems to offer the advantage of higher-order generalizations on Sufism's relations to politics. But such generalizations are diminished in value when we ask, as I have above, how political power was inscribed into the logics of human subject-formation.[9] Central to these logics were affect and memory; and it is literature that comprises their most complex formulation. A method adequate for this complexity cannot avoid close reading. It is such close reading that the chapters of this book offer.

The third discipline in which this book therefore intervenes is literary studies. The persistent problem with the body of literary critical work on Persian literature, whether of Mughal India or other pre-colonial contexts, has been an inadequate understanding of how imaginative literature *refers* to the world. Literary studies have tended to fall on two divergent sides of this question regarding the mode of literature's reference to the world, and accordingly have adopted two contrasting methods. The first has entailed the choice of texts whose generic logic determines that they name historically real places, persons and times rather than fictive ones. Hence the choice of narrative over non-narrative literature or the *mas̱navī* rather than the *ghazal* (the most prestigious of Safavid-Mughal genres) or *qaṣīdah*; and then of the historical *mas̱navī* rather than fictive and mystical ones; and of *taẕkirah*s or biographical dictionaries, travelogues and non-mystical autobiographies. These are all preferences for texts characterized by indexical modes of reference. Not that texts making such indexical reference to their historical world are unworthy of scholarly attention. Rather, it is my contention that to foreground only such texts is to miss those textual logics that may be less obvious to us today but were better known, more prestigious and therefore intensively cultivated in pre-colonial-century Persian literary culture. These were logics of genres that made *indirect* and often allegorical reference to their historical world. Here, Paul Losenksy's *Welcoming Fighani: Imitation and Poetic Individuality in the Safavid-Mughal Ghazal* is a pathbreaking exception and this monograph is partly indebted to it.

The other method, more characteristic of Persian- and Urdu-language scholarship, has been to directly address the more prestigious literary genres that I have referred to above but to account for their mode of reference to their historical world by now discredited nationalist explanations. The most conspicuous of these nationalist explanations is the geographical categorization of *ghazal* styles devised by the early twentieth-century Iranian literary critic, Muḥammad Taqī "Bahār" (1886–1951). Qājār Iran was not only geographically smaller than its Safavid predecessor, it had also lost the Safavid sense of a literary-cultural continuum with Mughal India. It was this geographically and culturally shrunken sense of Iranian identity that Bahār inscribed into his vastly influential study of poetic "styles" or *sabk*s, *Sabk shināsī* (Stylistics, 1942).[10] In this study he cited geographical and ethnic criteria to account for, distinguish chronologically between and hierarchize four *ghazal* styles: the *sabk-i khurāsānī* or the "Khurasani style" (10th–12th centuries), the *sabk-i 'irāqī* or the "Iraqi style" (13th–15th centuries), the *sabk-i hindī* or the "Indian style" (15th–18th centuries) and the *bāzgasht-i adabī* or "Literary Return" style (18th–19th centuries), which was centered in Qājār Iran and sought Neo-Classically to return to what was understood as the lost simplicity of the Khurasani style. It was thus that the time-taking metaphorical complexities of the most conspicuous Safavid-Mughal *ghazal* style, whose ethnically diverse practitioners had called it "Speaking Anew," came to be pejoratively denominated the "Indian Style." However, as Shamsur Rahman Faruqi and Rajeev Kinra have shown, there was nothing especially Indian about this style since even its detractors had cited poetic precedent, not ethnicity, to justify their criticisms.[11] However, Faruqi and Kinra's recuperations of pre-nationalist critical attitudes have only had limited effects on literary criticism from modern Iran, which mostly still retains Bahār's nationalist categorization of styles in some version or other.[12]

Modern Urdu literary scholarship on Mughal Persian literature is barely an exception to this trend. This is arguably because it inherits the loss of "self-confidence" with respect to Persian among South Asians that Shamsur Rahman Faruqi speaks of as having beset Indians from the early nineteenth century onward.[13] It is therefore not surprising that a century later the earliest modern history of Persian poetry, Shiblī Nu'mānī's *Shi'r al-'Ajam*, written in Urdu and published between 1908 and 1918, was as Irano-centric as it was.[14] Because it implicitly equated the quality of poetry with the political power of the court or dynasty patronizing it or ruling the region in which it was composed, it judged the poetry of politically enfeebled late Mughal Delhi poorly. What is more, its aesthetic criterion was a nativist version of European realism, so that the politically stronger the Islamic state in question was, the more realistic Shiblī judged its poetry to have been. Shiblī seems to have inaugurated a modern tradition in Urdu literary scholarship of evaluating Safavid-Mughal poetry – above all Speaking Anew poetry – negatively for the very ambiguity its authors and earliest readers had prized. An example of this trend among the most recent and valuable contributions to Bīdil scholarship in Urdu is Sayyad Aḥsan al-Ẓafar's magisterially assimilative two volume study, *Mirzā 'Abd al-Qādir Bedil: ḥayāt aur kārname.*[15] Aḥsan al-Ẓafar belongs to a tradition inaugurated in Urdu by Shiblī and his colleagues of literary criticism committed to the aesthetic and even moral evaluation of the work of literature in question. To this end, he quotes extensively from nearly all previous Persian, English and Urdu scholarship on Bīdil only to eventually concur with Nūr al-Ḥasan Anṣārī whom he quotes as writing of Speaking Anew poetry:

> The language used for expression is generally convoluted, allegorical, argumentative and to a great extent lifeless and dull. In the ghazal there is a lack of romanticism and fluency and an excess of a kind of philosophical despair. The over-use of allegory and ambiguity is the distinguishing feature of that period's poetry. The scope of the imagination was certainly widened by this tendency but the limits of words were overextended. The result was that the ghazal that has little scope for long-windedness and prolixity fell victim to ambiguity and convolutedness.[16]

Among the aims of this monograph is to challenge this long-standing characterization by offering an alternative explanation for the undeniable difficulties of Bīdil's style. I avoid the anachronistic judgments that have diminished the value of the Urdu and Persian literary scholarship I have discussed. Instead, I put these stylistic difficulties into relation with contemporaneous rhetorical categories and explain them as poetic responses to contemporaneous philosophico-theological problematics.

This is the point at which to pose three questions in descending order, passing from most general to most specific. What was the pre-history in the Islamic East of the Mughal dynasty's investment in Persian as a language of imperial power? What distinguished this Mughal investment in Persian from prior Indo-Islamic investments in it? And finally and most specifically, how did the three authors at the center of this book and their circles fashion themselves as authors by appropriating Persian and Indic literary canons? We will turn to these questions by turn.

Persian before and under the Mughals

Among the best-known features of Islamic civilization is the rise to literary status and spread of New Persian in the two centuries after the rapid Arab Muslim conquest of Iran. On the eve of this conquest Sasanid-ruled Iran is known to have used two distinct kinds of Persian: Pahlavi Middle Persian that was written in its own alphabet and used exclusively as an artificially preserved archaic language of the Sasanid bureaucracy and Sasanid Zoroastrian priesthood; and an unscripted language closely resembling New Persian in its grammar and much of its lexicon and spoken by the generality of people.[17] The Arab Muslim conquest destroyed the institutional foundations for Pahlavi Middle Persian but led to the elevation of the popular language of Iran or "proto-New Persian" to literary status.

It lies outside the scope of this Introduction to detail this elevation. It should suffice to observe that this process entailed modeling literature in New Persian mostly on an already prestigious Arabic-language canon of verse and prose genres; the modified use of the Arabic alphabet for writing it; and the patronage of New Persian literature by ethnically Turkic dynasties who sought thus to assert a cultural and imperial identity distinct to Arab ones. A crucial means to this imperial assertion of ethnic difference was the choice of the verse epic or *masnavī* genre that had no parallel in Arabic literary culture. Among the earliest of these Turkic dynasties were the Ghaznavids (977–1186) who thus patronized Firdawsī, the author of the famous epic, *Shāhnāmah* (Book of Kings, 977–1010), and whose eastern frontier included the Indian city of Lahore. The geography of the earliest efflorescence of Persian literature thus already included India. It was in keeping with this that all the Muslim dynasties – significantly also Turkic and Afghan in ethnicity – that ruled North India after the Ghaznavids adopted Persian as the language of court and patronized literary projects in it.

Although therefore in use from almost the very beginnings of Islamic rule in North India, Persian took on distinct imperial and aesthetic meanings under the later Timurids or Mughals (1526–1857). Unlike the pre-Mughal Islamic dynasties, the Mughals used – and mandated the use of – Persian alone in all documents of state.[18] This policy identified Mughal imperial expansion across regions with the already trans-regional status of the language. It also had the effect of identifying the Mughal court as the most prestigious arbiter of Persian literary authority. Underscoring this conflation of Persian literary canonicity with Mughal political power were the emperor Akbar's appointment of a succession of Iranian and Indian poets to the office of *malik al-shu'arā* (court poet), the migration of Iranian literati and intellectuals to wealthier Mughal courts and these courts' sponsorship of *tazkirah*s or biographical dictionaries of those who wrote Persian poetry.

The distinct aesthetic significance of the Persian poetic culture sponsored by the Mughals lay in its inheritance of the aforementioned legacy of Timurid Herat. This implied that the earliest collections in Mughal royal libraries were the results of the retrospective gaze cast by the Timurids of Herat over prior Persian poetry to synthesize and systematize that corpus. They also formed the basis on which the Persian poetic past was Spoken Anew in Mughal domains. A noteworthy but little studied feature of the Mughal "pursuit of Persian" was the character of its relations to spatially overlapping, socially famililar but semiotically dissimilar Indic linguistic-literary traditions. It was not only the explicit polytheism that formed the theological heritage of "this-worldly" (*laukika*) Sanskrit literary culture and the vernacular literary traditions that appropriated its legacy that distinguished them from Persianate literary culture.[19] It was also the absence in Persianate literary culture of any equivalent of *śṛṅgāra* or "the erotic aesthetic mood" that was the dominant "aesthetic mood" or *rasa* of Sanskrit and Sanskrit-informed literary traditions. By direct contrast, Persianate poetics elevated *firāq* or "erotic separation" to the status of dominant aesthetic mood. Accordingly, the Sanskrit "science of poetic figures of speech" or *alaṅkāraśāstra* long shared typologies for kinds of poems with those for kinds of heroines in the "science of sexual pleasure" or *kāmaśāstra*.[20] And yet, despite such semiotic divergences – or perhaps because of them – most Persian-language appropriations of Indic literary texts "domesticated" what they appropriated rather than letting it "foreignize" the semiotics of the Persian. Between what Lawrence Venuti has conceptualized as

> an ethnocentric reduction of the foreign text to target-language cultural values, bringing the author back home, and a foreignizing method, an ethnodeviant pressure on those values to register the linguistic and cultural difference of the foreign text, sending the reader abroad,[21]

the majority of Persian-language translations of Indic texts chose the former. This is true, for example, of the *Razmnāmah* (Book of War), the Persian translation Akbar commissioned in the 1580s of the Sanskrit *Mahābhārata*, as it is of Persian translations made outside the direct orbit of the court like Sa'dullāh Masīḥ Pānipatī's *Masnavī-i Rām va Sītā*, an early seventeenth-century Persian verse retelling in the *masnavī* genre of Valmikī's Sanskrit epic, *Rāmāyaṇa* (Rāma's Journey), composed around the second century BCE.[22] Those books of the *Mahābhārata* that relate to kingship and polity were translated in the *Razmnāmah* to convey the rhetorical atmosphere of texts in the tradition of Persianate royal ethics or *akhlāq*, clustering thickly with verses from Ḥāfiẓ and Sa'dī. Masīḥ's *Masnavī-i Rām va Sītā* is indebted for the poetics of its characters' inner states of being and its rhetoric of love and war to such canonical instances of the Persian *masnavī* tradition as Niẓāmī (d. 1209) and Firdawsī while its ingenious metaphors draw on the Speaking Anew *ghazal* tradition. This domesticating vector of Mughal India's Persian's appropriations of Indic linguistic-literary traditions complemented the political uses of Persian by the Mughals as a non-sectarian instrument of transregional imperial power.

However, by the time of the emperor Aurangzeb's death in 1707 such close relations between Persian poetry and Mughal polity had loosened. That is, the Mughal emperor's court had long abolished the office of court poet while increasingly assertive sub-imperial polities had begun to patronize Persian-language literati alongside literature in Braj, Urdu and other languages. By the time of Ārzū's death in 1756, two features of India's Persian literary culture – absent in the early Mughal period – had become well-established: the multiple and geographically dispersed locations in which Persian literary canonicity was formulated, mainly through the composition of *tazkirah*s or biographical dictionaries; and the status of Persian as only one of the two languages – the other being Urdu – in which Mughal imperial and sub-imperial courts patronized *sukhan*, Persian literary culture's own term for "literature." It is crucial to explicate the ontology of *sukhan* and the interpretative dispositions that went with it and the book's chapters do this with respect to each of the littérateurs in question. For now, we will turn to the last of the three questions posed above, namely how the three authors in question fashioned themselves as authors by appropriating Persian and Indic literary canons. We may answer this by offering a chapter outline of this book.

A chapter outline

Despite their shared affiliation to this city that they thought of as metonymic of the kingdom, the three thinkers in question did not all share the same conception of the relations between literature and polity. As Chapter 1, "Bīdil's portrait: ekphrasis as ascetic self-transformation," argues, Bīdil responded to the ambient crisis of Mughal political authority by fashioning himself into a Sufi exemplum of ascetic self-government. The first half of this chapter sets Bīdil within the networks of patronage that made such literary self-fashioning politically effective. That is, it recalls how the poet was not a solitary and world-renouncing Sufi but one whose pervasively mystical writings were variously addressed to the grandees of the Mughal state. The second half of the chapter examines the two main means by which he fashioned this politically effective literary persona: his employment of the tradition of rhymed and rhythmic prose and his kenotic poetics. *Kenosis*, an originally Greek term meaning "emptying," has been current in the contemporary humanities as designating the hollowing out of an individual's phenomal self to admit its displacement by a divine Self. While rhymed and rhythmic prose pervades Bīdil's prose oeuvre, kenosis takes genre-specific forms analyzed at various points in this book. Among the forms it takes in his autobiography, *The Four Elements* (*Chahār 'unṣur*), is the strange fading and flaring of a portrait of himself painted by a painter well known in Mughal ateliers, Bīdil's tearing up of the portrait and his own interpretation of the phenomenon. This chapter explicates the kenotic logic of this dense and poetry-studded narrative and of his interpretation of it in the context of his autobiography and Islamic courtly traditions of visuality. This explication serves as an introduction to Bīdil's kenotic voice. Chapter 2, "Bīdil's *tarjī'-band*: the author's kenotic chorus," extends the examination of this voice by making explicit the transformations he worked on the heritage of prior models of the *tarjī'-band*, a genre of stanzaic verse with an identical couplet at the end of every stanza. No *tarjī'-band*, this chapter argues, could be interpreted in the ways it might have been before Bīdil appropriated it for his self-empowering kenotic chorus. However, Bīdil's oeuvre is also characterized by its appropriations of its Indian and specifically Hindu locality, an appropriation not apparent in his *tarjī'-band*. Chapter 3, "A Hindu allegory of the Islamic philosopher-king: the tale of Madan and Kāmdī in Bīdil's *masnavī 'Irfān*," thus turns to this appropriation by explicating the narrative and poetic techniques by which, in the longest of his *masnavī*s – *'Irfān* (Gnosis) – he transformed the intertext of an Indic tale of long and multilingual currency. By translating or trans-coding this tale into the poetics of the Persian Sufi *masnavī* Bīdil asserted his authorial authority as a mastery of his multilingual milieu. He also presented his disciple-readers among the politically threatened ruling elites of Delhi with a new paradigm – identified with Bīdil himself – of ascetic self-mastery protected by a divine philosopher-king. In this sense, this chapter permits an explicit or thematic discussion of the relation between literature and the social, between poetry and polity. Through its interpretation of Bīdil's Islamic-Neo-Platonic adaptation of Hindu metempsychosis, it also returns to a theme only adumbrated in Chapter 1 – that of Bīdil's portrait as his body double. In this sense, this chapter closes the sequence of three chapters on Bīdil.

Bīdil's student, Sirāj al-Dīn 'Alī Khān "Ārzū," on the other hand, responded to Mughal Delhi's crisis of sovereignty, as Chapter 4 – "The local universality of poetic pleasure: Sirāj al-Dīn 'Alī Khān "Ārzū" and the speaking subject" – argues, by historicizing the canons of Persian-language literary scholarship. He did so in order to authorize what he understood as the temporal locality of a certain controversial *ghazal* style – Speaking Anew (*tāzah-gūyī*) – that had been current in Safavid Iran, Turkic Central Asia and Mughal India since the early 1500s. Moreover, this was a style in which his teacher Bīdil's *ghazal*s were considered to be the greatest threshold and model after Sā'ib Tabrīzī (d. 1676). By the theoretical authorization he gave this style, he defended his teacher's innovations but on grounds other than those of his teacher's. And indeed it could not have been otherwise for, as Chapters 1 and 5 show, the ground on which Bīdil appropriated literary canons for his purposes was a Sufi subjectivity that, through ascetic self-transformation, mystically perceived the perpetual Now (*ḥāl*). It was not a scholarly subjectivity that periodized the changes time and its contingencies wrought on language and literature. It is therefore perhaps no accident that Ārzū's apprenticeship to Bīdil was as brief as it was powerful. He says he met him only twice and benefited from both meetings.[23] And yet, his entry on Bīdil in his biographical compendium, *Majma' al-nafā'is* (Collection of Rarities, completed in 1750), is exceptionally long, running into twenty-nine pages in the print edition. In it he observes that "the people of India" – whom he tellingly identifies with Delhi – annually commemorate the anniversary of Bīdil's death by lighting lamps and distributing cooked food to the poor. We know from another contemporary witness that Ārzū himself organized these annual commemorations because "of his pedagogical relations with him" (*ba nisbat-i shāgirdīsh*), including a reading from his teacher's collected works (*kulliyāt*) as part of the ceremonies.[24] Before quoting extensively from Bīdil's verse oeuvre Ārzū adds: "Although he elevated poetry [*sukhan*] to a level where, like Ḥāfiẓ of Shiraz, it 'admits of no selection' [*intikhāb nadārad*] I for my part have selected the verses that I understood as far as I was able and set them down."[25] He underscores the comparison to the trans-temporal authority of Ḥāfiẓ by quoting the phrase famously repeated with respect to Ḥāfiẓ's verse by anthologists, namely that it was so unexceptionally or evenly excellent that it "admits of no selection." This was a comparison that, as explored in Chapter 5, "Khvushgū's dream of Ḥāfiẓ: building an ark with Ārzū and Bīdil," Bindrāban Dās "Khvushgū" would exploit to formulate his own authority as a poet and historian. Such popular Sufi reverence for Bīdil must have amplified Ārzū's own scholarly authority, even if the logics and genres Ārzū favored did not wholly coincide with Bīdil's. It needed an impetus other than Bīdil's to incite Ārzū to the historicism that distinguished his oeuvre. This incitement arrived from his encounter in Delhi with the prestigious Iranian émigré intellectual, Shaykh 'Alī Ḥazīn. Ḥazīn reacted to his own dispossession by the deposition in Isfahan of the Safavid ruling house, with whom he had been affiliated, by disparaging the Persian literary culture of India. By singling out Ḥazīn and his poetry for criticism, Ārzū performed his loyal defense of the Mughal sovereign whose gifts and welcome Ḥazīn had repudiated.[26] He also appropriated something of Ḥazīn's social authority for himself and his poetic-philological projects. But what interests me about these self-authorizations and the dispute that forms their social context is not their value for cultural history. Rather, they are important for my object of analysis only as an efficient cause for what far exceeded them in conceptual complexity: they allowed Ārzū to fashion his voice as that of a historicist philologist of the trans-regional prestige language of Persian. This meant that his attitude towards Persian literary history, as evidenced in his lexicography, manuals on poetic metaphor and syntax, poetry and his biographical compendium was diametrically opposite to Bīdil's by its categorical insistence on the periodicity of the Persian criterion of "linguistic purity" (*faṣāḥat*). In this sense, the two main littérateurs at the center of this book – as well as their respective but overlapping literary circles – represented disparate sets of relations between authorship and the temporality and canons of literary history.

The third littérateur, addressed in Chapter 5, Bindrāban Dās "Khvushgū," combined the models of his two main teachers, Bīdil and Ārzū. By this he fashioned his own authorial voice as a literary historian in the tradition of the *tazkirah* or Persian biographical compendium, a voice simultaneously indebted to Bīdil's invocations of trans-temporal mystical authority as well as to Ārzū's periodizing historicism.

Notes

1 Throughout the book I have followed Library of Congress conventions for transliterating Persian with Roman letters.

2 Paul E. Losensky, *Welcoming Fighani: Imitation and Poetic Individuality in the Safavid-Mughal Ghazal* (Costa Mesa, CA: Mazda Publishers, 1998), 164.

3 In this the retrospective gaze and prospective importance of Timurid literary culture is comparable to that of Late Tang China. Stephen Owen, *The Late Tang: Chinese Poetry of the Mid-Ninth Century (827–860)* (Cambridge, MA: Harvard University Press, 2009).

4 For a close reading of cases of the tension between innovation and imitation that formed a central preoccupation of Safavid-Mughal poetry, see Paul E. Losensky, *Welcoming Fighani: Imitation and Poetic Individuality in the Safavid-Mughal Ghazal*, 193–313.

5 A prominent instance of the invocation of Bīdil as a modernist exemplar is Sayyad Ḥassan Ḥusaynī, *Bīdil, Sipihrī va sabk-i Hindī* (Tehrān: Surūsh, 1387/2008).

6 Muzaffar Alam and Sanjay Subrahmanyam, *Writing the Mughal World: Studies on Culture and Politics* (New York: Columbia University Press, 2012), 3.

7 "My objective instead has been to create a history of the different modes by which, in our culture, human beings are made subjects." Michel Foucault, "The Subject and Power," *Critical Inquiry* 8: 4 (Summer 1982), 777–95.

8 Nile Green, *Indian Sufism Since the Seventeenth Century: Saints, Books and Empires in the Muslim Deccan* (Abingdon: Routledge, 2009).

9 Shahzad Bashir has addressed such subject-formation in Shahzad Bashir, *Sufi Bodies: Religion and Society in Medieval Islam* (New York: Columbia University Press, 2013).

10 Muḥammad Taqī Bahār, *Sabk-shināsī ya tārikh-i taṭavvur-i nas̱r-i Fārsī* (Tehrān: Parastū, 1337/1958).

11 Shamsur Rahman Faruqi, "Stranger in the City: The Poetics of Sabk-i Hindi," *Annual of Urdu Studies* 19 (2004), 1–94; and Rajeev Kinra, "Fresh Words for a Fresh World: *Tāza-Gū'ī* and the Poetics of Newness in Early Modern Indo-Persian Poetry," *Sikh Formations: Religion, Culture, Theory* 3: 2 (2007): 125–49.

12 A still influential Iranian nationalist reformulation of Bahār's categories that renames his "*sabk-i hindī*" "*sabk-i khurāsānī*" and thus re-appropriates it for modern Iran is Amīrī Fīrūzkūhī's preface to his edition of Sā'ib Tabrīzī, *Kulliyāt-i Sā'ib-i Tabrīzī* (Tehrān: kitāb-furūshī-i Khayyām, 1333/1954). A noteworthy recent attempt to clarify Fīrūzkūhī's nationalist obfuscation of categories by retrieving contemporaneous stylistic terminology is Javād Mihirbān, *Maktab-i nāzuk-khiyālī va naqd-i Bīdil* (Mashhad: nashr-i Tabīrān, 1390/2011). Mihirbān therefore persuasively terms the style *nāzuk-khiyāli* or "subtle imagination" but only to distinguish between its Iranian and Indian branches and then claim that the poetry of those of

its practitioners who were "of Indian origin" (*hindī al-aṣl*) was characterized by "a scattered dispersal of words, poor taste in the choice of words [and] grammatical deviations" (93). Mihirbān thus re-inscribes an Iranian nationalist essentialism into his analytical frame.

13 Shamsur Rahman Faruqi, "Unprivileged Power: The Strange Case of Persian (and Urdu) in Nineteenth Century India," *The Annual of Urdu Studies* 13 (1998), 3–30.

14 Shiblī Nu'mānī, *Shi'r al-'Ajam* (A'ẓamgarh: Shiblī Akaḍemī, 2002).

15 Sayyad Aḥsan al-Ẓafar, *Mirzā 'Abd al-Qādir Bedil: ḥayāt aur kārname: jild-i yekkum va duvvum* (Rāmpūr: Rāmpūr Raẕā Library, 2009). This study is based on the author's dissertation completed much earlier.

16 Aḥsan al-Ẓafar, *Mirzā 'Abd al-Qādir Bedil: ḥayāt aur kārname: jild-i duvvum*, 89.

17 Mahmoud Omidsalar, *Iran's Epic and America's Empire: A Handbook for a Generation in Limbo* (Santa Monica, CA: Afshar Publishing, 2012), 90–91.

18 Muzaffar Alam, "The Pursuit of Persian: Language in Mughal Politics," *Modern Asian Studies* 32 (1998), 317–49. It is well known that the Afghan dynasties who ruled North India patronized Avadhi – that they called by the generic name "Hindī" or "Hindavī" – as much as they did Persian.

19 On the "this-worldly" or *laukika* ethos of Sanskrit poetry or *kāvya*, see Sheldon Pollock, *The Language of the Gods in the World of Men: Sanskrit, Culture and Power in Premodern India* (Berkeley, CA: University of California Press, 2007), 13.

20 Deven M. Patel, "Shared Typologies of *Kāmashāstra*, *Alaṅkārashāstra* and Literary Critcism," *Journal of Indian Philosophy* 39 (2011), 101–22.

21 I derive this distinction between "domesticating" and "foreignizing" translation methods from Lawrence Venuti's exposition of Friedrich Schleiermacher's 1813 discussion of it, as referred to in Lawrence Venuti, *The Translator's Invisibility: A History of Translation* (New York: Routledge, 1998), 19–20.

22 Mullāh Masīḥ Pānipatī, *Rāmāyana: kuhantarīn hammāsah-i 'āshiqānah-i Hind* (Dehlī-i naw: Markaz-i tahqīqāt-i Fārsī, rāyzanī-i farhangī-i jumhūrī Islāmi-i Irān, 2009). This edition corrects the many scribal errors in the 1899 Munshī Naval Kishor lithograph edition but bears a title at odds with the one in Masih's own time, which, according to most extant manuscripts, was *Masnavī-i Rām va Sītā.*

23 Sirāj al-Dīn 'Alī Khān Ārzū, *Tazkirah-i majma' al-nafā'is: jild-i avval* (Islamābād: markaz-i taḥqīqāt-i Fārsī-i Irān va Pākistān, 2004), 240–41.

24 Dargāh Qulī Khān, *Muraqqa'-i Dehlī* (Ḥyderābād: maṭbu'a Tāj Press, 1973), 45.

25 Ārzū, Tazkirah-i Majma' al-nafā'is: jild-i avval, 241.

26 Mana Kia, "*Adab* as Ethics of Literary Form and Social Conduct: Reading the *Gulistān* in Late Mughal India," in (eds), Alireza Korangy and Daniel J. Sheffield, *No Tapping Around Philology: A Festschrift in Honor of Wheeler McIntosh Thackson Jr.'s 70th Birthday* (Weisbaden: Harrassowitz Verlag, 2014), 299.

Bibliography

Aḥsan al-Ẓafar, Sayyad. *Mirzā 'Abd al-Qādir Bedil: ḥayāt aur kārname: jild-i avval.* Rāmpūr: Rāmpūr Raẕā Library, 2009.

Aḥsan al-Ẓafar, Sayyad. *Mirzā 'Abd al-Qādir Bedil: ḥayāt aur kārname: jild-i duvvum.* Rāmpūr: Rāmpūr Raẕā Library, 2009.

Alam, Muzaffar. "The Pursuit of Persian: Language in Mughal Politics," *Modern Asian Studies* 32 (1998), 317–49.

Alam, Muzaffar and Subrahmanyam, Sanjay. *Writing the Mughal World: Studies on Culture and Politics.* New York: Columbia University Press, 2012.

Ārzū, Sirāj al-Dīn 'Alī Khān. *Tazkirah-i majma' al-nafā'is: jild-i avval.* Islamābād: Markaz-i taḥqīqāt-i Fārsī-i Irān va Pākistān, 2004.

Bahār, Muḥammad Taqī. *Sabk-shināsī ya tārikh-i taṭavvur-i naṣr-i Fārsī.* Tehrān: Parastū, 1337/1958.
Bashir, Shahzad. *Sufi Bodies: Religion and Society in Medieval Islam.* New York: Columbia University Press, 2013.
Dargāh Qulī Khān. *Muraqqa'-i Dehlī.* Hyderābād: maṭbu'a Tāj Press, 1973.
Faruqi, Shamsur Rahman. "Unprivileged Power: The Strange Case of Persian (and Urdu) in Nineteenth Century India," *The Annual of Urdu Studies* 13 (1998), 3–30.
Faruqi, Shamsur Rahman. "Stranger in the City: The Poetics of Sabk-i Hindi," *Annual of Urdu Studies* 19 (2004), 1–94.
Fīrūzkūhī, Amīrī. "Preface," in Sā'ib Tabrīzī, *Kulliyāt-i Sā'ib-i Tabrīzī.* Tehrān: kitābfurūshī-i Khayyām, 1333/1954.
Foucault, Michel. "The Subject and Power," *Critical Inquiry* 8: 4 (Summer 1982), 777–95.
Green, Nile. *Indian Sufism Since the Seventeenth Century: Saints, Books and Empires in the Muslim Deccan.* Abingdon: Routledge, 2009.
Ḥusaynī, Sayyad Ḥassan. *Bīdil, Sipihrī va sabk-i Hindī.* Tehrān: Surūsh, 1387/2008.
Kia, Mana. "*Adab* as Ethics of Literary Form and Social Conduct: Reading the *Gulistān* in Late Mughal India," in (eds), Alireza Korangy and Daniel J. Sheffield, *No Tapping Around Philology: A Festschrift in Honor of Wheeler McIntosh Thackson Jr.'s 70th Birthday.* Weisbaden: Harrassowitz Verlag, 2014.
Kinra, Rajeev. "Fresh Words for a Fresh World: *Tāza-Gū'ī* and the Poetics of Newness in Early Modern Indo-Persian Poetry," *Sikh Formations: Religion, Culture, Theory* 3: 2 (2007): 125–49.
Losensky, Paul E. *Welcoming Fighani: Imitation and Poetic Individuality in the Safavid-Mughal Ghazal.* Costa Mesa, CA: Mazda Publishers, 1998.
Masīḥ, Mullāh Pānipatī. *Rāmāyana: kuhantarīn hammāsah-i 'āshiqānah-i Hind.* Dehlī-i naw: markaz-i tahqīqāt-i Fārsī, rāyzanī-i farhangī-i jumhurī-i Islāmi-i Irān, 2009.
Mihirbān, Javād. *Maktab-i nāzuk-khiyālī va naqd-i Bīdil.* Mashhad: nashr-i Tabīrān, 1390/2011.
Nu'mānī, Shiblī. *Shi'r al-'Ajam.* A'ẓamgarh: Shiblī Akaḍemī, 2002.
Omidsalar, Mahmoud. *Iran's Epic and America's Empire: A Handbook for a Generation in Limbo.* Santa Monica, CA: Afshar Publishing, 2012.
Owen, Stephen. *The Late Tang: Chinese Poetry of the Mid-Ninth Century (827–860).* Cambridge, MA: Harvard University Press, 2009.
Patel, Deven M. "Shared Typologies of *Kāmashāstra, Alaṅkārashāstra* and Literary Criticism," *Journal of Indian Philosophy* 39 (2011), 101–22.
Pollock, Sheldon. *The Language of the Gods in the World of Men: Sanskrit, Culture and Power in Premodern India.* Berkeley, CA: University of California Press, 2007.
Venuti, Lawrence. *The Translator's Invisibility: A History of Translation.* New York: Routledge, 1998.

1 Bīdil's portrait

Ekphrasis as ascetic self-transformation

ba andāz-i taghāful nīm rukh ham 'ālamī dārad
chirā mustaqbal-i mardum chu taṣvīr-i farang āyī[1]

A spectacle, too, is your turning heedlessly away into a picture in profile.
Why face me like a European portrait?

The legacy of the Indo-Persian Sufi poet Mirzā 'Abd al-Qādir Khān "Bīdil" (1644–1720)[2] is conspicuous in the ongoing scholarly rehabilitation of the literatures of Mughal India, Safavid Iran and Turkic Central Asia. Once discredited for his stylistic complexities in Iran by the Neo-Classicism of the late eighteenth century, again in Soviet Central Asia by early twentieth-century "progressive" poetics, and increasingly unread in South Asia with the fading there of Persian itself, Bīdil's prodigious oeuvre has attained a new legibility as a result of critiques of nationalist literary historiographies. However, interpretations of his prose works that engage them in their formal specificity remain a desideratum.

This chapter reads an episode of ascetic self-transformation in Bīdil's autobiography, *The Four Elements* (*Chahār 'unṣur*), as an account that focuses in miniature on a concern with self-fashioning that pervades all his works. Indeed, the episode, as discussed in this chapter, can serve as a possible introduction to his oeuvre.[3]

An introduction to Bīdil's words and worlds: the portrait within the frame of a life

In 1116/1704, at his home Luṭf 'Alī Havelī, located outside the Dehlī Darvāzah or Delhi Gate and at a landing by the river Jamunā called Guzar Ghāṭ in the neighborhood of Khekaṛīyāñ on the south-east edge of Mughal Delhi or Shāhjahānābād, at the age of sixty-two, the Indo-Persian Sufi and prodigious poet Bīdil completed an autobiography which he had begun in 1094/1683, titled *The Four Elements*.[4] Into the fourth book or "Element" of this text he set an account of a portrait of himself painted around 1087/1677 by Anūp Chhatr, a painter famous for his portraits in the imperial Mughal ateliers of the time.

Initially refusing this painter permission to paint him, Bīdil finally yielded and was astonished at how the resulting portrait duplicated him like a mirror. After marveling at it for a decade, he fell ill. His friends visited him in his sickbed and one of them, leafing through his anthology of texts, came upon the painting. He exclaimed at how faded it was. Bīdil himself could barely make it out on the page. When he recovered his health, he opened the anthology to examine the faded portrait and was astonished and shocked, as his friends were, to see that it had recovered its brilliant colors. He tore up the painting. This chapter studies the meanings and functions of this ekphrastic[5] section of Bīdil's autobiography. In particular, this chapter offers a reading of the episode as a specific autobiographical appropriation of the semiotics he inherited from the Perso-Arabic literary tradition, an appropriation by which Bīdil fashioned his authorial authority as a Sufi in his milieu. This anecdote, however, is distinguished by its thematization of perception, the theory of which, partly adapted from the paradigmatic Andalusian Sufi thinker Muḥī al-Dīn Ibn 'Arabī (d. 637/1240), was central to Bīdil's concept of the imagination. As the imagination, understood as a subjective faculty always at work in the generation of mental images, forms the implicit subjective condition for the compound metaphors Bīdil was known for in his poetry, this study also aims to prepare the reader for encounters with Bīdil's poetry both in future chapters and independently.

But first, what does it mean to already denominate this text an "autobiography" as I have done? In what sense is it an autobiography that frames the ekphrastic representation of the author's visual portrait? Classical Persian has no word that might be a ready equivalent of the English "autobiography." However, the self-descriptor sometimes used by texts like Bīdil's that we today denominate "autobiographical" – *aḥvāl* – does disclose a dominant, though not exclusive, conception of the form taken by a retrospective summation of all or a large portion or one's own life. The word *aḥvāl* itself signifies "states of being" or "circumstances" and thus accounts for what we perceive as the anecdotal character of several biographical and autobiographical texts. This model of presenting a life entailed that an author assembled, sometimes under thematic sub-headings as in *The Four Elements*, more or less free-standing accounts of experiences that either he or those who participated in his conception of his own selfhood (typically ancestors, parents and teachers) had undergone. On this model, a life was thus told and read as a series of states of being rather than as a progressive accumulation. This reflected, as Dwight F. Reynolds says of medieval Arabic autobiographies:

> a widespread conceptualization of life as a sequence of changing conditions or states rather than as a static, unchanging whole or a simple linear progression through time. A life consists of stages dictated not merely by one's progression from childhood through youth to adulthood and old age but also by one's changing fortunes, which were often contrasted to those few areas of life in which genuine accrual over time was thought possible: the acquisition of knowledge and spiritual understanding, the creation of scholarly and literary works, and the fostering of offspring and students.[6]

It was therefore on the discursive scale of the anecdote that prior authoritative models of a life-account were cited and poetic tropes and prose styles employed. The ordering of textual units larger than the anecdote was, in effect, a freer authorial choice and tended to be idiosyncratic. That there was a much larger corpus of biographies than autobiographies in pre-nineteenth-century Persian and Arabic meant that there were relatively fewer models for autobiographies which thus facilitated such idiosyncratic ordering of meta-anecdotal textual units in autobiographies.[7] This is why the larger structure of Bīdil's autobiography conforms to no known autobiography from his lifetime or earlier. The four largest chapters corresponding to the elements of the title's *The Four Elements* thus invoke, not any particular autobiographical model, but, as will be discussed, Bīdil's simultaneous emphasis on his mortality – composed as he was, like all creatures of the four elements of fire, water, air and earth – and his power to command this mortal sphere as he ascetically commanded himself. The first chapter corresponding to the first element compiles anecdotes pertaining to his childhood and his earliest Sufi teachers; the second compiles anecdotes relating to the practice of poetry; the third presents anecdotes on ontological subjects that formed the main focus of Sufi thought and practice; and the fourth lays out anecdotes relating to personally witnessed remarkable events and mirabilia (*'ajā'ib*). It is to this last chapter that the anecdote mainly under discussion in this chapter belongs.

However, the reader not already informed of the topics of this text by its paratexts must await Bīdil's justification of his title for it in his preface to recognize it as an autobiography of a certain kind and form their hermeneutic expectations accordingly. There, he characterizes his text thus:

> A whiff in keeping with the fragrance and color of the garden of manifestations declares after traversing the stations of flower and thorn; and the veil-adorner of the countenance of diminutions and growths casts open the unveiled levels of his generosity – so it may not remain veiled what *this undrunken intoxication of the tavern of non-existence* [*'adam*] drank from the cup of the heedfulness [*i'tibār*] of being and what *this soundless melody from the party of Divine Oneness* [*vaḥdat*] heard from the lute of the distinctions of Manyness [*kas̱rat*] [my italics].[8]

Bīdil, speaking in his own name here, locates this text chronologically after a course of worldly experience ("after traversing the stations of flower and thorn"), characterizing himself as an item from the plenitude of the world's garden – a "whiff." He is also a "veil-adorner of the countenance of diminutions and growths." That is, he controls the display of creation itself, captured metonymically here by its trait of diminution and growth. This aggrandizing self-characterization leads us to ask whether Bīdil thinks he is God. I will return to this possibility – the possibility of theosis – later in this chapter. Confining ourselves to this passage for now, let us note that he characterizes his text as a generous disclosure to his reader. But what is being disclosed here?

Bīdil invokes two senses here: taste and hearing. He does so to declare that the text to follow will disclose what he – "the undrunken intoxication from the tavern of non-existence" – "drank from the cup of the heedfulness of being." He presents himself as caught between non-being and being. By a shift from singular to plural he maps this distinction onto the one between the One and the Many. The subsequent clause replicates this double feature by speaking of a passage from "soundless melody from the party of divine Oneness" to "the lute of the distinctions of Manyness." This rhetorical feature corresponds to a logical feature of his self-presentation, namely his simultaneous presence before his own creation and after it. This dual self-location in time allies him to a tradition of Persian-language poets, especially prominent from the sixteenth century onward, who authorized themselves by an Islamic-Neo-Platonic conception of creativity. According to this conception, creation was an emanation from the super-sensory One into the sensory Many that yet left the One undiminished. Claiming proximity with the One allowed poets to present themselves as circling around the back, as it were, of poetic predecessors to the primordial source of poetic topoi.

But to say this and no more is to read without an ear for the Persian original where the final syllables of these clauses of identical syllabic length rhyme with each other. Almost all of the prose in *The Four Elements* is thus externally or internally rhymed and arranged in symmetrically measured clauses, making various uses of the Perso-Arabic tradition of such "rhymed and rhythmic prose" (*saj'* or *nas̱r-i musajja'*). Here, the symmetry of these clauses in English, replicating the externally rhymed symmetry of Bīdil's clauses in Persian, align his "undrunken" or undistracted focus on the nothingness from which he came into being with his preoccupation – "soundless" or undivided by representations – with the Divine Oneness that brought him into being and that is the most real. The sentence's doubled and rhyming clauses therefore simultaneously introduce both the ontological frame of reference within which Bīdil's text becomes meaningful and the model reader who would ideally interpret this text in terms of such ontological commitments.

These details of Bīdil's style invite the following preliminary questions: what were the rhetorical antecedents for Bīdil's prose? What were its social effects? Given that autobiographical discourses in pre-nineteenth-century Perso-Arabic traditions possessed no generic unity, answering these two questions lets us better answer our opening question, namely what it means here to speak of an autobiography. Answering the former question will require a brief excursus on the specific genealogy Bīdil was invoking of the uses of "rhymed and rhythmic prose." Answering the latter will require a differentiated account of the social world such prose assumed. The following section will undertake the following tasks: trace the theological antecedents for Bīdil's style; recount the political crisis of his milieu and thus the political effects of his style on his three overlapping circles of readers; and speak of what the mimetic origins and aims of this style imply for the sense in which we may speak of autobiography here.

Let us first turn to the question of the rhetorical antecedents of Bīdil's style. Rhymed and rhythmic prose is as old as the Arabic language and thus older than the oldest Islamic Persian. We will not recapitulate its history here in either language but recall a scene from its earliest appearance in the Prophet Muḥammad's own life. In the Prophet's early Meccan career it was the *kāhin*s (pl. *kuhhān*) or soothsayers who uttered their divinations in such prose. The gradual spread of Islam brought an end to the *kuhhān* not only because of its claim that revelation had ceased with Muḥammad, "the seal of the prophets," but also because the Qur'ān as well as Muḥammad's own early appearances and rhymed and rhythmic proclamations closely resembled theirs.[9] It was this magical precedent as well as its prophetological negation that, despite its long-standing moral ambivalence, Sufis through the centuries had invoked by their rhetoric to variously empower themselves before their disciple-readers.[10] The pervasive use of such a prose style in Bīdil's milieu thus signals not only the prestige of the Sufi ethos across classes but also the general elite investment in the notion of linguistic utterance as isomorphic with the speaker's "balanced soul" (*ṭab'-i salīm, ṭab'-i mawzūn*).[11] Bīdil, in turn, invoked these early and contemporaneous antecedents by his prose style to authorize himself before his readers in politically dispersed and socially strained Delhi. His reader-disciples, in turn, would have discovered in such prose a rhetorical model signaling ascetic power. I will say more on this function of his style later by considering the precise social identities of these readers. But before I do so we must pause to consider a theological significance which Bīdil attached to this style that was peculiarly his own.

Central to understanding Bīdil's oeuvre is the recognition that it is a poetic interpretation – indeed a poetic enactment – of Ibn 'Arabī's theistic monism. Central to this monism was the idea that God created beings by breathing out their names. William C. Chittick:

> When the All-Merciful speaks, he articulates words in his Breath, so his Breath is the underlying stuff of the universe. It is the page upon which God writes out the cosmic book. The nature of the words that appear in the Breath is suggested by the etymology of the words *kalām*, "speech," and *kalima*, "word." Both derive from *kalm*, which the Arabic dictionaries define as *jarh*, which means to cut or wound. *Jarh* in turn is explained more generally to mean *ta'thir*, to leave traces and marks. Basing himself on these standard definitions, Ibn 'Arabī says that the divine speech leaves traces in the All-Merciful Breath. Each word is a "cut" or an "articulation," even though the Breath itself remains forever untouched and uncut.[12]

This breath – "the Breath of the All-Merciful" (*nafas-i raḥmānī*) – furnished Persian Sufi authorship, especially through 'Abd al-Raḥmān Jāmī's authoritative philosophical and poetic interpretations of it, with a mythic paradigm. Bīdil thus described his school friend's clove-scented breath that led him to compose his first verse as "the Breath of the All-Merciful."[13] But the key word by which he designated the complex of ideas surrounding this cosmogonic expiration of breath was *sukhan*, translatable as "poetic utterance." Though not a new word by any means, *sukhan* came to designate a theotic power in Bīdil's poetics that amplified in monist terms conventional Sufi understandings of it as a human imitation of the divine imperative in the Qur'ān that brought creation into being: *kun* or "Be!" "This establishes that *sukhan* is the spirit of creation [*rūḥ-i kāināt*] and the origin of the true nature of beings [*ḥaqīqat-i mawjūdāt*]."[14] He maintained that humans imitated the cosmogonic breathing of names better than other creatures because "the most comprehensive of [God's] names" was manifested in them, this distinction making them uniquely capable of *sukhan*.[15] However, not all humans were equal to this task. Only some who were endowed like the Prophet Muḥammad with the divine gift of a "balanced soul" (*ṭab'-i salīm*, *ṭab'-i mawzūn*) were capable of such imitation.[16] But what it meant to bear this gift and thus be capable of such imitation was borne out in the magical effects of such utterances.

Bīdil's first experience of the magical efficacy of his own *sukhan* occurred in the fortress of Mathura that, when he visited it, was afflicted by an army of djinns (*jinn*).[17] The fort-commander complained to Bīdil of how the djinns caused stones to fly in the fortress and fires to break out, making it uninhabitable. In response Bīdil composed on a sheet of paper with "a dry quill" (*qalam-i khushkī*) a couplet addressed to the djinns. He asked that this couplet, which requested the djinns "of another world" to leave for "another place," be placed on the tip of a spear and planted in the fortress. No sooner than the couplet-bearing spear was thus planted did the flying stones fall to the ground and the fires go out. Not once during Bīdil's visits to Mathura over the subsequent three years did the djinns show any sign of returning.

At the heart of this story is the correspondence between Bīdil's "dry quill" – that is, a quill without ink – and the bodies of the djinns who, according to conventional Islamic cosmology, were a rank of beings invisible to humans and made of fire. Bīdil's *sukhan* succeeded in dispelling these fiery creatures because he recognized and employed the elemental correspondence between dryness and fire. He says he chose a dry pen "so that it would correspond to the study of the subtle world [*'ālam-i laṭīf*] and so that the souls of those who practice writing of incomparability [*ṭabī'at-i tanazzuh-raqamān-i dabistān-i liṭāfat*] in the school of subtlety would raise no dust of ink."[18] He fought the fiery but invisible or subtle-bodied djinns with fiery but invisible or subtle-bodied writing and thus set his disciple-reader a model for such writing. Moreover, the rhythmic and rhymed couplet replicated the balanced character and yet fiery component of his soul, this controlled materiality of human and written signifiers enabling the illocutionary power of the verse. This episode thus contains within itself the elements necessary for an initial understanding of Bīdil's ontology of *sukhan* to whose praise and effects he devotes a section immediately after this episode.

But nothing of this episode's presentation of *sukhan* is peculiar to Bīdil. Its invocation of an elemental correspondence is at least as old as Ibn 'Arabī. To get at the specificity of Bīdil's attitude towards *sukhan* we may turn to how he formulated the Sufi theme of the superiority of gnosis or intuitive knowledge of the divine Real to dialectical or scholarly knowledge. His student and main hagiographer Khvushgū echoed this apologetics by presenting his teacher's early alienation from scholastic learning. Khvushgū writes that it was when, as a boy of eight in school, Bīdil witnessed two of his classmates squabbling over a point in Arabic grammar and finally coming to blows over it that his uncle, who also witnessed this, withdrew his nephew from school. His uncle remarked that: "the essence of humanity was dissolved" by such scholastic pettifoggery. Khvushgū: "Quitting the study of the Arabic sciences [*'ulūm-i 'arabiyyah*] from then on, he [i.e., Bīdil] cultivated the company of spiritually adept ascetics [*fuqarā-i sāḥib-kamāl*] and the study of distiches by the lords of spiritual states and words [*ash'ār-i arbāb-i ḥāl u qāl*]."[19] Regardless of how biographically accurate this report may be, what is relevant is that Khvushgū sees as worthy the substitution of scholarly disputation by "the company of spiritually adept ascetics" and speaks of this as continuous with "the study of distiches by the lords of spiritual states and words." In this contribution to the tradition of apologias for poetry inaugurated in Persian by Niẓāmī Ganjavī (d. 1209), then, *sukhan* displaced and rose above the petty egotism of dialectical learning by its formulation of intuitive knowledge, guided by Sufi masters, of the divine Real.

But this preference for *sukhan* as the verbal formulation of mystical states of being over scholarly debate should not be taken to mean a validation of undisciplined or formless expression. In his autobiography Bīdil presents a genealogy of and apologia for the formal elaborateness or the workliness of *sukhan* that is distinct to Niẓāmī's. He formulated this genealogy and apologia, as we will see, as a poetic response to a local reiteration in his North Indian milieu of a wider and older Sufi theological dispute. In the first section or Element of his autobiography he recounts a disagreement between two of his Sufi preceptors in Rānī Sāgar in his North Indian home province of Bihar.[20] One of them, Shāh Mulūk, adopts the practices of an extremist (*ghulluw*) and possibly antinomian tradition of Sufism by wandering naked and uttering ecstatic pronouncements (*shaṭḥ*). The other, Shāh Kamāl, calls for self-control as a distinguishing human trait, condemning such excesses and such frothing at the mouth as discourteous to the legacy of the prophets. These disputes may seem to some of us today like trivial quibbles over ritual minutiae. But they are, in fact, in line with a long Islamic tradition of Neo-Platonic concern with establishing the psychophysical conditions appropriate to one's recognition of one's own true self. Sufism was, in this sense, a tradition of ethical reflection on how embodied persons could best prepare themselves for self-recognition. Hinging therefore on the two divergent attitudes Bīdil describes amongst his two Sufi teachers, respectively, towards the permissibility or impermissibility of linguistic and corporeal signs – the one broadly permissive and the other broadly abstemious – were two distinct understandings of how ethical conduct yielded metaphysical insight. Shāh Mulūk conforms to the position the modern scholar Aḥsan al-Ẓafar identifies with the proponents of the doctrine of *vaḥdat al-vujūd* (Oneness of Being).[21] And Shāh Kamāl, as Aḥsan al-Ẓafar notes, appears to adhere to the rival group propounding *vaḥdat al-shuhūd* (Oneness of Witnessing). Both positions fundamentally entailed distinct if overlapping sets of assumptions on how human subjects related to the most Real. They therefore made distinct if overlapping sets of prescriptions on how human subjects were to conduct themselves with respect to this Real.[22] Bīdil himself refers to those who insist on the legal-moral necessity of restraint in signification as "musicians of knowledge in the assembly of witnessing" (*dānish-āhangān-i anjuman-i shuhūd*) while referring to himself at various points in his oeuvre as "one of those of oneness" (*az vaḥdatyānīm*).[23] Despite this self-identification, it is the ultimate difference Shāh Kamāl insists on between God and His creatures that forms the basis, as I will show below, for Bīdil's apologia for *sukhan*.

After Shāh Kamāl's criticism in Rānī Sāgar of ecstatic Sufi practice, Bīdil observes that Shāh Mulūk begins to drape himself in Shāh Kamāl's presence but reverts to nudity on his departure. Bīdil presents arguments in rhyming and elaborately metaphorical prose for both sides of this debate between "dervishes and the zealously abstinent" (*darvīshān va zāhidān*). Dervishes, exemplified by Shāh Mulūk, charge the zealously abstinent with a hypocritical, vain and fanatical concern with keeping up and enforcing pious appearances. The zealously abstinent, exemplified by Shāh Kamāl, criticize dervishes for being incapable in their ecstatic transports of heeding ethical injunctions (*takālīf-i shar'īah*) to proper conduct.

Immediately following this conclusion is a "subtle point" (*nuktah*). Bīdil typically uses this label throughout his autobiography to designate one of his counter-intuitive interventions or insights into an ontological matter. That he later compiled such subtle points into an independent collection titled *Subtle Points* (*Nikāt*) signals the importance he attached to them. Here, as often elsewhere, the subtle point allows Bīdil to mediate between rival positions in the foregoing debate. He offers a commentary on a *ḥadīs̱*, here a statement attributed to the Prophet Muḥammad, quoting a part of it, as was the convention, to stand for the whole: "I have with God an appointed hour" (*lī ma' allāh waqt*). The whole text of this Prophetic dictum appears with some variations in canonical Persian Sufi texts that he elsewhere lists as having read.[24] The fullest version of this dictum is: "I have with God an appointed hour [i.e., death] that neither His most proximate angel nor a messenger of God can help me evade."

Bīdil's entire commentary turns only on the word "with" separating "I" from "God" in the Arabic original:

> The point of this "with-ness" is the distinction between God and servant – that is, the comprehension of the status of two-ness and the discernment of the nature of I-ness and You-ness. In keeping with the distinction of this status he referred to the Absolute Unseen [*ghayb-i muṭlaq*] by the allusion [*ishārah*] of "general unity" [*aḥadiyyat*] and, to make apparent this result, through supplementary witnessing he brought forth the expression [*'ibārat*] "divine unity" [*vāḥidiyyat*].[25]

That is, Ibn 'Arabī or one or more of his interpreters or all of them taken together and referred to thus by the grammatically ambiguous "he" or "they" in this passage, distinguished between these two terms that both mean "unity." Chittick explains this difference by observing that whereas *aḥadiyya* refers to the unity of creatures with God without eliminating their servanthood, *vāḥid* – of which *vāḥidiyyat* is the substantive form – refers to none other than God and is one of His exclusive names in the Qur'ān.[26] On this point Ibn 'Arabī himself says:

> The Prophet said, "God is (*kān*) and no thing is with Him." The meaning is as follows: He is not accompanied by thingness, nor do we ascribe it to Him. Such is He, and there is no thing with Him. The negation of thingness from Him is one of His essential attributes, just as is the negation of "withness" (*ma'iyya*) from things. He is with the things, but the things are not with Him, since "withness" follows from knowledge: He knows us, so He is with us. We do not know Him, so we are not with Him.[27]

This distinction forms the basis of Bīdil's interpretation of the word "with" as a sign of the irreducible and hierarchical distinction between the Creator and his most favored human creature, between the most Real and its most accomplished human reality.

This was the very position that the founder in Mughal India of the Naqshbandiyyah Mujaddidiyyah Sufi lineage, Shaykh Aḥmad Sirhindī (1564–1624), had taken in his widely read letters. Explicitly anathematizing "the wicked heretics" who interpreted the expressions "dying to God" (*fanā*) and "subsisting in God" (*baqā*) as existential states, he insisted that these were in reality only states of perception or witnessing (*shuhūd*), not being (*vujūd*).[28] What was more real than these states was the abiding distance between God and human. "The servant is servant forever, and the Lord is Lord eternally," he wrote. This led him to uphold against the legal-moral laxity with which he charged the proponents of the "oneness of being" (*vaḥdat al-vujūd*) an insistence on adherence to the Sharī'ah. For to adhere to the ritual regimen of Islamic law was to practice the servant's submission to the divine master, bearing witness (*shuhūd*) to the Creator's ultimate transcendence of His creation. This is why Sirhindī and his votaries were called proponents of the "oneness of witnessing" (*vaḥdat al-shuhūd*). But what, we may ask, has all this to do with Bīdil?

The answer lies in the onto-theological status within this debate of signs. By aligning himself in the aforementioned commentary with what would have been recognized as Sirhindī's position, even as he identified himself as a proponent of the "unity of being," he appropriated both positions as an apologia for *sukhan*. He accomplished this by arguing that it was to bear witness to this *a priori* duality between Creator and creature by signifying it that Ibn 'Arabī or his tradition devised the allusion of "general unity" and the expression of "divine unity." On this interpretation, signs – both verbal and non-verbal – arise in response to the need to bear witness to a duality that founds creaturely mortality. Bīdil concludes that from the perspective of this duality Shāh Mulūk was insisting by his ecstatic unruliness on "negating the illusions of the limited entifications of the One" (*nafī-i awhām-i ta'ayyunāt*) while Shāh

Kamāl, by his insistence on decorum, was "establishing the nature of Oneness in the very order of Manyness" (*as̱bāt-i ẕāt-i_yek-tāyī dar 'ayn-i intiẓām-i kas̱rat*).[29] Both these positions were, he inferred, dependent on the hierarchical difference between the One and its supreme self-disclosure as the human subject – and so by extension on the signs by which this human subject signified the One. If the artifice of signs was a necessary creaturely recourse then so also were the artifices of clothing, ritual fasting and prayer. This is the heart of Bīdil's apologia for *sukhan*: the practice of workly language, of ingenious poetic artifice, is harmonious with Islamic orthopraxes as one of an ensemble of spiritual practices by which to testify to the distance that separates the world of creatures from what is most real. *Sukhan*, the verbal witnessing of the gap between Creator and creature, formed part of one's preparation for recognizing one's true self.

Bīdil's *Dīvān* includes two *ghazal*s with the end-rhyme (*qāfiyah*) *baḥs̱* or "disputation." The entirety of both *ghazal*s addresses the topos of the pettiness of scholarly disputation and advises against the damage it does to a Sufi ethics aimed at gnosis or an intuition of the most real. The *ghazal*s offer a succinct context in which to explicate his understanding of *sukhan*, so as a Sufi critique of scholastic knowledge, I will interpret the following three distiches from one of the *ghazal*s:

khwārī ast ba har kaj-mannish az rāst-ravān baḥs̱
bar khāk futad tīr chū gīrad ba kamān baḥs̱
dil shikva-yi ān ḥalqa-yi gīsū napasandad
har chand kunad āynah bā āynah-dān baḥs̱
jamī'at-i gawhar nakishad zaḥmat-i amvāj
bīdil ba khamūshān nakunand ahl-i zabān baḥs̱[30]

It's meanness for the cultivated to draw every crooked-natured fellow into disputation.
To the dust falls the arrow when it draws the bow into disputation.
The heart disapproves of the complaints of that ringlet of hair
Although the mirror disputes with the mirror-frame/knower.
The pearl's gathered intensity won't suffer waves.
Bīdil, speakers don't address the silent with disputation.

Noteworthy are the techniques by which Bīdil demonstrates the superiority of gnostic *sukhan* to scholasticism. The first distich makes a general claim in its first hemistich, using abstract nouns to make it. Its second hemistich exemplifies the claim of the first by a concrete analogy: that of the arrow that falls to the earth when it disputes with the bow. The is an instance of "the technique of exemplification" (*tarz-i tams̱īl*) widely popular among Speaking Anew poets, especially after Sā'ib Tabrīzī set authoritative examples of it. Ārzū, as Chapter 4 discusses, cited this technique as one that facilitated the comprehension of a distich's topos and so one that was avoided by those who sought to encrypt the topos instead. Bīdil's motivation in using it here is to make a poetic argument for the superiority of gnosis to scholastic dialectic by this concrete compound metaphor. But the metaphor does more than simply illustrate this idea. It discloses the relation between gnosis and scholastic dialectic as one in which the former suddenly and solitarily gains an advance on the latter.

The key image of the first hemistich of the second distich – the ringlet of hair – invokes both an image from the *ghazal*s of Ḥāfiẓ and a tradition of allegorical commentary on Ḥāfiẓ that was well developed by Bīdil's time. "Khatmī" Lāhorī, writing around 1617 in the same geographical region as Bīdil, composed what his renowned modern Ḥāfiẓ scholar-editor Bahā al-Din Khurramshāhī regards as the most useful of all commentaries on the *Dīvān* of Ḥāfiẓ. Bīdil's phrase "ringlet of hair" (*ḥalqa-yi gīsū*) occurs in near identical form in Ḥāfiẓ's *ghazal* 302 of Khatmī's commentary: "My ear and the friend's ringlet of hair./My face and the dust of the wine-seller's door."[31] Khatmī glosses "ringlet" thus:

> In [Sufi] terminology [this] is what they call "the firm rope" and also "the strongest handle." By "friend" is meant the noble guide who is the keeper of the aforementioned tavern who, in the second hemistich, he refers to as "wine-seller." Since, in the preceding distich, he had silenced the Sufi who had denied love with a conclusive proof in this couplet he inevitably encourages him to drink the wine of love, saying: since that wine will not come to hand without the assistance of the lofty guide of the tavern so, henceforth, it must be my ear and holding fast to the firm rope of the friend who is a means, my face and the expedient of the dust of that wine-seller guide.

In the context of this commentary the "ringlet of hair" in Bīdil's verse may now be glossed as symbolizing a tutelary gesture, here one that complains of or reproves the heart. The heart – a standard Sufi organ of intuition and conventionally symbolized by a mirror – disapproves of this teacher's reproof although, as the second hemistich implies, a mirror conventionally argues with its containing frame. That is, although a mirror seeks to slip out of its frame just as the Sufi's heart seeks to slip out of its corporeal container, this speaker's heart-mirror is antipathetic to argumentation. But Bīdil's arguably privileged meaning turns on a pun on *āynah-dān* that also translates as "mirror-knower," here referring to one who knows the heart or the Sufi preceptor whose ringlet of hair the disciple must hold on to. Such paronomasia was itself a technique called *īhām*, typically glossed in manuals of rhetoric as the use of a word or phrase with at least two meanings, one salient (*qarīb*) but less important and the other non-salient (*ba'īd*) but privileged by the poet. It had long been a conspicuous poetic technique of Sufi anagogy and Bīdil draws on it here to signal the superiority of intuition to intellection.[32]

The interlinear semantic connection (*rabṭ*) between the two hemistiches of the third and last distich turns on an implicit visual similarity between, respectively, the pearl's "gathered intensity" and silence, on the one hand, and the images of cresting waves and tongues curled in disputation on the other. Just as the gnostic pearl reposes in meditation far beneath the clamorous waves of the surface so do talkers spare the mystically silent their disputation.

If this *ghazal* is a synecdoche of Bīdil's vast *ghazal* oeuvre, it is in the sense that he seeks to present such *sukhan* as a series of technically masterful poetic "arguments." These were arguments for the social and epistemic superiority over other knowledges of an ascetically achieved intuition, in the tradition of Ibn 'Arabī's theistic monism, of what was most real. Such intuition was formulated in and transmitted by *sukhan*.

As to what *sukhan* as such a performance of sovereignty was responding to in the social world, we might begin by making the following observation: in a variety of overt and subtle ways the various scholarly and poetic projects of the Persianate elites of late Mughal Delhi register the strains on the Mughal court that was undergoing a dispersal of its formerly centered authority. Political authority in Mughal India had come to be dispersed into provincial fiefdoms, increasingly displaced after Aurangzeb (d. 1707) from the person of the emperor onto the nobility and crystallizing around powerful noblemen. Indeed, a prominent feature of the satire composed in Persian and Urdu in Mughal India of this period was its de-sacralization of the king's body and its attempts to capture in undignified fields of textual visibility the individual bodies of Mughal noblemen and women.[33] Exacerbating this erosion of royal authority from the late 1680s onward were the periodic Maratha raids from the Deccan into central Mughal territories and Jat insurrections in the region of Delhi. The later invasion of Delhi by Nādir Shāh of Iran in 1739 was perhaps only the most conspicuous of such assaults on Mughal sovereignty. It was such a Delhi that formed Bīdil's immediate readership and it was to this readership that his prose was immediately addressed.

This readership comprised three more or less overlapping circles of readers: the first imaginary and the second and third historically actual. In terms of their social identities and powers, hermeneutic abilities and locations, the three circles were: disciples imagined to be in training at a Sufi hospice; student-poets who were Mughal administrators of various ranks and frequented the poetry sessions at his home; and, finally, high-ranking courtly readers some of whom – like the emperor Aurangzeb himself and his Sufi intimate 'Āqil Khān "Rāzī," who was pay-master (*bakhshī*) and then governor (*ṣubah-dār*) of Delhi and secured Bīdil's career by mediating his access to the court – were littérateur grandees of the highest political status.[34]

The first of these circles was imaginary in the sense that no evidence exists to suggest that Bīdil was ever surrounded by disciples wholly engaged in nothing but Sufi practices. Nor did he ever inhabit a spatially distinct hospice that would conventionally have been the site of such relations. As we observed, he was buried in the courtyard of his own home and it was in this courtyard that his grave was venerated. However, his oeuvre – and especially his autobiography – adopts a conceit familiar in Sufi epistolography by assuming such an inner circle. Perhaps it was this conceit that allowed Central Asian readerships soon after his death to read his works as those of a hospice-based Sufi master. But no evidence exists of a historically actual readership of this sort in the Mughal Delhi of his lifetime.

The second circle which, in historical reality, mostly formed Bīdil's immediate readership included literati like Bindrāban Dās "Khvushgū" (d. 1756), Ānandrām "Mukhliṣ" (d. 1751) and Sirāj al-Dīn 'Alī Khān "Ārzū" (d. 1755) who transmitted Bīdil's poetry and authority to the third circle who, in turn, played a significant part in the dispersal of his works across social groups and to geographically far-flung places. This circulation of his writing depended on, and contributed to in turn, the broad Sufi ethos shared by individuals and groups across the two circles.

As in the case of some of his Indo-Islamic Sufi predecessors, the amenability of Bīdil's poetry to diverse interpretations and adaptations – its "polyphony" – can be accounted for by reference to this social diversity of reception.[35] Dargāh Qulī Khān, who visited Mughal Delhi from Hyderabad in 1738, that is eighteen years after Bīdil died, described how Ārzū who had been Bīdil's student in poetry annually organized a reading from Bīdil's *Dīvān* at his death anniversary or *'urs* (an Indian Sufi term cognate with the word *'arūs* for "bride" to signal the marriage of the saint's soul at death to God) on the third of the month of Safar in the Islamic calendar, a familiar memorial practice by which the living continued to benefit from the grace of dead Sufis. Over 100 of the city's foremost poets, including those who had been Bīdil's students, gathered in a circle around his grave to read from a manuscript of his collected works (*kulliyāt*) copied in his own "auspicious hand."[36] Among the most elite of his readers in the third circle was the pious emperor Aurangzeb who discovered ethico-spiritual import in Bīdil's poetry, quoting it in his letters to his sons one of whom, Muḥammad A'ẓam Shāh, employed Bīdil as superintendent (*darogha*) for twenty years.[37] Also in this high-ranking circle were Shukrullāh Khān, magistrate (*fawj-dār*) of Delhi and son-in-law to the aforementioned 'Āqil Khān, and his sons Shākir Khān and Mīr Karamullāh, all of whom long patronized the poet, bought him the house he lived in for thirty-six years until he died, were tutored by him in their poetry and corresponded extensively with him.[38]

Moving in between these two circles was the circle of those who held relatively minor Mughal offices but were better known as scholars and poets whose oeuvres were variously informed by Bīdil's teaching. This circle included individuals like his scholar-student Ārzū who, as I will demonstrate at length in Chapter 4, invoked rhetorical disciplines traditionally authoritative in Arabic in his Persian treatises in order to defend and authorize the oft-criticized difficulties of Bīdil's *ghazal* style. In addition to Ārzū were Bīdil's less known students, a significant number of them Hindus of Brahmin, Kāyastha, Khatri and Vaishya castes. One of them, the Mughal bureaucrat littérateur Bindrāban Dās "Khvushgū," referred to Bīdil with the panoply of reverential formulations characteristic of a Sufi disciple.[39] Another, Shiv Rām Dās "Ḥayā," composed a Persian prose description of the Braj region of Mathura and Vindravan whose geography was sacred to the popular Vaishnavite or Krishnaite piety of the region that was stylistically indebted to Bīdil's *The Four Elements*. Of this work and its author Khvushgū wrote:

> Having trained in his poetry under Mirzā Bīdil and received his pen-name from him, he speaks in his [i.e., Bīdil's] language. He wrote a prose work in the style [*ṭarz*] of the late Mirzā's *Chahār 'unṣur* called *Gulgasht-i bahār-i iram*. It describes the peculiarities of the Braj region – that is, the area of Mathura and Vrindavan [*bindrāban*] and all the special qualities of that land which is, in the religion of the Hindus [*mashrab-i hunūd*], the birthplace and the home of Krishna the avatar [*krishn-i avatār*], whom they consider the most perfect manifestation of the Infinite's attributes [*ṣifāt-i nāmutanāhī*]. I was delighted to read it.[40]

Lālā Ḥakīm Chand "Nudrat" (d. 1786?), yet another of Bīdil's Hindu students, composed a Persian *masnavī* translation of the tenth book of the *Bhāgvat Purānā* which narrates the life of Krishna, an incarnation of the god Vishnu. The rhetoric of this *masnavī* also suggests a debt to Bīdil's adaptation of Ibn 'Arabī's emanationist ontology in its conception of Krishna as a divine "manifestation" (*maẓhar*).[41]

These three social circles comprise Bīdil's implicit contemporaneous readerships. And yet, in keeping with Sufi precedent, Bīdil's oeuvre explicitly assumes only the first and imaginary kind of reader, that is, the disciple at the imaginary Sufi hospice. This is because Sufi convention assumed that it was only such a reader who could most radically achieve the ascetic aims of Sufi practice. Readers with this-worldly commitments, inevitably compromised in their asceticism, still discovered an orientation in such prose. The Sufi ethos shared by these identities also accounts for a trait of the rhetoric in the passage quoted earlier from *The Four Elements*, namely the impossibility of distinguishing between the metaphoricity and literalness of his sensory self-characterizations as a "whiff," an "un-drunken intoxication" and a "soundless melody." Bīdil, like all Sufis, seeks to *experience* the divine Real rather than only *know* it conceptually and discursively and so, in keeping with Sufi tradition, formulates such experiences in somatic terms.

Such somatic formulations refer not only to Bīdil's own experiences but are also aimed pedagogically at inducing a self-transformation in his reader-disciple who was normatively assumed to belong to the first of the three circles, that of the Sufi hospice. I will discuss the nature and functions of such Sufi reading practices with reference to a specific case in *The Four Elements* further on in this chapter. Here, to anticipate my discussion of this topic, I note that Sufis only undertook reading a revered text when, in the course of an apprenticeship to a Sufi preceptor, the apprenticeship had psychophysically oriented the disciple to the Real. It was at the end or in the course of such an apprenticeship that the Sufi undertook to read a text formulating disclosures of the Real. Such a reading was a reading with the body: the reader of *The Four Elements* would, in contemplating Bīdil's many failed attempts at intimacy with the divine Real, read it in the same somatic modes of wide-eyed astonishment and rolling-eyed drunkenness that characterized Bīdil's experience of the Real. This reader would be dispossessed of psychophysical self-control and re-constituted as no more than an effect of Bīdil's text just as Bīdil was no more than a psychophysical effect – a short-lived conjuncture of the four elements – of divine action.[42] We must recall that the four elements – fire, air, water and earth – formed what Islamic cosmologies such as Ibn 'Arabī's termed the world of "generation and corruption" (*kawn u fasād*). This was the world below the sphere of the moon – the sublunary world – that was constantly agitated by the mutually contrary motions of the spheres immediately around it, that of the seven planets which were observed to be moving (*al-kawākib al-sayyārah*) and that beyond it of the planets appearing stationary (*al-kawākib al-thābitha*).[43] Humans, like other creatures, were subject to these agitations. Yet, certain humans could master this agitation by the tempered practice of their ascetically achieved hidden or occult knowledge of the mimetic order connecting the twenty-eight letters of the alphabet to the twenty-eight lunar mansions. This group of humans thus formed a spiritual elite. Throughout *The Four Elements* Bīdil describes his theurgic powers to cure illnesses by writing amulets and poetry that numerically encoded auspicious planetary conjunctions. In his collection *Nikāt* (Subtleties), the seventh Subtlety (*nuktah*) advises his disciple-reader to exercise "moderation" (*i'tidāl*) in his asceticism (*riyāẕāt*) on the model of the prophets "none of whom practiced difficult asceticism except to the degree necessary for correcting the temperament [*mazāj*]."[44] The quatrain memorializing this advice states: "The body's foundation where the Names are at work/Remains standing a few days by wisdom of the soul [*ḥikmat-i ṭabi'ī*]./Don't strive overmuch at fasting and prayer for here/Balance in every matter is the perfection of Gnostics." The reference to "the body" here takes all creatures into its scope, as will be elaborated later. Here, it will suffice to note that, in keeping with Bīdil's "wisdom of the soul" or balanced mastery of his own body through his knowledge of the Names of God, his disciple Khvushgū lists the miraculous feats of strength his teacher was capable of at the height of his ascetic powers: wrestling a horse to the ground and rolling with it downhill, accidentally leaning on a wall and causing its collapse, beating a rider mounted on a thoroughbred in a race.[45] Evidently, Bīdil imagined himself to be a member of such a spiritual elite. His reader, by imitating Bīdil's practices, would come to enter the ranks of this elite and thus achieve, in turn, a brief mastery of the world of the four elements. This is the point at which the text's title – and my denomination of it as an "autobiography" – receives its justification: Bīdil is composed of the same intrinsically defective and mortal mixture of the four elements as all creatures. The logics of his self-presentation thus include all creatures in their scope. To the degree that his text presents so many instances of his brief mastery of this sphere of generation and corruption, he promises his disciple-reader similar command over all creatures. Surely, then, to all of his readers in politically threatened and socially strained late Mughal Delhi – from unnamed hospice disciple to storied courtly grandee – such Sufi asceticism was a paradigm of the will to power and a veritable metaphysics of sovereignty.

Surely, too, the rhymed and rhythmic prose of such asceticism was the linguistic register of the sovereign subject and signaled a mastery of "the world of generation and corruption."

Bīdil's stated spiritual-pedagogical aims and his participation – as evidenced in the passage quoted earlier – in Sufi rhetoric and practice should alert us to the peculiar sense in which this text constitutes an autobiography. Bīdil seeks to generously offer his Sufi reader an account of his own spiritual travails only insofar as these travails are imitative and imitable. It is because Bīdil sought to imitate the masters to whom he submitted himself that his disciple-reader might now hope to imitate Bīdil in turn by his intoxicated reading. This mimetic origin and aim imparts an iterative quality to the anecdotes which this text assembles, a quality that confronts most readers today with a particular stylistic difficulty. Dwelling on the reasons for this difficulty may furnish us with the hermeneutic expectations appropriate to Bīdil's account of his portrait. This is not a difficulty resulting from abstruse vocabulary since most of his lexicon derives from Persian literary and, particularly, Sufi traditions of prose and verse and thus assumes the reader to be conversant with this lexicon shared by several Sufi lineages. Indeed, where Bīdil introduces a technical term – typically from Ibn 'Arabī whose theophany everywhere informs Bīdil's thought – that he supposes this reader may not be familiar with or adequately comprehend, he glosses it at length.[46] Rather, the stylistic difficulty in question arises from the tension between his commitment, on the one hand, to writing of the particular events, experiences and encounters he underwent and, on the other, his commitment to simultaneously interpreting them as bearing an archetypal or mythic significance transcending their dateable and nameable particularity.

In this tension originates the difficulty Bīdil's modern reader must first confront at the level of the smallest unit of his language-use, the semantic level of the sentence: the mythic or archetypal character of the compound metaphors with which he articulates his references to particular, indexically named and sometimes dated events and experiences. He seeks, by this use of compound metaphors at this semantic level, to assimilate any particular event or experience – narrated at the discursive level of the larger linguistic unit of the anecdote – to the generality of a myth. I will confine myself to two examples, the first being the simultaneously historical and mythical figure of "Anūp Chhatr" himself. This proper name bore a historical referent several of whose paintings survive with his inscription. Som Prakash Verma thus notes in his entry on him in his *Mughal Painters and their Work: a Biographical Survey and Comprehensive Catalogue*:

> Anūp Chhatr seems to have begun his work at Shāh Jahān's court. At some stage he joined Dārā Shukoh's establishment, for min[iature] 6, a portrait of a lady in Dārā Shukoh's harem, is ascribed to "Rāi Anūp Chhatr Dārā Shukohi." He may well have received the title *Rāi* from his princely master. If so, its absence in later inscriptions is explained, for titles given by that Prince would not have been used after his fall.

> It would seem from miniatures nos. 1, 3–9 that portraiture was the forte of this painter. Fine lines and thin shading are characteristic of his drawings. In portrait-painting he prefers a flat background and the central figure is executed in a contrasting pigment.[47]

This entry corresponds in name, dates and description to the eponymous painter Bīdil describes as having painted his portrait around 1087/1677. And yet, Bīdil refers nowhere to the empirical particularity of the portrait or painter. Rather, he opens his description of Anūp Chhatr by declaring that "Mānī's soul, dust-dark, turned the color of his quill's dust and Bihzād's nature, in honor's veil, drew shame's dust upon itself at his skill."[48] These clauses – their mythic generality and interchangeability signaled by their end-rhymes – underscore that Anūp Chhatr becomes worthy of such mention not because he departs from his own two familiar mythic archetypes but because he excels them: Mānī (d. *c.*277), the Babylonian founder of Manichaeism, who was imagined in Firdawsī's *Shāhnāmah* (Book of Kings, *c.*339–400/1009–10), Niẓāmī's *Iskandarnāmah* (Alexander-book, *c.*586/1191) and poets in the Persian tradition after them as a painter and false prophet famed for his illusionistic paintings,[49] and the painter of Timurid Herat, Kamāl al-Dīn Bihzād (d. 941–42/1535–36), whom the Mughals had exalted to the status of a paradigmatic painter by this period.[50] Understanding the significations of this ekphrastic episode within its autobiographical frame therefore requires us to ask, not what kind of portrait the historical Anūp Chhatr probably painted, but how – or in what terms – the fact that he painted Bīdil's portrait at all comes to be formulated by Bīdil as autobiographically meaningful. To this question of the autobiographical significations of Bīdil's portrait – this chapter's orienting question – we will return at length.

A second example: when, in the course of the second Element, Bīdil borrows a private anthology of treatises by Sufi predecessors from his teacher Ḥaẓrat Shāh and gains his permission to copy and thus grow intimate with it, he adds a preface and verse afterword to it.[51] This afterword, quoted at length in this subsection of the second Element, reveals that reading the manuscript is pragmatically valuable only to those who already seek esoteric meaning or confirmation of truths already known. It is after spending time face to face with Ḥaẓrat Shāh and his companions that Bīdil becomes epistemically and ethically prepared to read a text venerated as a scented and flowering garden for its physical proximity to Sufi elders. And this prior orientation, in turn, determines that he treats every letter in the book as a symbolic short-hand for familiar moral lessons, warnings and virtues: the vertical stroke of the *alif* with which the Perso-Arabic alphabet begins symbolizes the upward yearning for transcendence and, after passing by way of interpretation through each intermediate letter, the concluding curve of the *ye* symbolizes writing's dissatisfaction with its own inadequacy to its divine referent, signaling this dissatisfaction by attempting to re-begin by curving back towards the beginning *alif*. The most likely paradigm for this instance of the occult Islamic "science of letters" (*'ilm al-ḥurūf*) was Ibn 'Arabī's *Kitāb al-Alif* (The Book of Alif) which articulated its author's theistic monism with a letter symbolism in which the Arabic alphabet's first letter, the vertical stroke *alif*, was already inscribed into all the letters that followed it as God was already contained in his creaturely manifestations.[52] Bīdil offers a condensed iteration of this topos in one of his *ghazal* distiches: "Love's self-praising mouth created unity./ In the quill-point of its mouth did our *mīm* contain an *alif*."[53] The reference is to the letter *mīm* in the Perso-Arabic alphabet that is made up of a circle joined to a vertically dropped *alif*-like stroke. Love, Ibn 'Arabī and Bīdil's cosmogonic force by which the phenomenal Many issue from the One, retains its unity even in multiplicity just as the letter *mīm*, appearing near the alphabet's end, still contains its beginning *alif*. Those of us today who read this autobiography seeking the particularity of Bīdil's individual experience must recognize that none of this is new to any reader familiar with how medieval Muslim, Jewish and Christian mystics read: an attitude towards reading as a confirmation of already known truths, as a resolution of familiar doubts and as an experience of the traces of a divine and absolute Author who generates a text in which, in Borges's words with reference to medieval Jewish Kabbalists, "the collaboration of chance was calculable as zero" and who thus saturates even the alphabet with His intentions.[54]

Myths for the Sufi reader

By such generalizing assimilations Bīdil's purported Sufi reader would read the episodes in Bīdil's life mythically while also learning to himself apply such a mythicizing hermeneutic to other texts and experiences. Just as there is no first time in myth so, too, is there no first time in Bīdil's life. This is why Bīdil composed in all but two genres of Persian prose – history (*tārīkh*) and biographical dictionary (*tazkirah*). Our observations on his mythicizing imperative allow us to explain these exceptions by arguing that these two genres would have committed him to chronological sequence and thus to temporal particularity. Indeed, this is why his *bayāẓ* or personal notebook of selected verses, too, ranks *ghazal*s composed in the same meter and rhyme not by chronology but aesthetic judgment as to which poet he regarded as having composed the best *ghazal* in that meter-and-rhyme scheme.[55] It is this persistent ahistoricism that also explains why, in *The Four Elements* too, none of his experiences unfold except as an iteration of the experiences of others famous in Islamic history or named by Bīdil as his teachers. They are "his" experiences only in this provisional sense that his iterations of them are the latest. Recognizing this iterative quality leads the reader to experience a blurring of Bīdil's identity with those of his teachers. These teachers include named men he meets face to face in geographical locations still extant on the North Indian map as well as those he encounters in dream-visions after their deaths or in their physical absence. Like Ibn 'Arabī and 'Abd al-Raḥmān Jāmī (d. 1492, Herat), Ibn 'Arabī's most widely diffused interpreter in Mughal North India, Bīdil becomes an author by ventriloquizing for teachers.[56] If he is yet distinguishable by a proper name, as his teachers were, it is because he strives to become a worthy ventriloquist for their voices.

We may distinguish three discursive levels on which Bīdil's teachers lay down patterns for him (or perhaps, authoritatively reiterate previously laid down patterns for him): at the level of the sentence or the semantic level; at the level of the anecdote or the discursive level; and at the level of *The Four Elements* itself, or at the narratological level. On the semantic level Bīdil's conformity to patterns is already evident in the quote from his preface where he speaks of his autobiography as a generous "unveiling" of "the countenance of diminutions and growths." This is a stock metaphor of the world as a bride unveiled. Elsewhere he submits apparently diverse experiences to a relatively small stock of compound metaphors drawn from semantic fields long familiar in Persian literature: drinking-parties, book-making and writing-equipment, physiology, horsemanship, painting, the alphabet and so forth. On the discursive level the ekphrastic anecdote under discussion partially conforms in its plot to the Sufi poet Rūmī's (d. 1270) initial refusal to be painted, followed by his excess in relation to any of the many portraits made of him.[57] I analyze this episode at length further on in this chapter and cite it here in brief only as an instance of a pattern on the discursive level. Some further instances of patterns on this level: an anecdote presenting a discussion of the ethical and ontological value of the opposed somatic states of sleep versus waking[58] conforms in the positions its interlocutors take to well-attested models in Islamic philosophical discourses on dreaming. An anecdote presenting disputations over doctrinal differences over the legal-moral validity of *ghulluw* or ecstatic Sufi practices versus sober self-control[59] rehearses familiar debates internal to Sufi traditions. Anecdotes presenting the thaumaturgical practices of traveling seated on water and curing the sick by breathing charms and poetry on them both have precedents in Sufi hagiographical literature on miracles.[60] Finally, on the narratological level, the most conspicuous pattern is that of the four chapters or "Elements" into which all the anecdotes are gathered, the text as a whole microcosmically replicating the primordial and long-familiar macrocosmic constellation of fire, air, water and earth.[61]

On all three levels these patterns furnish Bīdil and his presumed reader with myths for speech and action.[62] Reading the ekphrastic episode under discussion – like reading *The Four Elements* as a whole – with an attention to signs of Bīdil's individuality and self-determination must thus confront the resistance posed by its conformity to these mythic paradigms that constrain such individuality and self-determination.

The portrait

It is this mythicizing vector, then, that leads Bīdil to frame his ekphrastic anecdote with a distinction familiar from the Qur'ān and earlier Persian literature: whereas God alone acts independently and creates the world without technology, humans depend on Him for their actions and create what they do only by laboring to achieve a mastery of technology. And such action and mastery, Bīdil argues, misleads humans into the vanity of taking themselves for autonomous actors although they are, in truth, only ever mediums for divine action. Here he follows the precedent of 'Abd al-Raḥmān Jāmī who, in the third chapter of his *masnavī Yūsuf u zulaykhā* (1483), cites Qur'ān 6:76 on the Prophet Abraham's refusal to persist in his love for stars that set. This Qur'ānic exemplum confirms, in a word-play alluding to Jāmī's own affiliation to the Naqshbandī Sufi lineage, that despite the continually "renewed image" (*tāzah naqshī*) the planets presented to the eye by their various powers over and effects on the earth, they were unworthy of being "creators" (*naqshbandī*) in and of themselves for their command of such powers was derivative.[63] This primordial distinction in *The Four Elements*, probably inherited from Jāmī, that was first formulated in the preface to this Element[64] and again in this episode's opening passage, proleptically submits the subsequent account of Anūp Chhatr's portrait of Bīdil to a certain interpretation of human action and technology. On this interpretation, cosmicized in a *ghazal* fragment (*qiṭa'*) of nine distiches, creatures fail to comprehend their ultimate cause, mistaking their proximate causes for the ultimate one: the gardener forgets that it is rain and not his watering that causes a plant to grow; the mother cannot account by her womb for the fetus's miniscule transformations; the oyster dries out with astonishment at how a pearl knotted up in it without a thread; the ocean wonders why it sweats; and the sky why it cries.[65] This mistake defines the operation of the intellect (*'aql*) as an entrapment in proximate or secondary causes (*asbāb*). And technology, on this interpretation, prosthetically extends the intellect's entrapment in an exploration of secondary causality. To this, Bīdil opposes an "absorption in a place of bewilderment" (*mahv-i ḥayrat-khānah*). To comprehend "a little of this mystery" of the ultimate cause anterior to all technology is to become human. I should add in passing here that one of the aims of this interpretation of Bīdil's ekphrastic episode is to understand the sense in which, in Bīdil's thought, becoming human entails a comprehension of what traverses but exceeds the human.

Already interpreted by this critique of a rational investigation of causality, Bīdil's subsequent account of Anūp Chhatr's mastery of the skills of coloring (*rang-āmīzī*), drawing (*siyāh-qalamī*) and design (*gardah*) implicitly assigns them a morally ambivalent significance. They are positive signs of his miraculous status as a confidant of divine mysteries since his skills, Bīdil notes, excel all other known miracles (*mu'jizāt*). But they are also negative ones of his entrapment in a technologically exacerbated intellectual dependence on secondary causality. However, the negative significations come to be borne out only at the episode's end. At this point in the episode, Anūp Chhatr's painted images are simply described in a *ghazal* fragment as supra-real: his candle lights lamps and his moth-wing burns till the Day of Judgment; his drawn trees burgeon and bend with spring fruit; and the singing parrot of his magical theater never misses a note.[66] That is, his visual representations excel their mortal and defective originals in longevity and perfection of form. This, too, has a mythic antecedent in the Persian literary ideal of fiction's diegetic world as an inorganic and therefore immortal and superior simulation of organic and mortal beings.[67] This genealogy of fiction as an immortally famous verbal perfection of defective and mortal models is hardly peculiar to Persian and may be generalized to several traditional literary cultures – Sanskrit and Latin among them – wherein art relates to life as an idealization intended to immortalize both its maker and its model by fame. And it is in the form of such inorganic immortality that Anūp Chhatr, a long-time acquaintance of Bīdil, seeks to memorialize him, seeking his permission to paint his portrait in order "to create a bewildering text as a memorial [*nuskhah-i ḥayratī ba yādgār pardāzad*]." Bīdil would thus be perfected by being fictionalized in a portrait. That he denominates this painting a "text" (*nuskhah*) anticipates its later significance when we learn that, of this painting, only Bīdil's verbal description remains, this description thus assimilating the painting's characteristics of a bewildering memorial.[68]

At this point, however, he resists such fictionalization by refusing the painter permission: "Since the frivolity of such preoccupations did no more than polish amusement's mirror, the colorlessly traced self [*ṭabī'at-i bī-rangī*], barely sipped from favor's cup." And he adds in the course of a quatrain: "He to whom a deed is calamitous in origin [*aṣl*]/What pleasure might he derive from wandering a derivative's [*far'*] garden?" The technical references here to painting bear reflection. The "colorless tracing" (*bī-rang*) by which he metaphorizes his own self refers to the outline traced through perforated paper with charcoal pounce. It thus designated the *ṭarḥ* – a master artist's design or foundational drawing to which color was later added, often by junior painters in the workshop. It was this foundational drawing that formed, if the painting was inscribed, the empirical locus of the painting's authorship. As Gregory Minissale says:

> The composition of a picture in Mughal Indian art begins with *ṭarḥ*.... The main lesson to draw from this excursus into *ṭarḥ* is that it was treated as the superior aspect of image-making, reserved for senior artists and valued highly, much like the art of calligraphy, which similarly placed emphasis on proportion, line, and the relationship of parts to the whole in an overall pattern. *Ṭarḥ* was clearly related to the arrangement or grouping of figures and it was at this stage that proportional relationships were also worked out. This is undoubtedly because *ṭarḥ* is related to the art of writing in terms of proportion, unity, geometric precision and visual beauty, as opposed to merely coloristic charms.[69]

In formulating his refusal to grant his painter acquaintance permission to paint his portrait, Bīdil calls himself a "colorless tracing," reiterating his use of this image in his preface to *The Four Elements*:

> Since the purpose of the writing of these levels of the elemental quill is to set in order the intoxication with the world of possibility [*tartīb-i nash'a-i imkānī*], and the faintly traced outline [*gardah*] of the picture of these truths of the page of egotism [*man u mā*] is to compose a corporeal text [*tarkīb-i nuskhah-i jismānī*], wisdom ... distinguished it by naming it *The Four Elements*".[70]

The internally rhymed and balanced clauses of this sentence alert us to a semantic relation between "to set in order the intoxication with the world of possibility" and "to compose a corporeal text." This text constitutes the potentiality of a body that is a colorless tracing of Bīdil's nature. So, when Bīdil eventually yields to Anūp Chhatr's importunity and lets himself be painted, the resulting portrait is not only a picture within a picture, an instance of the *mise en abyme* so frequent in Mughal painting,[71] but also a deterioration from "the superior aspect of image-making" – the ideality and higher reality of a colorless geometric tracing when he was yet only a "possibility" – into the second-order reality of attributes or "coloristic charms."

Models of visuality

The valuation of the linear geometry determining the relative positions of bodies in the field of vision as superior to the bodies themselves aligns with a much older Islamic optical tradition, studied by Hans Belting and discussed with reference to Bīdil later in this essay, which subordinated the explanation of seen bodies to a theory of perception.[72] For now, it should suffice to note that the creation in the Islamic world of a theory of perception to the exclusion of what Belting calls "a theory of pictorialization" accorded with Bīdil's particular appropriation of Ibn 'Arabī's concept of theistic monism, called the "oneness of being" (*vaḥdat al-vujūd*) by his commentators. As Chittick notes, this concept has frequently been misunderstood to designate a kind of pantheism. But whereas pantheism entails the thesis that God inheres in all things and that all things are thus equally real, Ibn 'Arabī's "oneness of being" signified the unreality of all things except God.[73] The "unity" in question thus implies an equal unreality of all things with respect to the originating, limitless and divine Real that discloses itself in the forms of all things but, by this very self-limitation in form, conceals itself from our perception. Things, as Bīdil recurrently and variously formulates them throughout his voluminous corpus of *ghazal*s, are united in the simultaneous self-disclosure and self-concealment of the Real.[74] The blind, by this rationale that plays on Qur'ān 6:50, are equivalent to the seeing.[75] It is the optical logic governing his perception of the divine Real as a possibly delimited and therefore defective appearance of this Real that mainly concerns him rather than the nature of appearances themselves.

This explains the recurrence and significance of what Minissale calls the technique of the *mise en abyme* – literally "put into the abyss" – by which Mughal painting suggests the abyssal quality of the visible world. Replicating the literary technique of the *mise en abyme* found in Persian *ma̱snavī*s, a Mughal painting often duplicated itself within its pictorial world to induce a sense of the unreality of the visible universe through an infinite regress from frame to frame. Replicating such paintings, in turn, by his use of painting metaphors, Bīdil imputes a defective reality to his brilliantly detailed portrait by Anūp Chhatr even as he sets it within his autobiography's "faintly traced outline." Minissale:

> Simply put, the clue to the logic of the *mise en abyme* here may be found as long ago as Porphyry who reports that Plotinus was supposed to have refused to have a portrait painted of himself, objecting to the notion that he must consent to leave, as a desirable spectacle for posterity, "an image of an image." Plato's concept of an image "three times removed from reality" was certainly one that both Western and Islamic traditions are familiar with.[76]

This is why the theologically motivated iconoclasm of Persian visual culture took the form, not so much of a proscription on images as such, but of an anti-illusionism inscribed into the very aesthetics of image-making.

An anecdote from Shams al-Dīn Aḥmad Aflākī's (d. 1360, Anatolia) *Manāqib al-'ārifīn* (Virtues of the Gnostics), the foundational hagiography of Sufis of the Mevlevi order, on a painter's attempts to paint a portrait of the famous Sufi and poet Mawlānā Jalāl al-Dīn Rūmī (d. 1270) gives us an antecedent to Bīdil's iconoclasm-as-anti-illusionism. Here is Priscilla Soucek's plot summary:

> The … incident concerns a portrait Ayn al-Dawla paints of Mevlana himself at the request of one of the holy man's ardent admirers, Gurji Khatun, wife of the Seljuq ruler of Anatolia. She wishes to have a painting of Mevlana as a memento to console her when she is separated from him. To please her, her husband commissions Ayn al-Dawla to draw and paint such a portrait on a sheet of paper. Mevlana gives the painter permission to draw him. The artist puts his pen to the paper and produces an exquisite image, but when he compares it to Mevlana, the latter's appearance seems to have changed. He then takes a second sheet and makes another sketch, but each time that he captures Mevlana's image the latter seems to change. Finally after making twenty sketches he abandons his attempt to re-create an accurate likeness of Mevlana. On seeing the result of Ayn al-Dawla's efforts Mevlana compares himself to the limitless, ever-changing sea which cannot be immobilized. Gurji Khatun, however, accepts the paintings and takes solace in their contemplation.[77]

Gurji Khātūn settles for images only after they have been shown to be inadequate to their referent, after their character as illusions has been foregrounded. Their referent, Rūmī, exceeds any frozen portrayal of himself like a shoreless and shifting sea, a familiar characterization of the Qur'ān and thus suggesting that he has textualized himself on a Qur'ānic model. Equally at play here is Ibn 'Arabī's ontological idea of "the renewal of similars" (*tajaddud-i amsāl*), the idea that each body was substituted at each instant by another like itself by the divine One in whose essence all bodies were already contained.[78] The unperceptive, like 'Ayn al-Dawla, failed to glimpse these shifts though those who could, like Rūmī himself in this anecdote, could train the gaze of those who could not. It is by displaying his ever-shifting excess in relation to his portraits that Rūmī is imagined as having imparted this teaching. Like the infinite interpretations the Qur'ān generates, Rūmī's face enables his frozen portraits and yet exceeds them, their number – twenty – standing rhetorically for a shifting copiousness. As such, this anecdote would seem to contradict the illusionism at work in Bīdil's text since he marvels for ten years at the portrait from which he says he could not distinguish his mirror-image. But we will have to read Bīdil's anecdote to its end to recognize how it replicates Rūmī's anti-illusionistic iconoclasm at its end.

The portrait's correspondence to Bīdil's illness and recovery

At end of that decade, in 1099/1688, "in keeping with human infirmity, an illness overcame [my] helpless powers and, for seven months, laid me as low as the dust like a shadow." Here, with light and later amplified commentary, is what follows: Bīdil's friends visit him in his sickbed and one of them looks through his personal anthology of texts for a cure, presumably since he earlier and later describes such medicinal and apotropaic applications of his poetry. In leafing through this book he comes upon the portrait and exclaims in dismay at its faded colors. Bīdil, gazing at it in his illness, can barely make out its colors or image. Its eye-pupil has leaked into the surrounding blackness, its eyelashes have fallen away and its lips and mouth have all but vanished.[79] When he recovers his health, he returns to the painting to see why it had faded. This is what then occurs:

> All at once, like a lantern they uncover in a dark house from beneath a skirt or a lid lifted from a heated censer, the witness of the tent of the Unseen [*ghayb*] rent complacency's veil and, with a thousand rays, beauty's lightning beamed out. It was as if Bīdil, without a speaking tongue, was speaking and a departed spring, unveiling itself anew, was a smiling dawn.[80]

That is, the portrait has recovered its colors, disclosing this like a sudden stimulus to the eye or nose. The intensity of this stimulus seems to duplicate Bīdil in his portrait since he likens it to the negation of the conventional dumbness of pictures by a speaking image of himself. By this, the "witness of the tent of the Unseen rent complacency's veil." The familiar and mythicizing metaphor is that of a mystic-lover spying on or "witnessing" his divine Beloved, catching a blinding glimpse of Him in a state in which He is absent to the senses. Bīdil's word for this witness – *shāhid* – also means "martyr" just as the word 'martyr' itself also means 'witness' in Greek. Witnessing or looking and martyrdom or blinding coincide in Bīdil's rediscovery of his portrait as they do in several of his *ghazal* verses. The imagery and epistemic signification of a sudden sensory stimulus also recalls an earlier moment from the second Element when he describes the sudden advent of intuitive knowledge of the Real as a "helpless sneeze" that comes to him after a long period of smelling flowers which, in this metaphor, formulates attention to the bodies of the imaginal world.[81] Awareness of what is most real comes rarely and briefly as a shock to the body. The hairs stand on end on the bodies of Bīdil's friends. Never having experienced anything similar in the created or painted world, they find themselves unable to look further at the picture or hear anything more of it and collectively exclaim: "What calamity is this?" and "From where did this storm arise?" On recovering from his illness, he cannot bear to contemplate the painting again and tears it to bits, burying the bits in the ground. The formulaic phrase by which he describes this iconoclastic action – "I reduced it to a collar-rending" (*ba chāk-i garībān rasānīdam*) – cites the ecstatic Sufi practice of tearing one's own shirt or those of fellow practitioners open during a collective mystical transport. Specifically, the phrase cites Rūmī's formulation of the same spiritual practice: "If you seek the soul [*rūḥ*], rend your shirt, O boy/So you may swiftly attain purity./A Sufi is he who seeks purity/Not by woolen clothes, tailoring and fine patterning."[82] By his careful phrasing, Bīdil thus solicits an interpretation of his rending of his portrait as an action that is simultaneously iconoclastic and self-purifying, ridding him of his superficial attributes so he may become a Sufi. He and his friends then find themselves compelled by this "miracle of the world of the singular" (*jahān-i bī-chunī*) to admit to weakness as a condition traversing all creations, sentient and insentient.

Bīdil concludes this episode with a simultaneously self-effacing and self-aggrandizing set of statements that replicate his self-authorizing performance of self-effacement at the end of a subsequent episode in the same Element. There, he unintentionally and by his God-given powers brings a maid in his household back to life after she dies of an incurable illness. When witnesses praise him for this miracle (*khāriq*, *karāmat*), he briefly grows proud of his powers but then, admonishing himself, explains the event away with ostentatious modesty as no more than a fantasy (*tavahhum*).[83] Here, he argues: "The degrees of preparedness [*isti'dād*] are the manifestation of the mirror of the subtleties of the Invisible." "Preparedness" must be innate or given to be cultivated or else not even the best cultivation will improve a creature. The instances he cites of such "preparedness" suggest that he employs the word in line with Ibn 'Arabī and Jāmī to signify the soul's predisposition or preparedness to serve as a frame for the Real's self-disclosure: the natural generativity of even cut plants, the persistent natural barrenness of even watered salt-fields or the uncoerced natural lushness of fertile land.[84] His conclusion to the ekphrastic episode thus adds an item to this list of naturally generative creations: "Thus the truth of that portrait [*taṣvīr*] is among the distinctions of the Bīdilian nature [*az khavāṣ-i ṭīnat-i bīdilīst*] even as Bīdil, in the manner of a painted person, is bereft of the essence of awareness like the gleam of the eye's lights that is a ray of the pupil's traces even as the pupil remains bewildered in a veil of blackness."[85] The portrait was an unconscious effect of Bīdil's inner disposition (*ṭīnat*) just as the eye's pupil is unaware of the luminous rays it emits towards the selected object. But who, we should ask, selects the object? The answer, not formulated by Bīdil, must be: the Real. If the portrait shared an iconic relation with Bīdil's nature to fade or flare in keeping with his health it was not through Bīdil's active intention but by virtue of his God-given and unconsciously active "predisposition." But this also implies that it was God who, after limiting and thus concealing Himself in the form of Bīdil, gave His own delimited form the unconscious predisposition to select to participate iconically in the nature of a painted image of itself. That is, if the appearances of the Real are at least partly constituted by the human imagination and if humans themselves are constituted by the Real, then it must follow that the Real discloses and conceals itself *to* itself in the effects of the human imagination. God's cosmos constitutes a gigantic *mise en abyme*, as Minissale has suggested.[86]

This is the sense in which we may understand the importance to Ibn 'Arabī and his tradition of Allah's statement as Muḥammad transmits it in the famous Tradition (*ḥadīs̱*): "I was a hidden treasure and loved to be known." Ibn 'Arabī:

> That is, because one's self seeing is not like one's seeing oneself in another, which serves as a mirror for the seer. (The reason for this preference) is that the mirror reveals to the seer himself in a shape which is given by the substrate (*maḥall*) which one observes. If such a substrate does not exist and does not appear to the seer, he cannot see himself.[87]

This statement echoes Bīdil's own argument in his *mas̱navī 'Irfān*, his longest and most complex cosmogony that he completed in 1712 and was thus composing during the same years as he composed *The Four Elements*. In an early passage of this *mas̱navī* he argues for the necessity of bodies (*hiyulā, jism*) as signs (*naqsh*) by which the intellect (*'aql*) begins to grasp the coming into being or manifestation (*namū, shuhūd, ẓuhūr*) of the One in the Many.[88]

The heretical suggestion of metempsychosis

However, what distinguishes Bīdil's relation to the body of his own portrait from Rūmī's reported relation to the portraits of himself is that, unlike in Rūmī's case, the portrait itself changes in keeping with Bīdil. Rūmī's portraits are unambiguously frozen in comparison to his shifting appearance and thus dead. But Bīdil's portrait comes and stays alive in keeping with him. In terms of Bīdil's own explanation for this – namely that this was an unwitting effect of "the Bīdilian nature" (*ṭīnat-i bīdilī*) – this event suggests the possibility that his soul co-inhabited more than one body at once; his own body as well as that of the painting which, being mirror-like, was a duplication of his. There is here a suggestion of metempsychosis or the transmigration of the soul from one body to another (*tanāsukh*) that Bīdil would develop at greater length and with doctrinal specificity in his *mas̱navī 'Irfān*. It does not lie within the scope of this chapter to recount the reasons why metempsychosis has always been condemned as heretical in most Sunni and Shi'i traditions, only developing into a full-fledged ontology in radically marginal Islamic sects. A discussion of this heresy will form part of the topic of Chapter 3 that interprets Bīdil's *'Irfān*. Here, it should suffice to observe that Bīdil's cautiously creative adoption of this doctrine in that *mas̱navī* finds its echo here in his destruction of the body of his portrait double. By this action he conformed to such iconoclastic forbears as Rūmī but not without having claimed the reality of metempsychosis within the cautious brevity of an anecdote.

An excursus on the imaginal world of the body

What is the physiology and optics by which Bīdil explains the portrait as an effect of his own nature? In an earlier sub-section of the fourth Element, Bīdil discusses the body (*jism*) as "the Unbounded Interval" or "the Unbounded Imagination": "Thus, in truth, the body [*jism*] is the Universal Imagination [*barzakh-i kullī*] rays of whose real traces [*āsār-i vuqū'ī*] beam on these imaginal [*khiyālī*] places, and it sees the forms of its desired objects [*muqtazīyāt*] in this mirror."[89] The term *barzakh* which literally means "isthmus" conveys more than one technical sense in Ibn 'Arabī's cosmogony. Although "Universal Imagination" does not occur in Ibn 'Arabī's own terminology and maybe a term that Bīdil inherited from an unnamed commentator in Ibn 'Arabī's tradition, the context of Bīdil's use of the term allows us to explicate it. It here refers to bodies in general as imagined beings co-composed of relatively determined and shifting combinations of the spiritual (*laṭīf*) and corporeal (*kasīf*). These terms designate endpoints on a continuum of creations ranging between non-existence and *vujūd*, the being God bestowed on beings by disclosing Himself to Himself. The "soul" that, in this context, designates the totality of an individual's abilities to know as such, brings everything spiritual or intelligible and corporeal or sensible together through the imagination. To *know* beings by the imagination is also to grow conscious of or "find" God in His self-manifestations, this "finding" self-consciously at play in the Arabic trilateral root W-J-D shared by the words for "being" – *vujūd* – and "finding."[90] In this passage quoted from Bīdil, "the Universal Imagination" (*barzakh*) thus designates the corporeal which, as in Ibn 'Arabī, is interchangeable with the "imaginal" (*khiyālī* or *misālī*). William C. Chittick glosses this sense of *barzakh* in Ibn 'Arabī thus:

> The term designates intermediate reality, everything that shares the qualities of two sides, anything that needs to be defined in terms of other things. When imagination is understood in this broad sense, nothing in the cosmos escapes its ruling property. It is synonymous with *barzakh* or isthmus, a term that is applied to any intermediary reality ... the Shaykh more commonly employs the terms imagination and *barzakh* to refer to the domain that is intermediate between spirits and bodies, though he does not forget that spirits and bodies themselves belong to the realm of the Unbounded Imagination, so they can never escape the characteristic of intermediacy.[91]

The comprehensiveness of this sense of the imagination is closely related, for Bīdil, to the comprehensiveness of poetry's field of reference: "The *barzakh* of the subtle [*laṭīf*] and gross [*kasīf*] worlds He presented to awareness [*ba 'arz-i ash'ār āvardah*]."[92] In his punning original phrasing of "presented to awareness,, Bīdil exploits, as others had done before him, the common Arabic root underlying the word *ash'ār* for "to make known" and for "distiches." *shu'ūr* for "awareness" and *shā'ir* for "knower" or "poet." In speaking as a poet, Bīdil serves as God's medium for the "presentation" – rather than re-presentation – in the bodies of signs of the whole cosmos between non-existence and *vujūd*. His linguistic signs become the site of a theophany and he, through his imagination, implicitly embodies God's self-disclosure, undergoing a theosis arrested only by the epistemic unreliability of the imagination.

In what sense is the imagination epistemically unreliable? Answering this requires us to know that epistemic reliability, for Bīdil as for the tradition of Sufi metaphysics to which he belonged, designated perceiving "things as they are" (*ashyā kamā hiyāh*). The complete form of this Arabic phrase is a statement or Tradition attributed to the Prophet Muḥammad and addressed to God: "Lord, show me things as they are." Bīdil cites it a few times throughout his autobiography as well as in his *ma<u>s</u>navī 'Irfān* in abbreviated form to designate the goal of Sufi striving. Perception of "things as they are" was the same as knowledge of God's "names and attributes" (*asmā va ṣifāt*) contained in the Qur'ān. This implies the co-extensivity of metaphysical knowledge and knowledge of the Qur'ān, metaphysical inquiry and reading God's word. However, humans who seek such knowledge are kept from comprehending this co-extensivity because they are psychophysically unprepared to withstand such knowledge, being vulnerable in their bodies to fluctuations in food and weather. Such fluctuations give rise to an excess of black bile (*sawdā*) in an individual's temperament (*mazāj*), this humeral imbalance only giving rise to sensory cravings: the unbounded interval or imagination "sees the forms of its desired objects [*muqtaẕīyāt*]" reflected in the mirror of sense-perceptible bodies. And until satisfied by sense-perceptible bodies, these cravings cause hyperbolic imaginations of their desired objects: a thirsty man imagines an ocean. The water he sees and by which he slakes his thirst is no less imaginary for being sense-perceptible since everything available to the senses belongs to a defective and imaginal order of reality. Bīdil's frequent admissions throughout *The Four Elements* of failure to (re) achieve the intimacy he lost at birth with the Real also account for the melancholy thematization of such failures in his *ghazal*s, his imaginative creations. His student was thus to consider this goal an asymptotic one and imitate Bīdil even if only to fail differently. At any rate, the optics implicit in such veiled and thus intrinsically futile seeing crucially accounts for the logic of Bīdil's presentation of the ekphrastic episode under discussion.

Bīdil makes no explicit reference to the scientific authorities he draws on for his optics. Nor do his technical terms – few as they are – allow us to square his optics with that of a particular Islamic thinker. However, what does appear immediately evident is that his optics is based on what historians of optics would call an extramission theory: a model of explanation for vision that posits it as an effect of a process (variously understood as a power, sight rays, luminous rays) issuing from the eye outward towards the object seen.[93] The historiography of both Islamic and Western optics identifies the origin of the extramission model of explanation in the humeral optics of the Greek physician Galen (d. *c.*200 CE).[94] In both traditions, Galen's extramission theory was mainly favored by physicians while philosophers mostly tended towards the opposite intramission model of explanation. The popularity of extramission theory among physicians:

> is explained not simply by the fact that it had been taught by the 'Prince of physicians' and therefore found a natural audience among medical men, but also by the fact that it included anatomical and physiological detail not present in any other ancient theory of vision. If one's purpose was to treat diseases of the eye, what mattered was not so much the geometrical features of the perception of space as the anatomical features of the eye.[95]

This medically motivated pragmatism may also inform Bīdil's extramission optics given that he presents himself throughout his autobiography as healing the sick by his medicines, spells and poetry. However, the specificities of Bīdil's optics, as presented below, suggest that he inherited a version of Abū Yūsuf Ya'qūb bin Isḥāq Al-Kindī's (d. *c.*866, Baghdad) extramission theory that combined the Galenic extramission thesis with the thesis first put forward by Euclid – some of whose main postulates Al-Kindī undertook to strengthen by demonstration – that the rays issuing from the pupil traveled towards the seen object in straight lines.

Nūr al-Dīn Muḥammad 'Abdullāh Shirāzī's *'Ilājāt-i Dārā Shukūhī*, completed in 1646–47 in the same imperial Mughal circles as Bīdil moved in, was the most compendious medical encyclopedia of the time. Its author, Shirāzī, dedicated it to the Mughal prince Dārā Shukūh who had also patronized Anūp Chhatr and shared Bīdil's affiliation to the Qādirī Sufi lineage. Shirāzī's work, "perhaps the largest Persian medical work of encyclopedic character composed in India."[96] contains a chapter on optics that either formed the source of Bīdil's Al-Kindian extramission theory or, at least, formulated the canonical understanding of this theory. In Chapter 39 "on the explanation of vision, reflections, light, color and the difference between light and color," Shirāzī writes:

> Physicians are of three opinions regarding perception and the seeing of things. First: seeing occurs by imprinting. That is, seeing occurs when the seen form is imprinted in the eye. Second: seeing occurs because of the extramission of rays [*ba sabab-i bīrūn āmadan-i shu'ā'st*] from the eye in the form of a cone whose tip is closer to the eye. Its basis is the luminous ray and, in the science of conical geometry, is depicted thus: [diagram in red ink of a cone]. Third: seeing occurs because the transparent air between the eye and the seen object becomes affected [*mukayaf*] by the quality [*kayfiyat*] of the eye's ray [*shu'ā-i baṣar*]. For this reason, the air acquires the state of the eyes. This is the rule of Aristotle and Shaykh Abu 'Alī [Ibn Sinā].[97]

Bīdil employed a combination of the second and third explanations of vision to specify the terms in which seeing occurred within the faculty psychology he inherited from Ibn 'Arabī. That is to say, he offered an Al-Kindian interpretation and specification, most probably mediated by Shirāzī, of Ibn 'Arabī's account of perception.

The totality of sense-perceptible reality, Bīdil argues, radiates from the human eye:

> As to their having declared this vast city [of the Universal Imagination of the body] the size of a sesame seed and the assemblage of human nature [*ta'abīyah-yi ṭīnat-i ādam*], *this is a dying breath* [*ramaq*] *of the subtleties of the faculty of sight; that is, an effect of the sensation of the eye's pupil* in whose sky the form-giving faculty [*taṣavvur*] spreads imagination's [*takhyīl*] wings (my italics).[98]

The pronoun "their" refers either to Ibn 'Arabī in the respectful plural or collectively to him and his many glossators through whom Bīdil received this psychology. According to this tradition centered on Ibn 'Arabī, the vast interstitial world of the imagination that freely and fantastically "ensouls bodies" (*taravvuḥ-i ajsād*) and "embodies souls" (*tajassud-i arvāḥ*) or lets a person geographically bound to India envision himself in Turkistan by only closing his eyes comes into being as an effect on the air ("dying breath", "sky") of human sight. Here is how Ibn 'Arabī, punning on the Arabic word *insān* in both its senses of "human" and "eye-pupil," formulates the optical function of the "Perfect Man" (*al-insān al-kāmil*) in relation to Allah:

> As for his humanness, it derives from his comprehensive structure and his comprising of all the realities, (because) the human being (*insān*) relates to the Real (*al-ḥaqq* – God) as the pupil (*insān al-'ayn*) relates to the eye, and through the pupil seeing (*naẓar, baṣar*) occurs. Hence he is called *insān* (meaning human being and pupil), because through him the Real looks (*naẓara*) at His creation and has mercy (*raḥima*) on them.[99]

The effects on the air generated by Bīdil's gaze – implicitly and potentially the gaze of the Perfect Man – are retained in the "memory" or "preserving faculty" (*ḥāfiẓah*) and come to "imprint" the tablet of the "imaginal faculty" (*quvvat-i mutakhayyilah*) or "the faculty of the fantasy" (*quvvat-i vāhimah*).[100] And by the agency of the imagination, they are often fantastically transformed into "wild forms and unfamiliar places." Such fantastic visions, we must recall, are the effects of fluctuations in food and weather. This epistemology is therefore informed by an optics susceptible to physiological contingencies and thus to distortions of perception by way of the imagination. If the Real simultaneously discloses and conceals itself in corporeal forms, it is in the sense that its appearances do not always conform to geometrical laws. Rather, such appearances are inseparably suffused with the fantastic effects of the imagination and so cannot be reduced to value-free sensations.

How does his appropriation of Al-Kindī's extramission theory serve Bīdil? The use of this optics in the following *ghazal* distich – one of several by Bīdil on the "topos" (*maẓmūn*) – leads us to an answer:

> *ba andāz-i taghāful nīm rukh ham 'ālamī dārad*
> *chirā mustaqbal-i mardum chu taṣvīr-i farang āyī*

A spectacle, too, is your turning heedlessly away into a picture in profile.
Why face me like a European portrait?

The distich iterates a topos ubiquitous in Bīdil's poetry and the tradition of Sufi or Sufi-informed Persian poetry, one that we may term "the Beloved's self-disclosure" (*jilvah-i maḥbūb*), the divine Beloved's self-disclosure as radiance. The logic of the topos determines that the Beloved, who conventionally treats the ardent and abjectly supplicating lover-speaker with cruel disdain, here turns His gaze towards the lover and blinds him by His luminous self-disclosure, an idea central to Sufi authors in the Persian tradition from at least as early as Ḥakīm Sanā'ī (d. *c.*1130, Ghazni). The lover's desired vision thus blinds him even as he is granted it.[101] Negating this logic of seeing as blinding, the speaker in Bīdil's distich asks his divine addressee to turn away in the manner of a Mughal portrait-in-profile, using the technical term *nīm-rukh* for this format of portrait. This, it is implied, would spare him the blinding glare of a frontal portrait – here given its technical name of *mustaqbal* – such as Europeans had been known for since Mughal artists had been exposed to European portrait painting in the late 1580s.[102] Although I have translated the second hemistich as if it were only directly addressing the speaker, Bīdil in fact puns on the word *mardum* to signify the "eye's pupil" and "people" at once. Equally plausible here is what by this period would have been an intentionally archaic sense of *mardum* as "person" rather than "people," a signification befitting the singular rather than plural number of the speaker. But even taken simultaneously in its singular and plural senses as "person" and "people," *mardum* also functions as a bilingual pun across Persian and Arabic in translating the aforementioned Arabic synonym used by Ibn 'Arabī: *insān*, meaning "human" or a short-form for the all-encompassing "Perfect Man" as well as "eye-pupil." The divine Beloved would blind the speaker-lover by flooding his pupil, paronomastically identified with his own person, with light. Such light would radiate from His face and, particularly, from His eyes, thus cancelling the effect of the lover's own luminous sight-rays. The plea is thus a plea to be allowed to witness or direct his sight-rays towards the Beloved addressee without being blinded by an unbearably greater counter-light.

In citing for his purposes the Mughal painting technique – originally appropriated by Mughal imperial painters from European paintings and prints – of the outward gazing figure, Bīdil was appropriating one of its major functions. In Mughal painting, the outward gazing figure arrests our eye, interrupting what would otherwise be simultaneous or snapshot viewing to make us, instead, take time, viewing details within the picture consecutively.[103] This arresting function of the outward gazing figure draws the viewer into the picture's action, inducing self-consciousness in him as also seen rather than only seeing. Bīdil solicits our involvement in the picture-frame of his autobiography, arresting our attention by looking out at us as we look at him. We – the structural equivalents of his Sufi reader-viewer – are fixed by his gaze that, when he tears his painting up, is refined to luminous rays stripped of bodily anchor.

This ekphrastic invocation of the eye's arrest replicates "the technique of the imaginary" (*tarz-i khiyāl*), a *ghazal* technique of semantic encryption of which Bīdil was a major practitioner. His student, Sirāj al-Dīn 'Alī Khān "Ārzū" (d. 1756), described its practitioners as "recent masters" (*muta'khirīn*) who sought "abstruseness and subtlety," "going so far as to use improbable and abstruse comparisons so that the mind comprehends the topos [*ma'nī*] after much contemplation and endless thought, the meaning being one unknown to those who know poetry."[104] Bīdil's couplet, quoted above, requires the reader-listener to be informed of the technical names for two kinds of portrait formats, names that were relatively historically new and arguably restricted to the Mughal courtly elite, to recognize the compound painting metaphor encrypting the primordial topos of "the Beloved's hierophany."

Bīdil, then, appropriated what was probably Shirāzī's version of Al-Kindī's extramission theory to scientifically authorize his characterization of himself in terms of a classical poetic topos as the hierophanic divine Beloved. More precisely, it was "the Bīdilian nature" – a curiously transpersonal and objectifying formulation of the ability with which he claims he was naturally endowed – that served as a locus for the Beloved whose luminous sight-rays physically transformed the painting in iconic correspondence with changes in the health of the "Bīdil" who identifies himself as such.

The iconoclastic hypotext beneath Bīdil's ekphrastic hypertext[105]

But why, if it was God who disclosed and concealed Himself to Himself in Bīdil's body and portrait, did Bīdil tear up the portrait? I will argue in this concluding sub-section that by this iconoclastic action, Bīdil modifies a certain canonical earlier scene of ekphrasis known to him from the Persian literary-mystical tradition, namely Rūmī's famous account of the painting contest between the Greeks and the Chinese. Bīdil's account of his portrait is in this sense a hypertext laid over the hypotext of Rūmī's famous episode from the end of the first book of his *Masnavī-i ma'navī* describing the painting contest. At this point, we may note in passing the prominence of Rūmī's *Masnavī* in Bīdil's milieu: his mentor 'Āqil Khān Rāzī composed a commentary on it as did his student, Shukrullāh Khān, at Rāzī's urging.[106] Khvushgū notes that "several matters that the Mawlavī of Rūm had expounded in his *Masnavī* and Shaykh Ibn 'Arabī in his *Fuṣūṣ al-ḥikam* he [i.e., Bīdil] employed [*bastah*] fully with commentary, elaboration, novel comparisons and immeasurable vividness in his own poetry."[107] Rūmī himself had precedents for this scene in Abū Ḥāmid al-Ghazālī (d. 504/1111) who used a closely similar plot in his *Iḥyā' 'ulūm al-dīn* (Revivification of the Religious Sciences) and then in Niẓāmī Ganjavī who, in his *Iskandar-nāmah* (Alexander-Book, *c.*590/1194), adapted the same plot to his own purposes. However, as I will explicate later, on account of Rūmī's extended emphasis on the metaphysical significations of color, it is his use of the plot of the painting contest rather than those of his predecessors that forms Bīdil's most germane hypotext, a mythic template for Bīdil's ekphrastic account.

Towards the end of the first book of his *Masnavī*, Rūmī calls for an overcoming of the mere intellectual hoarding of scholarship in favor of the intuitive knowledge of the Real that comes of spiritual poverty. To illustrate this, he relates a story about a competition between the Greeks and the Chinese in the art of the painting.[108] Each claims to be superior in the art of painting, Rūmī's original word for which – *naqqāshī* – is cognate with *naqsh*, a polysemic noun meaning "image" and "imprint" and thus related by a self-conscious etymology to the arts of writing. (Throughout Bīdil's autobiography, *naqsh* also signifies "creature," thus implicitly characterizing the Creator as writer and painter). The Chinese ask the Emperor who arbitrates the competition for "a hundred colors," daily receiving the colors they ask for. By contrast, "The Greeks said neither image [*naqsh*] nor color [*rang*]/befits this task, but only a removal of verdigris [*zang*]." Rūmī's rhyme phonemically identifies "color" (*rang*) with "verdigris" (*zang*). The heart was conventionally symbolized by the mirror and the heart's attachments by the rust-like verdigris that forms on polished surfaces like mirrors. Polishing color away thus symbolized detaching the heart from its attachments and improving its power to reflect what shone into it: "Color is like a cloud and colorlessness a moon." When the painting is complete, the Chinese confound the emperor's intellect (*'aql*) and understanding (*fahm*) with their painted image while the Greeks who have only polished their wall on the opposite side of the same room to reflect the Chinese painting "steal the [Emperor's] eyes from their sockets."

Rūmī here interprets his own anecdote by identifying the Greeks with "those Sufis" who are "without rote-learning, books and unskilled [*bī-hunar*]." The Chinese, by implied contrast, command such exoteric knowledge as the Sufi Greeks are bereft of. Whereas color and form symbolize the limits with which knowledge is articulated, a heart polished of all colors is able to reflect the limitless. The Chinese skills appeal only to limited faculties in the Emperor (intellect, understanding) while the reflection of their images in the Greek mirror – signifying Gnostic intuition of the Real – strain the Emperor's sensory limits, stealing his eyes from their sockets. Rūmī even suggests that such a perfectly reflective heart is "He Himself." Rather than disparaging book-learning, this anecdote calls for its interiorization through the cultivation of a perfect receptivity. Such cultivation would culminate in a superior miniaturization in the heart of "the images [*nuqūsh*] of the seven heavens," that is, a perfect integration of macrocosm with microcosm.

Also among the significations of color in Rūmī's anecdote is technology. In asking for paints, the Chinese demand technology to prove their skills, thus furnishing the mythic prototype for Anūp Chhatr's technical mastery of the skills of painted illusion. By contrast, the Greek method of polishing color off the wall pares away the effects of the technological exacerbation of what I earlier noted was an entrapment in the secondary causality with which scholarship and exoteric knowledge concerns itself. In this sense, the Greek method stands for the spiritual poverty of the Sufis and the Chinese one for the amassing of scholarship. In tearing up and burying his own painted portrait even as he verbalizes it in his autobiography, Bīdil models his action on the iconoclastic erasure of color by the Greeks. Earlier in this essay, we had noted the citation of another of Rūmī's spiritual teachings in Bīdil's use of the formulaic phrase "a collar rending" in his description of his tearing up of his portrait, amplifying this citation as a paring away of the superficiality of Sufi clothing in favor of the spirit. Here, he implicitly cites Greek iconoclasm as canonized by Rūmī and strips himself of the density of attributes gathered in the course of a lifetime ever since his soul "shone like the sun from the emanation of Pre-Eternity" and took on a body in "the land of appearances."[109] We must bear in mind that Bīdil claims near the beginning of the first Element that he wrote this autobiography to compensate for the shame of his soul becoming flesh.[110] Here is how Jāmī – whose interpretations of Ibn 'Arabī's thought, as I earlier noted, were influential in Bīdil's Indian milieu – speaks of color as embodiment:

> Although the child of Adam, because of corporeality, has extreme density, in terms of spirituality he has the utmost subtlety. He takes on the property of everything towards which he turns, and he receives the color of everything to which he attends.... Moreover the generality of creatures, because of their intense conjunction with this corporeal form and their perfect preoccupation with this material figure, have become such that they do not know themselves apart from it and cannot make the distinction.... So, you must strive to conceal yourself from your own gaze.[111]

Bīdil, in his fascination with his own portrait, "became such that he did not know himself apart from it." Alerted to the iconic relationship between his body and his portrait by his illness, he "strives to conceal himself from his own gaze" by tearing up his portrait or, by extension, discoloring and disembodying himself to leave behind only the faintly traced outline of his autobiography.

Conclusion

'Abd al-Qādir "Bīdil", titled the "father of meanings" (*'abul ma'ānī*), inaugurated a new threshold in the *ghazal* stylistics that called itself "Speaking Anew" (*tāzah-gūyī*). This stylistics originated throughout the Indo-Persian world in the 1500s and, by Bīdil's lifetime, had attained a semantic complexity and polysemic density sometimes compared to the contemporaneous European aesthetic of the Baroque.[112] It has long been noted that this deepening stylistic density was an effect of its practitioners' attempts to variously reflect on the cumulative literary heritage of Persian in their own poetry.[113] Bīdil's *ma<u>s</u>navī*s, quatrains, stanzaic poems and *ghazal*s comprise canonical instances of this reflexive stylistic thematization of the Persian poetic past. However, the extant scholarship on his oeuvre does not specify how his poems constitute dense imaginative re-formulations of his own expository interpretations of certain Islamic philosophical, scientific, theological and visual traditions. Inasmuch as these interpretations mostly appear in the course of what he characterizes in the opening lines of his first Element as an autobiographical clarification of the divinely authored and pre-written text of his own embodied soul, his poems are also autobiographical formulations.[114] This chapter began by explicating the mythic senses and spiritual-pedagogical contexts in which *The Four Elements* is an autobiography. The rest of the chapter has argued that recognizing Bīdil's individuality depends on recognizing the philosophical-theological theories he adapts and the myths he renews. The iconoclastic anti-illusionism Bīdil inscribes into his verbal portrait of his painted portrait presents us, as it would have its Sufi reader, with the gift of a new iteration of the myth of Islamic iconoclasm. Receiving this gift, we may turn or return to his poems to read them – as we read his *ghazal* distich that forms this chapter's epigraph – as so many self-erasures of images beamed from Bīdil's eye.

Notes

1 'Abd al-Qādir Khān Bīdil, *Kulliyāt-i Bīdil: jild-i duvvum* (Tehrān: mu'assasah-i intishārāt-i Ilhām, 1386/2007), 1364.
2 For a general introduction to his life and oeuvre, see www.iranicaonline.org/articles/bidel-bedil-mirza-abd-al-qader-b (accessed on August 3, 2013).
3 For a brief and general encyclopedia entry on *Chahār 'unṣur*, see: www.iranicaonline.org/articles/cahar-onsor-four-elements-an-autobiographical-work-in-prose-by-the-poet-and-sufi-abul-maani-mirza-abd-al-qader-bi (accessed on August 3, 2013).
4 'Abd al-Qādir Khān Bīdil, *Chahār 'unṣur*, in *Āvāz'hā-i Bīdil* (Tehrān: mu'assasah-i intishārāt-i Nigāh, 1386/2007), 335–676. I derive the information on his place of residence from Bindrāban Dās Khvushgū, *Safīnah-i Khvushgū: daftar-i thālith* (Patna: idārah-i taḥqīqat-i 'Arabī va Fārsī, 1959), 109. He relates that Bīdil was buried in his home on a platform (*chabutra*) he had had built for himself in around 1710. At some point over the following two decades, sadly for us but perhaps in keeping with the poet's own poetic preoccupation with the world's evanescence, his home and grave that would have been located in what is today Daryā Ganj in the heart of Delhi fell into ruin and, by the late 1780s, were deserted. For a brief and general encyclopedia entry on *Chahār 'unṣur*, see: www.iranicaonline.org/articles/cahar-onsor-four-elements-an-autobiographical-work-in-prose-by-the-poet-and-sufi-abul-maani-mirza-abd-al-qader-bi (accessed on August 3, 2013).
5 I gloss "ekphrasis," for the purposes of this chapter, by W.J.T. Mitchell's initial and most general formulation of it: "the verbal representation of a visual representation." See W.J.T. Mitchell, "Ekphrasis and the Other," in *Picture Theory: Essays on Verbal and Visual Representation* (Chicago, IL: University of Chicago Press, 1994), 151–81.
6 Dwight F. Reynolds, *Interpreting the Self: Autobiography in the Arabic Literary Tradition* (Berkeley, CA: University of California Press, 2000), 4.
7 I owe this suggestion to Dwight F. Reynolds, who makes it with reference to medieval Arabic autobiographies.
8 Bīdil, *Chahār 'unṣur*, 341. Bīdil uses the word *i'tibār* in one of Ibn 'Arabī's technical senses that William C. Chittick translates as "take heed." I have therefore translated it as "heedfulness." Likewise, my translations of *vaḥdat* as "Oneness" and *kas̱rat* as "Manyness" are indebted to Chittick. William C. Chittick, *The Sufi Path of Knowledge: Ibn 'Arabi's Metaphysics of the Imagination* (Albany, NY: State University of New York Press, 1989), 165, 202, 25.

9 "Kāhin," in M.Th. Houtsma (ed.), *E.J. Brill's First Encyclopedia of Islam, 1913–1936*, Vol. 4 (Leiden: Brill Academic Publishers, 1993), 624–26.

10 A much-imitated early instance of such Sufi uses of rhymed and rhythmic prose in Persian is Khwājah Abdullāh Anṣārī (d. 1089, Herat), *Munājāt va guftār-i pīr-i Herāt* (Kābul: Thālith, 1390/1970). On the long-standing moral ambivalence of *saj'* in classical Arabic literary culture and the shifting evaluations of *saj'* in the Qur'ān – all but two of whose 114 chapters have rhyme – see Devin J. Stewart, "Saj' in the Qur'ān: Prosody and Structure," in *Journal of Arabic Literature* 21: 2 (1990), 101–39.

11 How widespread this prose style was in Bīdil's ambient milieu may be seen in Nūr al-Ḥasan Anṣārī, *Fārsī adab ba 'ahd-i Aurangzeb* (Delhi: Indo-Pershyan Sosayṭī, 1969). This text may be read as an anthology of prose and verse composed during Aurangzeb's reign.

12 William C. Chittick, *Ibn 'Arabi: Heir to the Prophets* (Oxford: Oneworld, 2005), 59.

13 Bīdil, *Chahār 'unṣur*, 352.

14 Ibid., 531.

15 Ibid., 529–30. I translate *ghayb-i muṭlaq*, in keeping with Chittick, as "Absolute Unseen." Chittick, *The Sufi Path of Knowledge*, 164.

16 Bīdil, *Chahār 'unṣur*, 534. For a thematization and discussion of "the Breath of the All-Merciful" and the privileged status with respect to it of a Sufi elite or "those who know the Truth" (*ḥaqīqat-āgāhān*), see 486–88.

17 Bīdil, *Chahār 'unṣur*, 442–44.

18 I translate *tanazzuh*, because it is cognate with *tanzīh*, in keeping with Chittick's translation of the latter term as "incomparability." The term itself is conventionally contrasted with *tashbīh* or "similar" in Islamic theology before, in and after Ibn 'Arabī.

> The Shaykh al-Akbar constantly alternates between these two points of view. He maintains that true knowledge of God and creation can only come through combining the two perspectives. He commonly refers to them as (the declaration of God's) incomparability (*tanzīh*) and (the declaration of His) similarity (*tashbīh*).
>
> Chittick, The Sufi Path of Knowledge, 68

19 Khvushgū, *Safīnah-i Khvushgū*, 106.

20 Bīdil, *Chahār 'unṣur*, 358–67.

21 Sayyad Aḥsan al-Ẓafar, *Mirzā 'Abd al-Qādir Bedil: ḥayāt aur kārname: jild-i duvvum* (Rāmpūr: Rāmpūr Raẓā Library, 2009), 459.

22 For an exposition of such overlapping spiritual practices, see David W. Damrel, "The 'Naqshbandi Reaction' Reconsidered," in David Gilmartin and Bruce B. Lawrence (eds), *Beyond Turk and Hindu: Rethinking Religious Identities in Islamicate South Asia* (Gainesville, FL: University Press of Florida, 2000), 176–98.

23 Bīdil, *Chahār 'unṣur*, 366. For his self-identification as one of those who adhered to *vaḥdat al-vujūd*, see Aḥsan al-Ẓafar, *Mirzā 'Abdul Qādir Bedil: jild-i duvvum*, 459.

24 The *Ḥadīs̱* appears in Jāmī's *Nafahāt al-uns* (Breaths of the Intimate), Farīd al-Dīn 'Aṭṭār's (d. 1221) *Tazkirat al-awliyā* (Memorial of God's Friends) and elsewhere in the Persian Sufi canon. Bīdil remarks elsewhere in his autobiography on his familiarity with both of these texts by Jāmī and 'Aṭṭār.

25 Bīdil, *Chahār 'unṣur*, 365.

26 Chittick does not himself offer direct translations of these two terms, so I have made these translations in keeping with his explication of the difference. Chittick, *The Sufi Path of Knowledge*, 244–45.

27 Chittick, *The Sufi Path of Knowledge*, 88.

28 Muhammad Abdul Haq Ansari, *Sufism and Sharī'ah: a Study of Shaykh Aḥmad Sirhindī's Effort to Reform Sufism* (Leicester: The Islamic Foundation, 1986), 55.

29 Bīdil, *Chahār 'unṣur*, 367.

30 'Abd al-Qādir Khān Bīdil, *Kulliyāt-i Bīdil: jild-i avval* (Tehrān: intishārāt-i Ilhām, 1386/2007), 762–63.

31 *gūsh-i man u ḥalqa-i gīsū-yi yār/rū-yi man u khāk-i dar-i mai-furūsh.* 'Abul Ḥasan 'Abd al-Raḥmān "Khatmī" Lāhorī, *Sharḥ-i 'irfānī-i ghazal'hā-i Ḥāfiẓ: jild-i sivvum* (Tehrān: nashr-i Qaṭrah, 1378/1999), 1954.

32 Though glossed only in the semantic context of the distich, *īhām* was recognized as applicable to textual units larger than a distich. One of the most famous instances of such an employment of *īhām* on a textual scale larger than a distich is Farīd al-Dīn 'Aṭṭār's *The Conference of the Birds* (*Manṭiq al-ṭayr*) whose lord of the birds – the Sīmurgh – bears a name that is a pun on the identity of the thirty birds who have journeyed to see him since *sī* means "thirty" and *murgh* "bird." Another equally famous use of *īhām* as the master signifier of a *ma<u>s</u>navī*'s semiotics is 'Abd al-Raḥmān Jāmī's *Yūsuf u Zulaykhā*, whose plot turns on the double meaning of the noun *'azīz* which, in that *ma<u>s</u>navī*, saliently means "mighty" and non-saliently "beloved." Both *ma<u>s</u>navī*s are significantly Sufi ones.

33 The mixed Persian-Urdu oeuvre of Ja'far Zatallī, its macaronic quality itself a lexemic and phonemic subversion of Persian rhetorical norms of "linguistic purity" (*faṣāḥat*), was the most prominent textual locus of this de-sacralization of the bodies of the Mughal ruling classes from emperor to soldier. Ja'far Zatallī, *Zatal-nāmah, Kulliyāt-i Ja'far Zatallī* (Delhi: Anjuman-i taraqqī-i Urdu, 2011), especially his mock roster of the king's daily activities, "Akhbārāt-i siyāhah-i darbār-i mu'allā" on 53–78. Also in the emperor Aurangzeb's employ was the satirist Ni'mat Khān "'Ālī" whose *Vaqā'ī* mockingly and often obscenely described the emperor's long-drawn Mughal siege of the Qutbshāhī fort of Golkonda in 1687. Ni'mat Khān 'Ālī, *Vaqā'ī* (Kānpūr: Naval Kishor, 1873). For an account of factional formations centered on powerful nobles, see Satish Chandra, *Parties and Politics at the Mughal Court: 1707–1740* (Delhi: Oxford University Press, 2002), 278–92.

34 Khvushgū, *Safīnah-i Khvushgū*, 13. Khvushgū states that Bīdil was indebted for his mastery of Sufism (*taṣavvuf*) to Rāzī's command of Sufi terminology and topics. 'Āqil Khān "Rāzī" authored a number of works in verse and prose on Sufi topics, among them a prose exposition, titled *<u>S</u>amarāt al-hayāt*, of the sayings and lessons of his teacher, a Shaṭṭāri Sufi called Burhān al-Dīn Rāz-i Ilāhī. Nūr al-Ḥasan Anṣārī, *Fārsī adab*, 523.

35 I derive this understanding of "polyphony" from Thomas de Bruijn, *Ruby in the Dust: Poetry and History in Padmāvat by the South Asian Sufi Poet Muḥammad Jāyasī* (Leiden: Leiden University Press, 2012), 20 and 205–75.

36 Dargāh Qulī Khān, *Muraqqa'-i Dehlī*, (Ḥyderābād: Tāj Press, 1973), 44–45 and 10–11. In keeping with Sufi practice, Bīdil's handwriting was considered a sanctified trace of his personhood. Bīdil, in turn, describes how Ḥaẓrat Shāh, one of his Sufi masters, had copied out Bīdil's *ghazal* fragment in his own "auspicious hand" and sent it to another Sufi to seek his help in giving Bīdil further spiritual guidance. Bīdil, *Chahār 'unṣur*, 481.

37 Khvushgū, *Safīnah-i Khvushgū*, 108, 115. In Bīdil's collection of letters, *Ruqa'āt*, letter 200 is addressed to Qābil Khān Munshī, secretary to the emperor Aurangzeb. It recalls that seven years previously the emperor had expressed his interest in reading Bīdil's work and conveys Bīdil's gratitude to the emperor for having read the "text of prose" Bīdil had sent him by way of a gift. In general, the letters in this collection comprise an invaluable window into Bīdil's literary field. In particular, they let us infer the shifting interactions between his Akbarian poetry, otherworldly postures and the implications of both in the political power and patronage of the tumultuous late Mughal milieu. 'Abd al-Qādir Khān Bīdil, *Ruqa'āt*, in *Āvāz'hā-i Bīdil* (Tehrān: mu'assasah-i intishārāt-i Nigāh, 1386/2007), 29–182. For letter 200, see 128–29.

38 Khvushgū, *Safīnah-i Khvushgū*, 17. Besides the other features that recommend it, this volume of Khvushgū's *Safīnah* contains such precious and mostly reliable social and biographical information on the Persian literary culture of Khvushgū's Delhi, including anecdotes about the everyday lives and interactions of poets. I characterize them as reliable on the condition that they are understood, as I noted in my Introduction, to be invested in exalting Delhi.

39 Khvushgū, a long time student of Bīdil in poetry and other spiritual practices, refers to him in his verse marking Bīdil's death as "that holy threshold," a "guide" and "a prophet, an assistant, a leader" in "poetry" (*sukhan*). Khvushgū's other descriptions of Bīdil, especially the spectacles of his miraculous strength, conform on many points to Sufi hagiographical tropes. Khvushgū, *Safīnah-i Khvushgū*, 103–25.

40 Ibid., 183–84. For a discussion of Bīdil's central role in authorizing Hindu self-inscriptions into the Persian literary tradition, see Stefano Pello, "Persian as a Passe-partout: The Case of Mirzā 'Abd al-Qādir Bīdil and his Hindu Disciples," in A. Busch and T. de Bruijn (eds), *People in Motion, Ideas in Motion: Culture and Circulation in Pre-Modern South Asia* (Leiden: Brill, 2013).

41 Lacchmī Nārāyan "Shafīq," *Tazkirah-i gul-i ra'nā* (Ḥyderābād: 'Ahd-āfarīn Press, 1967), 167. Bīdil's Vaishnava students who composed Persian accounts of the sacred landscape of the Braj region very likely took for a model Bīdil's own admiring description of the locality. He describes Mathura and its varieties of Hindu ascetics and pilgrims in rhapsodic rhyming prose as a land still traced by the melancholy of Krishna's parting, universalizing Krishna by a verse that identifies him with the Sufi cosmogonic principle of Love. Bīdil, *Chahār 'unṣur*, 482.

42 A visual representation of such Sufi reading may be seen in a British Library painting numbered 7573, folio 25r, completed around 1611 in Mughal imperial circles by Muḥammad Riẓā and inserted, significantly, into a copy of the *Dīvān* of Ḥāfiẓ. It depicts the poet-theologian Imād al-Dīn Faqīh (d. 1371) letting the *Dīvān* of Ḥāfiẓ drop from his hand as he and his pupils fall into an ecstasy.

43 Titus Burckhardt, *Mystical Astrology According to Ibn 'Arabi*, trans. Bulent Rauf (Louisville, KY: Fons Vitae, 2001), 16. Bīdil's own most extended explication of his understanding of this sublunary sphere appears in Bīdil, *'Irfān*, in *Kulliyāt-i Bīdil: jild-i sivvum* (Tehrān: mu'assasah-i intishārāt-i Ilhām, 1386/2007), 65–104. For an exposition of this distinction between apparently moving and stationary planets as it is implicit in Jāmī's *Yūsuf u Zulaykhā*, a *masnavī* interpreting Ibn 'Arabī's theistic monism and widely read and cited in Bīdil's milieu, see Muḥammad bin Ghulām Muḥammad, *Sharḥ-i Yūsuf u Zulaykhā* (MS BW Ivanow 0064, Redpath Library, McGill University, Montreal), fl. 10–11. The commentator was a member of the Chishtiyyah Niẓāmiyyah Sufi lineage of Multan. He completed the commentary in 1819 and included glosses from three earlier commentaries as well as dictionaries of Persian and Arabic.

44 Bīdil, *Nikāt*, in *Āvāz'hā-i Bīdil* (Tehrān: mu'assasah-i intishārāt-i Nigāh, 1386/2007), 194.

45 Khvushgū, *Safīnah-i Khvushgū*, 110–11.

46 An example may be found in the sub-section of the fourth Element given to an exposition of the technical terms for the "soul" considered in its positive aspect as *rūḥ* (the negative typically being denominated *nafs*). Bīdil, *Chahār 'unṣur*, 598.

47 Som Prakash Verma, *Mughal Painters and their Work: A Biographical Survey and Comprehensive Catalogue* (Delhi: Oxford University Press, 1995), 61–62.

48 Bīdil, *Chahār 'unṣur*, 615.

49 For a study of the Persian literary imagination of Mānī, see Priscilla Soucek, "Nizami on Painters and Painting," in Richard Ettinghausen (ed.), *Islamic Art in the Metropolitan Museum of Art* (New York: The Metropolitan Museum of Art, 1972), 9–21.

50 David J. Roxburgh, "Kamal al-Din Bihzad and Authorship in Persian Painting," *Muqarnas* 17 (2000), 119–46.

51 Bīdil, *Chahār 'unṣur*, 477–80.
52 Ian Richard Netton, *Allah Transcendent: Studies in the Structure and Semiotics of Islamic Philosophy, Theology and Cosmology* (London: Routledge, 1994), 270–71.
53 *yek-tāyī āfarīd lab-i khud-sitā-i 'ishq/dar nuqṭah-i dahan alifī dāsht mīm-i mā*. Bīdil, *Kulliyāt-i Bīdil: jild-i avval*, 328.
54 Jorge Luis Borges, "The Mirror of Enigmas," in *Labyrinths* (New York: New Directions, 1964), 209–12. Bīdil's immediate source for this conception of a text as always-already taking into account any possible interpretation of it and thus as made up even in its letters of the signifying traces of the absolute Author is Ibn 'Arabī. As Ian Almond writes:

> Whether it is Ibn 'Arabī's mystical reinterpretation of the date of Almohad's victory over the Christian armies in 1194, or the Shaykh's understanding of a man figure (the Perfect Man, *al-insān al-kāmil*) from the letters of the Prophet Muḥammad's name, the all-encompassing infinity of the Divine Mind anticipates every Koranic nuance, every so-called "chance" or "coincidence", every hermeneutic variation as one more unspeakable development in the Infinite Will.

Ian Almond, *Sufism and Deconstruction: A Comparative Study of Derrida and Ibn 'Arabi* (New York: Routledge, 2004), 65.
55 'Abd al-Qādir Khān Bīdil, *Bayāẕ-i Bīdil*, MS ADD. 16802, 16803, British Library, London.
56 Ibn 'Arabī said: "I swear by God, I say nothing, I announce no judgment that does not proceed from an inbreathing of the divine spirit in my heart." This is an internal quotation from Carl Ernst, "The Man without Attributes: Ibn 'Arabi's Interpretation of Abu yazid al-Bistami," *Journal of the Muhyiddin Ibn 'Arabi Society* XIII (1993), 1–18. Following upon Ibn 'Arabī, Jāmī declares in his preface to his *The Gleams* (*Lawā'ih*):

> This is a treatise named *The Gleams* on the explanation of the gnostic sciences and the meanings. It has gleamed forth from the tablets of the secret hearts and spirits of the lords of gnosis and the masters of tasting and finding in appropriate expressions and lustrous allusions.

Sachiko Murata, *Chinese Gleams of Sufi Light: Wang Tai-yu's Great Learning of the pure and Real and Liu Chih's Displaying the concealment of the Real Realm; with a new translation of Jami's Lawā'ih from the Persian by William C. Chittick* (Albany, NY: State University of New York Press, 2000), 134.
57 Priscilla Soucek, "The Theory and Practice of Portraiture in the Persian Tradition," *Muqarnas* 17 (2000), 103.
58 Bīdil, *Chahār 'unṣur*, 464–67. Falling asleep seems to have interested Sufis because it was a state of being that the sleeper entered unintentionally and thus rehearsed the Sufi problematic of how to act without the vanity of willing the action. The earliest Persian-language precedent for this Sufi discussion of sleeping and waking is 'Alī bin 'Us̱mān al-Jullābī al-Hujvīrī (d. *c.*1073–77, Lahore), *Kashf al-mahjūb: The Oldest Persian Treatise in Sufism*, trans. R.A. Nicholson (London: Luzac, 1936), 352–54. This discussion itself summarizes earlier Sufi views of the topic and was composed roughly contemporaneously with 'Abdul Karīm ibn Hawazin Qushayrī's (d. 1072, Nishāpūr) equally paradigmatic Arabic-language *Risālah al-Qushayriyya* that also discusses the topic.
59 Bīdil, *Chahār 'unṣur*, 357–67.
60 Ibid., 374–75 and 353–54.
61 A canonical earlier instance of such an autobiographical appropriation of the elemental schema for literary ends, in this case to order a lifetime's output of *ghazal*s into four *dīvān*s corresponding in quality to the four elements, may be found in Amīr

Khusraw's *Dībāchah-i dīvān-i ghurrat al-kamāl*, his preface to his eponymous *Dīvān* of *ghazals* completed in 1298. Amīr Khusraw, *Dībāchah-i dīvān-i ghurrat al-kamāl* (Lahore: maṭba'-i 'Aliyyah, 1975). The elemental schema was not only a rhetorical device but continuous with classical Islamic pharmacology. Y. Tzvi Langermann, "Another Andalusian Revolt? Ibn Rushd's Critique of Al-Kindi's Pharmacological Computus," in Jan P. Hogendijk *et al.* (eds), *The Enterprise of Science in Islam: New Perspectives* (London: MIT Press, 2003), 351–52. A medically aimed exposition of the possible mixture of the elements that was contemporaneous with Bīdil and underwritten by a Sufi metaphysics may be seen in *'Ilājāt-i Dārā Shukūhī*, composed between 1642–43 and 1646–47 in his own courtly circles and the largest Persian medical encyclopedia of Islamic India. Nūr al-Dīn Muḥammad Abdullāh Shirāzī, *'Ilājāt-i Dārā Shukūhi* or *Ṭibb-i Dārā Shukūhī*, MS 6226, Kitāb-khānah-i majlis, Tehrān, fls. 47v–47r. See also Bīdil's medical references to the elements in his letters praying for his patron's good health. Bīdil, *Ruqa'āt*, in *Āvāz'hā-i Bīdil*, 49, 50.

62 It is the failure to grasp this mythicizing motivation that has led Nabī Hādī, the author of major modern critical study of Bīdil, to despair of Bīdil's style and condemn it for its obscurity, settling for mere plot summaries and thematic descriptions of his works as if these were solutions to such perceived obscurity. Nabī Hadī, *Mirzā Bedil* (Urdu) (Delhi: Ejukeshnal Pablishing Haus, 2009; first published in 1982), especially 70–75. Hādī's negative evaluation of Bīdil's style derives from his commitment to a conception of literary realism first canonized by the Reformist Urdu critic Muḥammad Ḥusayn Āzād in the late nineteenth century, one that anachronistically demands that written prose replicate the supposed verisimilitude of a spoken idiom. His frustration over Bīdil's failure to conform to this referential ideal leads him to try and resolve this difficulty by offering a plot summary of *The Four Elements*, an exercise antithetical to the mythicizing aims and recursive temporality of Bīdil's text that begins and concludes by emphasizing its author's failure to achieve intimacy with the Real and thus the circularity of spiritual arrest rather than the linearity of spiritual development. A possible incitement to this methodological error is that the first Element begins with an account of Bīdil's birth, misleading him as well as the critic Salāḥ al-Dīn Saljuqī into taking this as a sign of a chronologically linear emplotment of his life thereafter. Salāḥ al-Dīn Saljuqī, *Naqd-i Bīdil* (Persian) (Tehrān: Muḥammad Ibraḥīm Shari'atī Afghānistanī, 1388/1968), 461–63. Abdul Ghani, by contrast, notes the anecdotally staggered character of Bīdil's autobiography and the non-narrative order of its four chapters. However, he does this only in the course of a summary of the text's topics, abandoning analysis in favor of summarizing comprehensiveness. In doing so, he assigns the ekphrastic episode relating to Anūp Chhatr no more than a passing mention as one of the miracles characteristically included in a Persian prose work's concluding chapter. But such short shrift not only pretends to conventionalize what was intended to be read as unconventional, it also misses an opportunity to understand Bīdil's aesthetics and ethics in ways deeper than any summary listing of his oeuvre could achieve. This said, Abdul Ghani's book remains the most comprehensive bio-bibliographical introduction to Bīdil in English. Abdul Ghani, *Life and Works of Abdul Qadir Bedil* (Lahore: United Publishers, 1960). Siddiqi's 1975 PhD dissertation on Bīdil's *'Irfān* mostly comprises an account of the poet's life and age, culled heavily from Ghani's work. Its later portions anticipate my exercise in setting Bīdil's poetry within its cosmological-theological contexts but offer little insight into how the poem appropriates and encrypts these ideas. Moazzam Siddiqi, "An Examination of the Indo-Persian Mystical Poet Mirzā 'Abdul Qādir Bedil with Particular Reference to His Chief Work *'Irfān*" (PhD diss., University of California, 1975). A measure of how far the study of Bīdil in North America has come since 1975 is Kovacs's insightful doctoral interpretation of Bīdil's 1667 *masnavī Muḥīt-i a'ẓam*. Hajnalka Kovacs, "The Tavern of

the Manifestation of Realities: The Masnavi Muhit-i Azam by Mirza Abd al-Qadir Bedil (1644–1720)" (PhD diss., University of Chicago, 2013). The most comprehensive study of Bīdil's oeuvre in any language is the two-volume study in Urdu by Sayyad Aḥsan al-Ẓafar, *Mirzā 'Abd al-Qādir Bedil: ḥayāt aur kārname: jild-i yekkum va duvvum* (Rāmpūr: Rāmpūr Raẓā Library, 2009). However, Aḥsan al-Ẓafar fails to recognize the literary and visual traditions implicated in the ekphrastic episode under discussion. For a tabulation of and commentary on Bīdil's codicological metaphors in his vast corpus of *ghazals*, see Ḥamīdreẓā Ghelīchkhānī, *Iṣṭilahāt-i nuskhah-pardāzī dar dīvān-i Bīdil-i Dihlavī* (New Delhi: Center for Persian Research, Office of the Cultural Counselor, Islamic Republic of Iran, 2011). This study has the merit of recognizing the importance for modern criticism of what Bīdil's student Ārzū already remarked on as the focus of poetic creativity in his milieu, namely that poets sought, not to devise new "figures of speech" (*ṣanā'i-i badī'ī*) like poets in the past, but "new comparisons and metaphors" (*tashbīh va isti'ārah*). Ghelīchkhānī argues that Bīdil's metaphorical use of technical terms, such as from the art of book-making, accounts for the initial obscurity of Bīdil's style. However, inasmuch as Bīdil submits such metaphorical novelty to the mythic logics of traditional topoi (*maẓāmīn*), we must also put his initial obscurity down to what I have called his mythicizing motivations. For Ārzū's formulation of this recognition, see Sirāj al-Dīn 'Alī Khān Ārzū, *'Aṭiyah-i kubrā*, in *'Aṭiyah-i kubrā va Mawhibat-i 'uẓmā* (Tehrān: Firdaws, 1381/2002), 51.

63 Nūr al-Dīn 'Abd al-Raḥmān bin Aḥmad Jāmī, *Haft awrang: jild-i duvvum* (Tehrān: Mirās̱ maktūb, 1378/2013), 21. I owe my understanding of Jāmī's play on *naqsh* and *naqshbandī* to the commentary by Muḥammad, *Sharḥ-i Yūsuf u Zulaykhā*, fl. 12.

64 Bīdil, *Chahār 'unṣur*, 587–88.

65 Ibid., 614.

66 Ibid., 615.

67 Sa'dī's *Gulistān* (The Rose Garden, 1258, Shiraz) famously describes its own genesis in the author's response to a friend's sense of the imminent seasonal death of a rose garden, prompting Sa'dī to create a literary rose garden immune to autumn. Abū 'Abudullāh Musliḥ al-Sa'dī, *Kitāb-i Gulistān* (Tehrān: Chāp-khānaḥ-i Gulshan, 1360/1942), 2–16. This remained an ideal of fiction imbued with magic in the Persianate world at least as late as 1837 in Sikandarabad in North India when a student of the Persian-Urdu poet Ghālib (d. 1869), Bālmukund "Be-ṣabr," described the nature of his Urdu narrative poem in similar terms. Bālmukund Be-ṣabr, *Masnavī Lakht-i jigar*, (New Delhi: Anjuman-i taraqqī-i Urdu, 1999), esp. 103–05.

68 In addition to Bīdil's indication, internally marked by his own given dates, that he spent over twenty years composing *The Four Elements*, such pervasive signs of proleptically and analeptically motivated word-choices confirm that his plans for the logic of textual presentation minutely accounted for the semantic level of the sentence, the larger discursive level of anecdotes and then the grossest narratological one of books or Elements. Such evidence of long-term planning contrasts with the relative speed with which he composed his prodigious output of around three thousand *ghazals*.

69 Gregory Minissale, *Images of Thought: Visuality in Islamic India: 1550–1750* (Newcastle: Cambridge Scholars Press, 2006), 59–60. Also, on the foundational drawing as the empirical site of a painter's authorship, see David J. Roxburgh, "Kamal al-Din Bihzad and Authorship in Persian Painting," *Muqarnas* 17 (2000), 119–46.

70 Bīdil, *Chahār 'unṣur*, 342.

71 Minissale, *Images of Thought*, 230–42.

72 Hans Belting, *Florence and Baghdad: Renaissance Art and Arab Science*, trans. Deborah Lucas Schneider (Cambridge, MA: Harvard University Press, 2011).

73 Chittick, *The Sufi Path of Knowledge*, 79–80.

74 In this originates Bīdil's evident attachment in his *ghazals* to the topos (*maẓmūn*) of blinking as alternating between states of divine self-disclosure and self-concealment.

75 The relevant sentence from the Qur'ān 6:50 reads "Is the blind equivalent to the seeing?" Bīdil is drawing here on Ibn 'Arabī who, in his *Futuḥāt al-makkiyyah* (Meccan Revelations), said that with respect to true knowledge www.ibnarabisociety.org/articles/mr_introduction.html#_ftn24

76 Minissale, *Images of Thought*, 234.

77 Priscilla Soucek, "The Theory and Practice of Portraiture in the Persian Tradition," *Muqarnas* 17 (2000), 103.

78 Chittick, *The Sufi Path of Knowledge*, 96–97. Also, Aḥsan al-Ẓafar, *Mirzā 'Abd al-Qādir Bedil: jild-i duvvum*, 642.

79 The interlocking of prose and verse in classical Persian literary culture, an economy of bound and unbound language lost through English colonialism, may be judged by Bīdil's *ghazal* adaptation of this episode in the following distich: "One must await the fled colors./The painter's brush spilled its eyelashes in my portrait." Although I translate the first person pronoun conventionally as "I," Bīdil literally says "we" (*mā*). That this first person plurality is no mere convention throughout his oeuvre becomes apparent when we recognize the transpersonal quality of the self who speaks. This transpersonal self forms the subject of Chapter 2. Bīdil, *Kulliyāt-i Bīdil: jild-i avval*, 413. Bīdil thematizes the mutual convertibility of prose and verse in letter 35, addressed to his main patron Shukrullāh Khān, of his *Ruqa'āt*. Bīdil, *Ruqa'āt*, in *Āvāz'hā-i Bīdil*, 48.

80 Bīdil, *Chahār 'unṣur*, 617–18

81 Ibid., 463.

82 Jalāl al-Dīn Rūmī, *Masnavī-i ma'navī: daftar-i panjum* (Tehrān: Pizhmān, 1373/1994–95), 362–63.

83 Bīdil, *Chahār unṣur*, 623.

84

> The voluntary acts of men occur through the power of God alone, but only after that power has descended to their planes and has become manifest within them and become determined in accordance with their predispositions. Men possess no power beyond this.

'Abd al-Raḥmān Jāmī, *The Precious Pearl: al-Jāmi's 'Al-Durrah al-Fākhirah' together with its Glosses and the Commentary of 'Abd al-Ghafur al-Lārī* (Albany, NY: State University of New York Press, 1979), 66. Since I have followed Chittick's translations of Ibn 'Arabī's terminology I have preferred his translation of *isti'dād* which is "preparedness." Chittick, *The Sufi Path of Knowledge*, 91.

85 Bīdil, *Chahār 'unṣur*, 619.

86 Minissale, *Images of Thought*, 231–33.

87 Binyamin Abrahamov, *Ibn al-'Arabī's Fuṣūṣ al-ḥikam: An Annotated Translation of "The Bezels of Wisdom"* (New York: Routledge, 2015), 16.

88 'Abd al-Qādir Bīdil, *'Irfān*, in *Kulliyāt-i Bīdil: jild-i sivvum* (Tehrān: mu'assasah-i intishārāt-i Ilhām, 1386/2007), 65–68.

89 Bīdil, *Chahār 'unṣur*, 604.

90 Chittick, *Ibn 'Arabi: Heir to the Prophets*, 36–38. Hans Wehr glosses *vujūd* as "finding, discovery; being; existence; presence; whereabouts; stay, visit." Hans Wehr, *A Dictionary of Modern Written Arabic* (London: MacDonald and Evans Ltd, 1980), 1050.

91 William C. Chittick, *The Self-Disclosure of God: Principles of Ibn 'Arabi's Cosmology* (Albany, NY: State University of New York Press, 1998), 332.

92 Bīdil, *Chahār 'unṣur*, 602.

93 The characters imperial Mughal painters sometimes located just outside the margins of paintings looking into the frame or out of it sideways or at us, the viewers, are visual instances of the penetrative power of the gaze. Their eye-rays pierce the frames separating pictorial and non-pictorial reality, sometimes, as Minissale remarks, making us wonder who is watching who: "In Shah Jahan period-painting,

the use of the outward gazing figure is a clever way to pique the interest of the viewer and to play a game of illusion versus reality." Gregory Minissale, "The Dynamics of the Gaze in Mughal Painting," *Marg* 58: 2 (December 2006), 57.

94 David Lindberg, *Theories of Vision from Al-Kindi to Kepler* (Chicago, IL: University of Chicago Press, 1976).

95 Lindberg, *Theories of Vision*, 33.

96 www.iranicaonline.org/articles/sirazi-nur-al-din-mohammad-abd-allah

97 Shirāzī, *'Ilājāt-i Dārā Shukūhī* or *Ṭibb-i Dārā Shukūhī*, 158.

98 Bīdil, *Chahār 'unṣur*, 602.

99 Abrahamov, *Ibn al-'Arabī's Fuṣūṣ al-ḥikam*, 18.

100 Bīdil, *Chahār 'unṣur*, 603.

101 Of Bīdil's several *ghazal* distiches on this topos, the following one articulates the identity of blindness and sight in desire for the Beloved's hierophany with perhaps the most condensed compound metaphor: "The lightning of longing for a vision charred my eyes' veils./Waiting peeled my almonds at last" (*pardah-i chishmam ba barq-i ḥasrat-i dīdār sūkht/intizār ākhir muqashhar kard bādām-i marā*). Almonds, by a conventional topos (*maẓmūn*), were metaphors for the beloved's eyes. Peeled almonds are white and so, in Bīdil's "topos-elaboration" (*maẓmūn-āfrīnī*), resemble blind eyes. However, the phrase "white-eyed" (*sapīd-chishm*) also means "staring brazenly." Brazen staring and blindness thus coincide in longing to behold God. Topos-elaborations on this metaphor of the eyes as almonds occur throughout Bīdil's *Dīvān*, signaling the importance of visuality to his oeuvre. Bīdil, *Kulliyāt-i Bīdil: jild-i avval*, 417.

102 Gregory Minissale, "Seeing Eye-to-Eye with Mughal Miniatures: Some Observations on the Outward Gazing Figure in Mughal Art," *Marg* 58: 3 (March 2007), 40–49.

103 Ibid., 42. Minissale writes of the outward gazing figure in Mughal painting: "no written description of its use is extant in Mughal historical documents." Insofar as Bīdil's *The Four Elements* and his *ghazal*s constitute "Mughal historical documents," this chapter calls attention to evidence to the contrary.

104 Ārzū, *'Aṭiyah-i kubrā*, 67.

105 "Hypotext" and "hypertext" are terms coined in Gerard Genette, *Palimpsests: Literature in the Second Degree* (Lincoln, NE: University of Nebraska Press, 1997). A hypotext is a later text that transforms an anterior text – a hypertext – in citing it in any of many possible ways. The densely allusive quality of traditional Persian literature makes it especially amenable to the use of Genette's terminology.

106 Anṣārī, *Fārsī adab*, 317.

107 Khvushgū, *Safīnah-i Khvushgū*, 115. Khvushgū's use of the verb *bastan* for "employed" in this passage discloses his perception of his teacher's *ghazal*s as a commentary on Ibn 'Arabī and Rūmī since the complete form of the verb at work is *maẓmūn bastan* or "the employment of a *ghazal* topos."

108 Jalāl al-Dīn Rūmī, *Ma̱snavī-i ma'navī: daftar-i avval* (Tehrān: Pizhmān, 1373/1994–95).

109 This is a quotation from Bīdil's chronogram commemorating the date of his own birth: 1054/1644. The chronogram, as indeed all of the rest of his oeuvre, bespeaks one of his overriding aims, which was to fashion his authorial authority as kenotic recovery of his divine origin. Bīdil, *Kulliyāt-i Bīdil: jild-i avval*, 285.

110 Bīdil, *Chahār 'unṣur*, 346.

111 Jāmī, *Lawā'ih*, in Murata, *Chinese Gleams*, 143–44.

112 Ricardo Zippoli, *Chirā sabk-i Hindī dar dunyā-i gharb sabk-i Bārūk khwāndah mīshavad?* (Tehrān: Anjuman-i farhangī-i Itāliyā, bakhsh-i bāstān-shināsī, 1984).

113 Paul E. Losensky, *Welcoming Fighani: Imitation and Poetic Individuality in the Safavid-Mughal Ghazal* (Costa Mesa, CA: Mazda Publishers, 1998), 100–64. And Shamsur Rahman Faruqi, "Stranger in the City: The Poetics of Sabk-i Hindi," *Annual of Urdu Studies* 19 (2004), 1–94.

114 Bīdil, *Chahār 'unṣur*, 345.

Bibliography

Abrahamov, Binyamin. *Ibn al-'Arabī's Fuṣūṣ al-ḥikam: An Annotated Translation of "The Bezels of Wisdom"*. New York: Routledge, 2015.

Aḥsan al-Ẓafar, Sayyad. *Mirzā 'Abd al-Qādir Bedil: ḥayāt aur kārname: jild-i avval va duvvum*. Rāmpūr: Rāmpūr Raẓā Library, 2009.

'Ālī, Ni'mat Khān. *Vaqā'ī*. Kānpūr: Naval Kishor, 1873.

Almond, Ian. *Sufism and Deconstruction: A Comparative Study of Derrida and Ibn 'Arabi*. New York: Routledge, 2004.

Anṣārī, Khwājah Abdullāh. *Munājāt va guftār-i pīr-i Herāt*. Kābul: Thālith, 1390/1970.

Ansari, Muhammad Abdul Haq. *Sufism and Sharī'ah: A Study of Shaykh Aḥmad Sirhindī's Effort to Reform Sufism*. Leicester: The Islamic Foundation, 1986.

Anṣārī, Nūr al-Ḥasan. *Fārsī adab ba 'ahd-i Aurangzeb*. Delhi: Indo-Pershyan Sosayṭī, 1969.

Ārzū, Sirāj al-Dīn 'Alī Khān. *'Aṭiyah-i kubrā va Mawhibat-i uẓmā*. Tehrān: Firdaws, 1381/2002.

Belting, Hans. *Florence and Baghdad: Renaissance Art and Arab Science*, trans. Deborah Lucas Schneider. Cambridge, MA: Harvard University Press, 2011.

Be-ṣabr, Bālmukund. *Masnavī Lakht-i jigar*. New Delhi: anjuman-i taraqqī-i Urdu, 1999.

Bīdil, 'Abd al-Qādir Khān. *Bayāz-i Bīdil*. MS ADD. 16802, 16803, British Library, London.

Bīdil, 'Abd al-Qādir Khān. *Chahār 'unṣur*, in *Āvāz'hā-i Bīdil*. Tehrān: mu'assasah-i intishārāt-i nigāh, 1386/2007, 335–676.

Bīdil, 'Abd al-Qādir Khān. *Kulliyāt-i Bīdil: jild-i avval, duvvum, sivvum*. Tehrān: mu'assasah-i intishārāt-i ilhām, 1386/2007.

Bīdil, 'Abd al-Qādir Khān. *Nikāt*, in *Āvāz'hā-i Bīdil*. Tehrān: mu'assasah-i intishārāt-i nigāh, 1386/2007, 185–322.

Bīdil, 'Abd al-Qādir Khān. *Ruqa'āt*, in *Āvāz'hā-i Bīdil*. Tehrān: mu'assasah-i intishārāt-i nigāh, 1386/2007, 29–182.

Borges, Jorge Luis. "The Mirror of Enigmas," in *Labyrinths*. New York: New Directions, 1964, 209–12.

de Bruijn, Thomas. *Ruby in the Dust: Poetry and History in Padmāvat by the South Asian Sufi Poet Muḥammad Jāyasī*. Leiden: Leiden University Press, 2012.

Burckhardt, Titus. *Mystical Astrology According to Ibn 'Arabi*. Louisville, KY: Fons Vitae, 2001.

Chandra, Satish. *Parties and Politics at the Mughal Court: 1707–1740*. Delhi: Oxford University Press, 2002.

Chittick, William C. *The Sufi Path of Knowledge: Ibn 'Arabi's Metaphysics of the Imagination*. Albany, NY: State University of New York Press, 1989.

Chittick, William C. *The Self-Disclosure of God: Principles of Ibn 'Arabi's Cosmology*. Albany, NY: State University of New York Press, 1998.

Chittick, William C. *Ibn 'Arabi: Heir to the Prophets*. Oxford: Oneworld, 2005.

Damrel, David W. "The 'Naqshbandi Reaction' Reconsidered," in David Gilmartin and Bruce B. Lawrence (eds), *Beyond Turk and Hindu: Rethinking Religious Identities in Islamicate South Asia*. Gainesville, FL: University Press of Florida, 2000, 176–98.

Dargāh Qulī Khān. *Muraqqa'-i Dehlī*. Hyderābād: Tāj Press, 1973.

Ernst, Carl. "The Man without Attributes: Ibn 'Arabi's Interpretation of Abu yazid al-Bistami." *Journal of the Muhyiddin Ibn 'Arabi Society* XIII (1993), 1–18.

Faruqi, Shamsur Rahman. "Stranger in the City: the Poetics of Sabk-i Hindi," *Annual of Urdu Studies* 19 (2004), 1–94.

Genette, Gerard. *Palimpsests: Literature in the Second Degree*. Lincoln, NE: University of Nebraska Press, 1997.

Ghani, Abdul. *Life and Works of Abdul Qadir Bedil*. Lahore: United Publishers, 1960.

Ghelīchkhānī, Ḥamīdreẕā. *Iṣṭilahāt-i nuskhah-pardāzī dar dīvān-i Bīdil-i Dihlavī*. New Delhi: Center for Persian Research, Office of the Cultural Counselor, Islamic Republic of Iran, 2011.

Hādī, Nabī. *Mirzā Bedil*. Delhi: Ejukeshnal Pablishing Haus, 2009.

Houtsma, M.Th. *E.J. Brill's First Encyclopedia of Islam, 1913–1936*. Vol. 4. Leiden: Brill Academic Publishers, 1993.

al-Hujvīrī, 'Alī bin 'U̱smān al-Jullābī. *Kashf al-mahjūb: The Oldest Persian Treatise in Sufism*. London: Luzac, 1936.

Jāmī, Nūr al-Dīn. 'Abd al-Raḥmān bin Aḥmad. *The Precious Pearl: al-Jāmi's 'Al-Durrah al-Fākhirah' together with its Glosses and the Commentary of 'Abd al-Ghafur al-Lārī*. Albany, NY: State University of New York Press, 1979.

Jāmī, Nūr al-Dīn. 'Abd al-Raḥmān bin Aḥmad. "*Lawā'ih*," in Sachiko Murata, *Chinese Gleams of Sufi Light: Wang Tai-yu's Great Learning of the pure and Real and Liu Chih's Displaying the concealment of the Real Realm; with a new translation of Jami's Lawā'ih from the Persian by William C. Chittick*. Albany, NY: State University of New York Press, 2000, 128–210.

Jāmī, Nūr al-Dīn. 'Abd al-Raḥmān bin Aḥmad. *Haft awrang: jild-i duvvum*. Tehrān: mirāṯ maktūb, 1378/2013.

"Khatmī," 'Abul Ḥasan 'Abd al-Raḥmān Lāhorī. *Sharḥ-i 'irfānī-i ghazal'hā-i Ḥāfiẓ*. Tehrān: nashr-i Qaṯrah, 1378/1999.

Khusraw, Amīr. *Dībāchah-i dīvān-i ghurrat al-kamāl*. Lāhor: maṭba'-i 'aliyyah, 1975.

Khvushgū, Bindrāban Dās. *Safīnah-i Khvushgū: daftar-i thālith*. Patnā: idārah-i taḥqīqat-i 'Arabī va Fārsī, 1959.

Kovacs, Hajnalka. "The Tavern of the Manifestation of Realities: The Masnavi Muhit-i Azam by Mirza Abd al-Qadir Bedil (1644–1720)." PhD diss., University of Chicago, 2013.

Langermann, Y. Tzvi. "Another Andalusian Revolt? Ibn Rushd's Critique of Al-Kindi's Pharmacological Computus," in Jan P. Hogendijk and A.I. Sabra (eds), *The Enterprise of Science in Islam: New Perspectives*. London: MIT Press, 2003, 351–52.

Lindberg, David. *Theories of Vision from Al-Kindi to Kepler*. Chicago, IL: University of Chicago Press, 1976.

Losensky, Paul E. *Welcoming Fighani: Imitation and Poetic Individuality in the Safavid-Mughal Ghazal*. Costa Mesa, CA: Mazda Publishers, 1998.

Minissale, Gregory. *Images of Thought: Visuality in Islamic India: 1550–1750*. Newcastle: Cambridge Scholars Press, 2006.

Minissale, Gregory. "The Dynamics of the Gaze in Mughal Painting," *Marg* 58: 2 (December 2006).

Minissale, Gregory. "Seeing Eye-to-Eye with Mughal Miniatures: Some Observations on the Outward Gazing Figure in Mughal Art," *Marg* 58: 3 (March 2007), 40–49.

Mitchell, W.J.T. "Ekphrasis and the Other," in *Picture Theory: Essays on Verbal and Visual Representation*. Chicago, IL: University of Chicago Press, 1994.

Muḥammad, bin Ghulām Muḥammad. *Sharḥ-i Yūsuf u Zulaykhā*, MS BW Ivanow 0064, Redpath Library, McGill University, Montreal.

Netton, Ian Richard. *Allah Transcendent: Studies in the Structure and Semiotics of Islamic Philosophy, Theology and Cosmology*. London: Routledge, 1994.

Pello, Stefano. "Persian as a Passe-partout: The Case of Mirzā 'Abd al-Qādir Bīdil and his Hindu disciples," in Allison Busch and Thomas de Bruijn (eds), *People in Motion, Ideas in Motion: Culture and Circulation in Pre-Modern South Asia*. Leiden: Brill, 2013.

Reynolds, Dwight F. *Interpreting the Self: Autobiography in the Arabic Literary Tradition*. Berkeley, CA: University of California Press, 2000.

Roxburgh, David J. "Kamal al-Din Bihzad and Authorship in Persian Painting," *Muqarnas* 17 (2000): 119–46.

Rūmī, Jalāl al-Dīn. *Ma̱snavī-i ma'navī: daftar-i avval*. Tehrān: Pizhmān, 1373/1994–95.

Rūmī, Jalāl al-Dīn. *Ma̱snavī-i ma'navī: daftar-i panjum*. Tehrān: Pizhmān, 1373/1994–95.

Sa'dī, Abū 'Abudullāh Musliḥ al-. *Kitāb-i Gulistān*. Tehrān: chāp-khānah-i Gulshan, 1360/1942.

Saljuqī, Salāḥ al-Dīn. *Naqd-i Bīdil*. Tehrān: Muḥammad Ibraḥīm Shari'atī Afghānistanī, 1380/2001.

"Shafīq, Lacchmī Nārāyan. *Taẕkirah-i Gul-i ra'nā*. Ḥyderābād: 'ahd-āfarīn Press, 1967.

Shirāzī, Nūr al-Dīn Muḥammad Abdullāh. *'Ilājāt-i Dārā Shukūhi* or *Ṭibb-i Dārā Shukūhī*, MS 6226, Kitāb-khānah-i majlis, Tehrān, Iran.

Siddiqi, Moazzam. "An Examination of the Indo-Persian Mystical Poet Mirzā 'Abdul Qādir Bedil with Particular Reference to His Chief Work *'Irfān*." PhD diss., University of California, 1975.

Stewart, Devin J. "Saj' in the Qur'ān: Prosody and Structure," *Journal of Arabic Literature* 21: 2 (1990), 101–39.

Soucek, Priscilla. "Nizami on Painters and Painting," in Richard Ettinghausen (ed.), *Islamic Art in the Metropolitan Museum of Art*. New York: The Metropolitan Museum of Art, 1972, 9–21.

Soucek, Priscilla. "The Theory and Practice of Portraiture in the Persian Tradition," *Muqarnas* 17 (2000), 97–108.

Verma, Som Prakash. *Mughal Painters and their Work: A Biographical Survey and Comprehensive Catalogue*. Delhi: Oxford University Press, 1995.

Wehr, Hans. *A Dictionary of Modern Written Arabic*. London: MacDonald and Evans Ltd, 1980.

Zatallī, Ja'far. *Zatal-nāmah, Kulliyāt-i Ja'far Zatallī*. Delhi: anjuman-i taraqqī-i Urdu, 2011.

Zippoli, Ricardo. *Chirā sabk-i hindī dar dunyā-i gharb sabk-i bārūk khwāndah mīshavad?*. Tehrān: anjuman-i farhangī-i Itāliyā, bakhsh-i bāstān-shināsī, 1984.

2 Bīdil's *tarjī'-band*

The author's kenotic chorus

Through an interpretation of an ekphrastic episode from Bīdil's autobiography the last chapter disclosed an ambition that pervades his *The Four Elements*: an iconoclastic self-transformation, playing on a diversity of mythic models, into a locus for the divine Real. I suggested at various points in that chapter that his oeuvre of verse, too, shared this ambition. This chapter will develop this suggestion by arguing, mainly with reference to his *tarjī'-band* – a genre of stanzaic verse with an identical couplet at the end of every stanza – that Bīdil appropriated canons specific to each genre of verse in which he wrote in order to present distinct logics of his kenosis. *Kenosis* literally means "emptying" in Greek and is current in English language scholarship on diverse theologico-mystical traditions for an emptying of the self so it comes to be inhabited by God.[1] It here covers the varieties of ascetic self-erasure and apotheosis metaphorically conveyed in Chapter 1 by Bīdil's destruction of his portrait. Woven into this interpretation of his *tarjī'-band* are readings of his *ghazal* couplets and passages of his *masnavīs*, disclosing similarities and differences between the logics of self-transformation in each genre.

But first, here are two justifications for this arguably idiosyncratic choice of his *tarjī'-band* over his other poems as my main object of analysis in this chapter. These are necessary justifications because Bīdil has been remembered in biographical dictionaries (*tazkirahs*) and modern literary criticism on him mainly for his *ghazals* and then occasionally for his four longest *masnavīs*. Almost none of this corpus of biographical and scholarly writing has analyzed or even addressed his *tarjī'-band*. What, then, commends this poem to our attention here? First, its metonymic representation at the level of its themes of the rest of Bīdil's oeuvre: this poem, twenty-six printed pages and thirty-four stanzas long and the only one he composed in this genre, shares a gnostic cosmogony, cosmology, psychology and narrative itinerary with his four longest *masnavīs*, his vast corpus of *ghazals*, over three thousand quatrains (*rubā'īs*), *tarkīb-bands* (another stanzaic form with a differing couplet refrain at the end of every stanza) and panegyrics (*qaṣīdah*). However – and this is the second justification – it is shorter than any of the four aforementioned *masnavīs* because it abbreviates the cosmogony and correlated genesis of the human soul that his longest *masnavī*, *'Irfān* ("Gnosis," completed in 1712), details in all its stages. This abbreviation makes it more amenable to the analytical scope of a chapter than the entirety of one of the *masnavīs*. Indeed, Chapter 3 closely reads only one section of *'Irfān*. Counter-intuitively, this abbreviation also permits us to submit it to a more comprehensive textual analysis than his *ghazals*. Although any one of his *ghazal* distiches is obviously shorter than his *tarjī'-band*, it demands to be interpreted with an attention to its relations to the rest of his *ghazal* corpus which, taken as a coherent whole as it ought, is larger than a chapter can do justice to. This hermeneutic criterion of interpreting the part in consonance with the whole also places his huge corpus of quatrains outside the scope of this chapter. Notwithstanding these limitations, the following discussion will include analyses of a selection of Bīdil's verses from these other genres, adumbrating a frame of reference within which they could later – and by other scholars – be interpreted more comprehensively.

It is a curious feature of Bīdil's oeuvre that, if read with an attention to its concepts alone, it yields, relative to Ibn 'Arabī the appropriation of whose tradition was discussed in Chapter 1, a sparse grid of concepts or terms.[2] This terminological sparseness is an effect of the mainly propaedeutic aims of his oeuvre as well as of the almost exclusively poetic rather than expository genres in which he chose to write. It was to convey – or rather to induce – certain ideal psychophysical dispositions in his disciple-reader that he employed a range of poetic techniques throughout his vast corpus. In social practice, as I noted in Chapter 1, these readers were dispersed across the three overlapping social spaces of the imaginary hospice, his domestic literary assembly and the imperial court. They would have come to inhabit such dispositions in keeping with their varying degrees of literary-spiritual training and their social settings. Normatively, however, these dispositions were conceived with the hospice-based Sufi reader in mind as initial "states" (*aḥvāl*) that would prepare the reading or listening subject for a graduated progress towards an intuitive experience of the divine Real. The riches of Bīdil's vast oeuvre thus lie not so much in his overtly named and semantically stable web of concepts – these being relatively meager in any case – as in the poetic techniques by which he iterated and reiterated this relatively small stock of core theses.

What are these theses? Fundamental among them is a distinction that frames his oeuvre, namely the distinction between the most real and transpersonal Self and a personal and phenomenal one. Like several others in his Persianate milieu he inherited this originally Neo-Platonic distinction from the Andalusian Sufi thinker Ibn 'Arabī (d. 1240). Chapter 1 explicated Bīdil's specifically visual appropriations from Ibn 'Arabī. In doing so, it also disclosed how terminologically uneven and doctrinally broad this appropriation was. In this Bīdil was anticipated by Jāmī's (d. 1492, Herat) poetic expositions of Ibn 'Arabī's thought. This terminological unevenness may also be explained, as noted above, by the pedagogical motivations of Bīdil's *tarjī'-band* and indeed of much of his oeuvre that was – and must be read as – a poetic propaedeutic to the Sufi journey into oneself and the Real. The technical terms Bīdil uses mostly cluster in the discursive sections of his *masnavīs* that expound cosmogonic and ontological developments or notions and that are only a few of the ramifying web of terms structuring Ibn 'Arabī's thought and practice. The greater part of his *masnavīs*, as indeed his *ghazals*, is taken up with metaphorical explorations and presentations of states of being. Occasionally, through a conceit typical of Sufi littérateurs, he appears to self-effacingly mock the poetic technique and craft that distinguish his famously difficult style. Yet, his poetic oeuvre variously conforms, as we will note below, to the heritage of each of the genres in which he wrote. As such, each of his poetic compositions is intended pedagogically to orient the reader who is bewildered (*ḥayrat, ḥayrānī, taḥayyur*) – the affect in his oeuvre accompanying a frustrated desire for ontological ascent – by the Real's manifestation as beauty towards the possibility of attaining intimacy with – and self-annihilating identification with – the source of this beauty. Moreover, this source is already contained within and envelops the reader's inquiring self. Bīdil:

aī sham' āfiyat-kadah taslīm-i nīstīst
kashtī-nishīn-i kām-i nahang-i khvudīm mā[3]

Shelter, O flame, lies in submitting to nothingness.
We sail in the hull of our whale's maw.

As Bahram Jassemi says of the first necessary condition for Sufi journeying in Ibn 'Arabī:

> The mystical journey is the form of practice of the Sufi way (*tarīqa*). Every person who feels awakened and has begun to marvel at Being (*ḥayrah*) accordingly feels called to begin to follow the way of the transcendent. And this is only the beginning. The Sufi learns first to know himself, since an insight gained without knowledge of who he is cannot be a true witnessing of the Divine. For this the adept seeks a *shaykh* (or is 'called' by the *shaykh*) who can help him to change his inner structure by means of re-education, to conform to the Unseen and to develop the taste (*zauq*) he requires for the long journey.[4]

In Bīdil such *ḥayrat* or marveling bewilderment is directed at the multifarious beauty (*ḥusn*) in which the Real, as discussed in Chapter 1, discloses and delimits Itself at once. The first step in such a progressively deepening experience of the Real or the One is the same as the incipience of self-knowledge or the recognition that the Real constitutes one's true Self. Bīdil's oeuvre therefore comprises a generically diverse panoply of techniques and pedagogical prescriptions to this end.

Beauty is the human's blinding inner perception of the emanation of the Many from the One that is already within the human. On the question of just *how* the Many emanated from the One, Sufis in Ibn 'Arabī's tradition were distinguished from certain theologians and philosophers. Jāmī noted that Ash'arite

Muslim theologians believed it possible for multiple effects to issue from a single cause because of their doctrine of the immediate causal dependence of all contingent beings on God.[5] He contrasted this position with that of Islamic-Neo-Platonic philosophers who, he observed, argued it was impossible for the truly One to issue in the Many except through the mediacy of the first emanation ("the First Principle"). The Sufi position, which was also his own, was a qualified acceptance of both positions. It was qualified in the sense that Sufis admitted the Ash'arite doctrine of the emanation of the Many from the One but not directly. Rather, they insisted on the mediated or indirect emanation of the Many from the first emanation of the One. In this they "differed from them [i.e., philosophers], however, with respect to the First Principle's being really one for, as has been said, they affirm of him Attributes (*ṣifāt*) and relations (*nisab*) which differ from Him in the mind (*'aqlan*) but not in the external world (*khārijan*)."[6] That is, the Sufis in Ibn 'Arabī, Jāmī and Bīdil's tradition distinguished between the *external* unity of God's Attributes and relations with God and their *mental* difference from Him. Since most humans grasped only the mental multiplicity of God's Attributes and relations, the task of Sufi pedagogy was to have them recognize the true or external identity of these Attributes and relations with God. A broad aim of Bīdil's poetic corpus is to effect shifts in the reader's states of mind towards this recognition. Bīdil:

namūd-i z̲arrah t̲ilsim-i ḥuẓūr-i khvurshīd ast
kih guftah ast farāmūsh kardah'ī mā rā[7]

The mote's coming into view is a talisman of the sun's presence.
Who ever said You forgot me?

The reader learns on this model to recognize the sun in each of its motes. Bīdil's *tarjī'-band* presents itself to readers who bear such mote-like phenomenal selves as a pedagogical means to self-recognition and thus self-transformation into the sun. Reading Bīdil, who speaks here both as himself and as all other Sufis and especially those who had used this genre before him, the reader may be alerted to the phenomenality of his personal self and undertake to ascetically cultivate his attention to the true Self. This would entail learning to train an ascetic attention on the iridescent multiplicity of the created world. By this each of its beings, typically imagined as a mirror fogged in its reflection of the true Self by the verdigris of egotism, would come to disclose its origin in the One. Through this pedagogically supervised ascetic paring away of his attention to the attributes (*ṣifāt*) of the divine essence (*z̲āt*) or the true self, the reader would overcome the false sense of mineness or ownership which such attributes detain him in. And a relinquishing of such ownership would disclose the divine essence itself as inherent in himself. The guiding text of this process of ascetic self-transformation is the Prophetic dictum (*ḥadīs̲*) that is precious to all Sufis and is quoted in part to stand for the whole at the end of the *tarjī'-band*: "He who knows himself knows his Lord." But this summary of Bīdil's core theses fails by its very intellectualism and abstraction. It is not to *what* is conveyed but to *how* it is conveyed – to the manifold poetics or logics of Bīdil's self-presentations – that we must turn for a concrete sense of how he fashioned his authorship as a Sufi poet by re-fashioning the Sufi heritage of the *tarjīʻ-band.*

Tarjīʻ, a verbal noun derived from the Arabic root *rajʻ* meaning "to return" or "turn around," in turn means: "Causing to return or recur; uttering the ejaculation from the Kur'ān, *innā li'llāhi wa innā ilaihi rājiʻūna*, 'Verily we belong to God, and verily to Him we shall return.' "[8] In poetry it refers to the generic trait of the refrain or returning identical couplet or *band* – literally "interstitial space" – at the end of every stanza and before the next. The theological meaning in the foregoing dictionary gloss alerts us to the recursive logic relating the phenomenal, personal self to the most real transpersonal one. The recursive movement in both these senses, poetic and theological, is justified by the assumption of the chronological priority of the couplet refrain in relation to the rest of the poem. The first stanza does not open with the couplet refrain and thus precedes the refrain's first textual appearance. However, the refrain itself is first disclosed to Bīdil, who names himself as the speaker of the poem, as a "testimony" (*gavāh*) to the priority of the truth of theistic monism over the dispersed multiplicity of creaturely identities, a testimony whose authorship he does not explicitly and exclusively claim.[9] In this sense, the refrain takes logical and chronological priority over the rest of the poem. This double priority of the refrain allows Bīdil to employ it as an arrest or check on the sequential character or narrativity that characterizes his *masnavī* expositions of his cosmogony. His *tarjīʻ-band,* as we will be remarking, rhythmically returns to the refrain to qualify any sense of gnostic progress that might have gathered in the preceding stanza. For this reason it embodies in the very recursivity of its form what his *masnavīs* narrate and briefer verse forms imagistically condense: namely, the human's continual lapses into forms of egotism from an ideal evacuation of one's false self to give place to the divine true Self, a theotic evacuation I have called *kenosis*. This articulation of kenotic failure with poetic form allies Bīdil's *tarjīʻ-band* with his *Four Elements* whose four-part elemental structure, we must recall from Chapter 1, signaled his predisposition to sin. Any gnostic progress achieved by the iconoclastic destruction of his portrait stood qualified by its place within a frame of four elements. This formal resonance with the text at the center of Chapter 1 further justifies the priority this chapter gives to his *tarjīʻ-band.*

If Bīdil's poem in question shares a poetics of kenotic failure with his autobiography, then is this poem autobiographical too? What is the voice in which the poem is spoken? Who speaks in the poem? This question cannot be answered except by attention to the spiraling structure of the *tarjīʻ-band* and the shifting functions of the couplet refrain that variously returns at the curve-end of each spiral. Here are the opening and concluding passages of the first stanza, concluding with the couplet refrain that I here italicize to distinguish it from the preceding text:

We are companions [*ḥarīfān*] in the assembly of secrets
Drunk on the cup of witnessing union [*dīdārīm*]
Upwellings of the ocean of divinity [*lāhūtīm*]
Dawn emanations of the world of lights.
Effect and act of the Real are manifest by us.
Undoubtedly are we presentations of the secret of manifestation.
Self-disclosing is the Real by our robes.
Unavoidably do we bear a coruscation of colors.
Sometimes are we the cup, sometimes clear wine
Sometimes the cup-bearer, sometimes intoxication
Sometimes insane, sometimes the essence of wakeful awareness
Sometimes drunk, sometimes sober
Sometimes are we maddened by our own works
Sometimes vexed by our own deeds
Sometimes over-spilling ourselves like a flood
Sometimes firmly founded like a mountain [...]
Our yearning, despite colorlessness,
Grows acquainted with color to make us rose gardens.
Faith and heresy are just so much talk or else
We are the rosary itself, the sacred thread itself.
To prattlers from the classroom of conviction.

Do we present these two hemistiches as testimony:

The world is nothing but a self-disclosure of the Friend.
This talk of "I" and "us" is a self-same addition to Him.

[*kih jahān nīst juz tajallī-i dūst*
īn man u mā hamān 'iẕāfat-i ūst].[10]

The stanza is spoken in the first person plural, a grammatical feature emphasized by the use of the attached pronoun for "we" – "*īm*" – for the end rhyme of every distich's second hemistich. With this feature the poem begins by already announcing the plurality of individuals it contains: "We are companions in the assembly of secrets." The word *ḥarīfān* that is here translated as "companions" is also translatable by "rivals," thus including its opposite within its semantic field. The antonymy anticipates the inclusion of the contradictory plenitude of attributes within the choral speaker. This coruscation of opposites is also an allusion to what scholarship on Ibn 'Arabī has recognized as the two contradictory aspects of his God in relation to His creation: His incomparability (*tanzīh*) to it and similarity (*tashbīh*) to it.[11] While the imagination (*takhyīl*) is able to comprehend God's immanence in the beings that issue from His "names and attributes" (*asmā va ṣifāt*), the intellect (*'aql*) comprehends His transcendence in relation to His creation. "Our" nature is thus a site for the quicksilver oppositions of the self-disclosures of the Real. It is these self-disclosures or hierophanies that are the referent of the word *tajallī* in Bīdil's couplet refrain. In his book glossing Sufi technical terms Ibn 'Arabī defines *al-tajallī* as "that which is revealed to [men's] hearts from the lights of the Transcendent [or Hidden] (*min anwār al-ghuyūb*)."[12] This definition specifies the inner and individual locus of God's appearances and thus also accounts for the diversity of His appearances, a diversity as infinite as human individuals and their abilities to imagine Him through prayer.

This inner contradictoriness implies that we "unavoidably [...] bear a coruscation of colors." Here, as in Chapter 1, "colors" bear the pejorative connotation of a distracting and limited accident upon the substance of a thing. Included in these accidents – metaphorized above as the multiplicity of foam on the single ocean's surface – are the identities of container and contained (cup and wine), both dark intoxication and its clear cause and sartorial markers of theological difference (rosary and sacred thread). All of these are equally unreal in relation to the one divinity from which they issue, an unreality to which the readers of this poem, identified here as "prattlers," are inattentive in their "talk of 'I' and 'us'." It is to silence them and teach them to turn their attention to the One at the origin of the Many that the speakers invoke the couplet refrain as "testimony." The Persian original uses the compound verb *gavāh āvardan*, literally to "bear witness," a formulation signifying fetching what already exists rather than devising it. The "we" of the formulation "Do we present these two hemistiches as testimony" leaves open the possibility of Bīdil's participation in a collective authorship of this distich. The text of the refrain thus first appears to be of ambiguously multiple authorship. Who exactly is the author of the testimonial text of the refrain?

To answer this we must read this first stanza as a proleptic achievement of the sought identification with the Real that will be related in the thirty-fourth and very last stanza. It is in this sense that we are tracing a spiral, the destination being the most superior of the many iterations of the beginning. In this last stanza Bīdil addresses himself by name thus: "Of the elements is your apparent structure/Though you are purer than these/But admixture has its effects/For impossible is patience with them." He discovers the purity of the Self within in the "guiding text" (*dalīl*) of the aforementioned Prophetic dictum – "He who knows himself knows his Lord" – which is here quoted in part because its full form was familiar: "*He who knows himself* is your sufficient guide/So you know that you are the singular divine essence [*z̤āt-i_yektā'ī*]." Even as an elemental and thus inevitably sinful and frail conjuncture, he is the protean or "colorful" hierophany of the Friend. The Qur'ānic model cannot be missed here: God speaks throughout the Qur'ān in the first person plural. The author of the couplet refrain thus proves to have been Bīdil himself and comprehends all the stages traversed in Sufi self-transformation to look back from the vantage point of the final and highest stage of theotic kenosis at his earlier "colors" or limited attributes.

An excursus on the dialectic of author and speaker

But as anyone familiar with the poetics of Sufi texts knows, the *author* is not the same as the *speaker*. Rather, an individual fashioned his authorial authority through a dialectical relation between author and speaker. This can be made sharply apparent by reference to an untitled prose piece by Ghanī Kashmīrī (d. 1669), Kashmir's most famous Persian-language poet, in self-defense against the charge of literary theft and in accusation of a scribe for his lapse.[13] An acquaintance of Ghanī's who happened to be studying a copy of the *Tārīkh-i Badāyūnī*, a famous Persian-language book of history completed by a scholar associated with the emperor Akbar's court, 'Abdul Qādir Badāyūnī, in 1596 – that is, possibly half a century before Ghanī wrote – discovered in it a distich that had recently grown famous as Ghanī's.[14] The acquaintance alerted Ghanī to this discovery and thus to the possibility that Ghanī might be considered to have stolen the distich from Badāyūnī's book of history. At this, Ghanī resolved to keep silent and compose no more poetry until his name was cleared of dishonor and asked his friends to set his name down beside the distich wherever they found it written for it was, in truth, his own. When, finally, Ghanī came upon and studied closely an older copy of the *Tārīkh* and did not find the distich in question in it, he summoned the scribe who had made the allegedly incriminating copy of the *Tārīkh.* After "much importuning and endless reproofs" the scribe confessed that the original copy he had copied had not contained the distich and that he had nonetheless interpolated it into his copy of the *Tārīkh* because it had "fitted the occasion." Disgraced, the scribe was debarred from literary assemblies and Ghanī, his name cleared of dishonor, concludes his piece by requesting his readers, who are earlier explicitly addressed as practitioners of the Speaking Anew (*tāzah-gūyī*) stylistics of the Persian *ghazal*, not to blame the poet for the scribe's fault when they suspected "the interpolation of topos-theft."

Remarkably, Ghanī aggressively protected his claims to the authorial ownership of his own poetry to the same degree that, in his poetry itself, he was pervasively concerned as a Sufi with the kenotic erasure of his selfhood and property. This was a dialectical contradiction. These two attitudes were dialectically related in that any kenotically achieved poetic formulation depended for its valuation on public knowledge of the empirical individual who undertook such kenosis. It was by the communal acclaim of a named and known individual's ascetic practice that the verbal results of that practice were judged as to the sincerity of their professions of poverty and self-effacement. The paradigm for this dialectic lay, of course, in the philologico-ethical discipline of *Ḥadīs̱* that verified the attribution to – we might say authorship of – the Prophet Muḥammad of exemplary statements and deeds. This is not the place to elaborate on this prophetological paradigm for the poet's dialectically contradictory insistence on his authorship and proclamations of kenosis. However, I have made the argument in brief because it lets us conceptualize the difference between Bīdil's *authorship* of the *tarjī'-band* and the choral *voice* in which he *speaks* it.

Despite the approximate terminological resemblance, this distinction between author and speaker is not a version of the distinction current in contemporary literary criticism between author and narrator. The latter distinction, originating as it does in Structuralism and its narratological applications, maintains a gap between signification and reference, between the level of signs and that of the world they refer to. Moreover, it is by methodologically excluding the world of reference that Structuralism is able to achieve systemic coherence and closure in its analyses of sign-systems.[15] By contrast, the discussion in Chapter 1 of Bīdil's authorship of *sukhan*, focusing on his literary appropriation of a prominent theological distinction of his time, involved us, not in Structuralist analysis, but in literary and cultural history. The *author* may thus be conceptualized as the embodied individual who is empirically verified in a community's prosopographical discourses on him as *owning* a corpus of texts. In this sense the author is one of the forms of personhood recognized in a community. The *speaker* may be conceptualized as any number of *personae*, typically archetypal (e.g., *fakhriyyah* or "boastful," *inkisāriyyah* or "self-abasing," abject lover, magician, posthumous voice from the grave...), that the author, depending on his communal acclaim or reputation, is able to assume in the corpus of texts communally validated as his own.

Chapter 1 studied Bīdil's authorship as his autobiographical appropriation, addressed as mimetic model to a disciple, of a historically attested famous painter's portrait of him. It disclosed how he adapted a variety of poetic and painterly myths to signal at once the individuality of his life as a series of inner states and its membership in multiple intellectual, poetic and mystical trajectories of thought and practice. This chapter asks who, on the basis of the limited theosis he presents himself as achieving in his disciple's gaze, he presents himself to be when he *speaks* in his *tarjī'-band.* It asks, in other words, what *voice* he adopts in this poem. This question cannot be answered without recourse to literary history because the voice he adopts in this poem assumes, like all classical Persian literature, the reader's awareness of a "family resemblance" with prior models in this genre.

The littérateur Khvushgū, who was one of Bīdil's longest serving student-disciples in poetry as in other Sufi practices, has left us in his entry on Bīdil in his biographical dictionary *Safīnah-i Khvushgū* (mostly composed between 1724 and 1735) what is perhaps the most valuable first-hand account of his teacher's activities. However, it is to his entry on the great thirteenth-century Sufi poet Fakhr al-Dīn 'Irāqī (d. 1289) that we must turn. Here, taking advantage of the rhetorical trait of digression that seems to have become characteristic of eighteenth-century biographical compendia, he remarks with reference to the poem in question at the center of this chapter that Bīdil had composed a *tarjī'-band* in imitation (*javāb*) of Fakhr al-Dīn 'Irāqī's. Stated formally, such digressions were rhetorical techniques by which to make the past present. This specifically entailed characterizing a life and its works in ways that assigned it a stake in the biographer's milieu, techniques that will not be discussed here but that form the main object of analysis in this book's final chapter. For now, we will confine our attention to

Khvushgū's observation that Bīdil's competitive imitation of 'Irāqī's "very famous" *tarjī'-band* comprised seven hundred couplets "and the humble compiler Khvushgū, too, has tested his mettle by imitating [*tatabbu'*] it."

This poetic affiliation to 'Irāqī places Bīdil in a lineage of poetic interpreters of Ibn 'Arabī. Having spent twenty-five years in Multan as a disciple of Bahā al-Dīn Z̲akariyā, an Indian association that evidently made him valuable for Khvushgū's purposes and accounts for Khvushgū's relatively long six-page entry on him, 'Iraqī had studied in Konya under Ibn 'Arabī's main disciple, Ṣadr al-Dīn Qūnavī (d. 1274). William C. Chittick writes: "'Irāqi's short mixed prose and poetry classic, *Lama'āt*, was inspired by Qūnavī's lectures on Ibn 'Arabī's works." On the commentaries on this work Chittick adds: "The most famous of the commentaries, Jāmī's *Ashe'at al-lama'āt*, also sees the work mainly in terms of the teachings of Qūnavī and his school."[16] If a significant portion of 'Irāqī's oeuvre comprised an interpretation of Ibn 'Arabī's monism and if Jāmī who influentially mediated the transmission of Ibn 'Arabī's thought to India composed a commentary on 'Irāqi's work, then Bīdil's competitive imitation of 'Irāqī's *tarjī'-band* implicates a veritable tradition of poetic interpretations of Ibn 'Arabī.

The couplet refrain of 'Irāqī's *tarjī'-band* is, as Khvushgū's quotes, "That/For with the heart's eyes do not look upon anyone but the Friend/Whatever you see, know that it is a manifestation of Him [*kih ba chishmān-i dil mabīn juz dūst/har chih bīnī bidān kih maẓhar-i ūst*]." This refrain, too, condenses the Neo-Platonic pedagogical aim of the poem as a whole, namely to train its reader's gaze to recognize the One inherent in its Many emanations. Khvushgū's own *tarjī'-band* written in competitive imitation of his teacher's and 'Iraqī's shares these traits and confirms that Bīdil was playing on what was by then an established tradition of *tarjī'-band* expositions of Akbarian theistic monism. Khvushgū proudly notes that his own couplet refrain in imitation of his teacher's was:

> That to meet the needs of the Friend's conquering beauty
> Darkness and light were the rising light of His face
>
> *kih baḥr-i hājat-i ḥusn-i farrukh-i dūst*
> *z̤ulmat u nūr maṭla'-i rukh-i ūst*

– yet another formulation of an Akbarian and Neo-Platonic emanationist inheritance.

But this would not be much of a tradition had it comprised only the names of 'Irāqī, Bīdil and Khvushgū. It is probable that Khvushgū named 'Irāqī as Bīdil's only predecessor in this generic formulation of Akbarian monism either because he did not know of the others whose *tarjī'-band*s Bīdil was working variations on, or because he took Bīdil at his word when he declared 'Irāqī to have been his model. At any rate, the tradition in question also comprised others who composed *tarjī'-band*s as well as a more diffuse and wider group of yet others who composed poetry in other genres but also to formulate such theistic monism in emanationist terms. Conspicuous among those who, after 'Irāqī, found the stanzaic form and couplet refrain of the *tarjī'-band* a valuable means by which to expound and repeatedly reinterpret an ontological characterization of the world as a multiform emanation of God's single light were Nāṣir Bukhārī, a contemporary of Ḥāfiẓ from fourteenth-century Transoxiana, and Ni'matullāh Valī (d. 1531) whose *tarjī'-band* was most probably an imitation of Bukhārī's.[17] Bukhārī's *tarjī'-band* uses the following the couplet refrain:

For the world's a ray of the Friend's face
All of creation's His shadow

kih jahān partow ast az rukh-i dūst
jumlah-i kayināt sāyah-i ūst

Ni'matullāh Valī's couplet refrain:

For everywhere in the world and all that's in it
Is an image of a ray of the Friend's face

kih sarāsar-i jahān u har chih dar ū ast
'aks-i yek partow'īst az rukh-i dūst

Both refrains paratactically balance the comprehensiveness of the "world" with the particularity of the "Friend's face." Were we to agree with Erich Auerbach's famous postulate of an isomorphism between syntax and degrees of social complexity, we could relate such paratactical simplicity to the simplicity or non-composite nature of the One whence the Many emanated.[18]

Among the aforementioned poetic formulations of such monism that did not take the form of the *tarjī'-band* but formed a strand in Bīdil's inheritances are Ḥāfiẓ's (d. *c.*1390) *ghazal* couplet:

No difference between the love of the hospice and the tavern.
Whatever the place, there is a ray of the Beloved's face.

dar 'ishq-i khānqāh u kharābāt farq nīst
har jā kih hast partow-i rū-yi ḥabīb hast.[19]

Ḥāfiż, in turn, possibly had in mind Farīd al-Dīn 'Aṭṭār (d. 1221) one of whose *ghazal* couplets declares:

Wherever the world is adornment
It is a ray of Your world-adorning face

chun jahān har jā kih hast ārāyishī
partow az rū-yi jahān-ārā-yi tu'st.[20]

This long trajectory of the onto-theological use in poetry of light imagery transforms a Qur'ānic hypotext even as it is sanctioned by it. Verse 88 of Chapter 28 of the Qur'ān, a verse Ibn 'Arabī quotes frequently throughout his works, declares: "Everything will be destroyed except His face. His is the judgment and to Him you will be returned." In this Qur'ānic verse the word "returned" – *turja'una* – is recognizably cognate with the *tarjī'* of *tarjī'-band.* This is no semantic coincidence, for Bīdil and his predecessors employed the stanzas of the *tarjī'-band* to signal a continual dissolution of the ontological postulates of each stanza into the couplet refrain that variously asserted the judgment of the One from whose light the Many emanated. And *tarjī'*, we must recall from our opening discussion of the term, means "Causing to return or recur; uttering the ejaculation from the Kur'ān, *innā li'llāhi wa innā ilaihi rāji'ūna*, 'Verily we belong to God, and verily to Him we shall return.'" This gloss alerted us to the simultaneously poetic and theological return conveyed by the word. In the context of our discussion of the Akbarian uses of the *tarjī'-band* it signals the priority of the refrain that repeatedly submits the multiplicity of each stanza to the ontological priority of the luminous face of the Real.

At the poetic origin of this use of repetition to inscribe the idea of onto-theological return to God into poetic form is Ibn 'Arabī's use of what Denis McCauley has termed "the ultra-monorhyme" in a few poems in his *Dīvān.* McCauley:

> It was traditionally considered bad style to use the same rhyme-word twice in close proximity, a flaw that is known as *īṭā'.* However, Ibn 'Arabī's *Dīwān* contains a few poems in which the same rhyme-word is used not only twice in a row, but throughout the entire poem.[21]

Ibn 'Arabī broke this rule of rhyme propriety in order to inscribe into the phonemic texture of his poems the ontological anteriority of the One and divine Real over its manifestations in the Many. McCauley:

> Ultra-monorhyme is a useful device to drive this point home: every verse similarly comes back to God. At each turn, Ibn 'Arabī seems to embark on a new line of thought, only for the second hemistich to pull him back to God.[22]

Also among the probable hypotexts transformed by Bīdil's employment of the refrain is the account of Abū Yazīd al-Bistāmi's (d. 875) account of his nocturnal ascent on the Prophet Muḥammad's model – his Ascension (*mi'rāj*) – as described in a text attributed to Junayd of Baghdad (d. 910) but probably composed after Junayd's death, *The Quest for God* (*al-qaṣd ilā allāh*).[23] Modeled on the Prophet Muḥammad's ascent through the seven heavens to God's throne as well as on the ascensions of the Jewish prophet Enoch and the Harranian ascension narratives circulating in the Late Ancient Near East, this ascension narrative makes comparable use of a refrain. Al-Bistāmī refuses to accept the invitation of the angels in each heaven to remain in that heaven. Instead, he heeds his ontological intuition (*ma'rifa*) by declaring that "my goal is other than what you are showing me" before pressing on to the next heaven. In each heaven al-Bistāmī is reported to have declared that the angels of that heaven disclosed to him "dominion that would wear out the tongue to describe and depict". This sentence or a close variation on it re-appears in this account of each heaven, each time referring negatively to a higher degree of reality. For the stake of all such ascensions is, as Michael A. Sells says, "to become more purely intellectual, more angelic, or more deeply human."[24] By citing this hypotext, then, Bīdil signaled his participation in a prophetological tradition of ascensions that intensified a given attribute. On al-Bistāmī's model Bīdil intensifies his ontological intuition by repeating the couplet refrain in progressively intensified senses.

Also reinterpreted in the couplet refrain and the *tarjī'-band* as a whole are three heritages of light imagery: at the greatest chronological distance is the Late Ancient Gnostic heritage that adapted the ancient Greek notion of "light as a metaphor for truth" to assign light an ontological value.[25] Light was no longer a metaphor but the most perfect being itself entrapped in the darkness of matter. Light now acquired a history and the human was an actor in a larger drama of the retrieval of primordially squandered light. Possibly inheriting this imagery but equally possibly employing it independently is the Qur'ānic formulation of the Creator God as "the light of the heavens and the earth."[26] The third heritage was Neo-Platonic and Islamic emanationism. Emanationist ontologies, whether Greek or Islamic, conceived of God as the most perfect grade of reality that remained undiminished even as derivative grades of reality serially cascaded out of it. As such, these ontologies differed from the Qur'ān's emphasis on the creative aspect of God by emphasizing His transcendent one. The highest grade of reality was ultimately unknowable to the derivative ones and thus only formulated by a negative theology even though certain of its aspects – such as its unity – were known and positively assertable.[27]

This ultimate unknowability generated a rich vocabulary of apophasis in Islamic as in other emanationist traditions, an apophasis that Ibn 'Arabī paradigmatically transformed in his vast oeuvre. Two features of his thought were central to this transformation. The first was his theistic monism – designated "oneness of being" (*vaḥdat al-vujūd*) by his commentators – whereby all apparently derivative grades of reality were, as we have observed in Chapter 1's discussion of the *mise en abyme*, only God's manifestations of Himself to Himself. This implied, as Ian Netton has observed, a radical synonymy underlying the provisionally distinguished names for these derivative grades of reality. Apophasis, in this Akbarian frame of reference, was no longer a function of simply the Neo-Platonic ineffability of the most Real but of the radical monosemy of all nouns, which were names for God, and all verbs which formulated his Self-manifestations. Bīdil's couplet refrain thus rhythmically underscores the dissolution of the names and actions distinguished in each stanza into the "hierophany of the Friend."

The second of these features was the centrality of the human to this ontology, a centrality that distinguished it from Late Ancient Gnosticism wherein the human was subservient to the history of light. In Ibn 'Arabī's self-contained and circular ontology the human was privileged, on the Qur'ānic paradigm, as the most perfect of creatures. This perfection rested not only on its place as the ontological culmination of a sequence running from minerals to plants and animals but also on its unequalled ability to know the most Real. This ability, though ultimately falling asymptotically silent before God's transcendence, especially characterized an elite of teachers of whom Bīdil, ventriloquizing for Ibn 'Arabī and the aforementioned practitioners of the *tarjī'-band*, was one.

This explains the central importance of the metaphysical distinction between the human's phenomenal and true Self discussed earlier. The human, more than any other creature, is able to surpass the particularism of his phenomenal self to recognize his true one. This is why one of Ibn 'Arabī's most widely read interpreters, Maḥmūd Shabistarī, in his richly commentated upon didactic Persian verse encyclopedia of fifteen stock questions regarding Sufi topics and their answers, *Gulshan-i rāz* (The Garden of Mystery, 1317, Tabriz), glosses the word "I" (*man*) thus:

> When the absolute Being [*hast-i muṭlaq*] is expressed [*'ibārat*]
> By the word "I" do they express [*'ibārat*] it.
> When the Real, by entification [*ta'ayyin*], was made an entity [*mu'ayyin*]
> You called it by the expression "I."
> You and I are presentations [*'āriẕ*] of the Divine Essence of Being [*ẕāt-i vujūd*]
> We're gratings in the lamp-niches of Being [*vujūd*].[28]

We have veered far from our discussion of the *tarjī'-band* itself. But this divagation into Bīdil's poetic and theologico-philosophical inheritances has brought us to a juncture at which we may return to the poem prepared to understand the centrality of the human to its ontology and pedagogy. The poem itself asserts this centrality only in the tenth stanza. Before that, the stanzas abbreviate cosmogonic topics expounded at greatest length in Bīdil's *masnavī 'Irfān* (Gnosis, 1712), the longest of Bīdil's *masnavīs*. Since the second stanza condenses this emergence of the human in a primordial partition – here imagined as a wave – from Eternity – imagined here as an ocean – it is worth retracing it. As we do so, we will also remark on how the couplet refrain shifts in meaning in each of its textually identical reappearances. As discussed in Chapter 1, the human, like all other created things, is at once a disclosure and delimitation of the eternal Real. However, it is distinguished among these by its ability to inquire into its beginningless (*azalī*) incipience in the Real. In Bīdil's Akbarian cosmogony Subsistence (*baqā*) passes into the delimited human form of knowledge (*'ilm*) that comprises the "names" (*asmā*) of Real. These names, being potentialities, enter delimited forms in, or are "entified" as, "things" (*ashyā*). The first of these things here is "the skies" (*āsmān'hā*) that, growing denser, yield the four elements (*'anāṣir*) in squared opposition. These include the primordial oppositions of light and darkness and numbers. The elements give rise to the minerals (*jamād*) which, when shaken, yield "plants" (*nabāt*). "Then the animal [*ḥayvān*] came into being and after that the human [*insān*]./It came to be named Adam and Eve." The "human kind" (*naw'-i insānī*) comes to be distinguished into the sects of "infidel, Zoroastrian, the faithful and Christian," a formulaic characterization of ontologically tertiary sectarian difference. Bīdil suggests the tertiary or ontologically deficient character of such sectarian differences in the very next couplet: "Oneness [*vaḥdat*] expended itself in an upwelling of multiplicity./Silence was converted into the color of sound." I will return ahead to the meta-poetic implications of this analogization of cosmogony with speech. At this point, we must note that the stanza culminates in the observation that the "possible" (*mumkin*) emerges from the "necessary" (*vujūb*) through "the melody of our contemplation" – that is Bīdil's contemplation which, given his choral voice, includes that of his predecessors in the tradition of Akbarian poetry. The world comes into being, then, because the divine Real or the true Self issued into limited actuations by contemplating itself. Chapter 1's exposition of Bīdil's uses of the *mise en abyme* offered a visual analogue to this monist autogenesis. The intellect (*'aql*) is ignorant of why "meaning" should be "trapped in words" – that is, the Real in its limited actuations.

> Since we fell into an ocean of bewilderment
> Our Nonmanifest nature [*bāṭin*] heard Love calling
> That [*kih*] the world is nothing but a self-disclosure of the Friend
> This talk of "I" and "us" is a self-same addition to Him.[29]

Here, the particle *kih*, articulating Love's pronouncement with the foregoing stanza, introduces direct speech. But this is only one of its many functions for it is grammatically ambiguous, an ambiguity that Bīdil, on the model of the aforementioned poets who employed the *tarjī'-band* in the Akbarian tradition, richly exploits. Here is Steingass's summary of the particle's grammatical functions:

> for Persian, the particle *ke*, either as relative and interrogative pronoun (*kāf-i mauṣūl, kāf-i istifhām* respectively), or as conjunction, in which latter case again it either stands in the sense of because, &c. (*kāf-i ta'līl*), or introduces a direct speech (*kāf-i mūfājat*).[30]

If the previously discussed first stanza introduces the "testimony" of the refrain by the *kih* of direct speech or quotation, the second uses the same quotational function to present the refrain as Love's riddling call to "our Nonmanifest nature" (*bāṭin-i mā*). The third, fourth, fifth and ninth present it in its conjunctive form as a check on idle talk and futile action. The sixth employs it again in its conjunctive form but as a leveler of silence and speech; the seventh and tenth do so in its quotational form as a formulation of the ontological truth transcending petty limited identities and values; the eighth as a "stratagem" (*ḥaylah*) by which to avoid entrapment in particularistic manifestations of the Real and so on, each semantically distinct setting of the same grammatical particle re-contextualizing the refrain text and thus pointing ahead to its new meanings. The paradigm for this semantically ever-shifting framing of an identical sign-sequence lies not only in Ibn 'Arabī's aforementioned "ultra-monorhyme" but also in the Qur'ān whose unique variety of "internal rhyme" (*saj'*) and especially monorhyme have been interpreted as facilitating its semantic inexhaustibility.[31] By this formal invocation of Qur'ānic polysemy Bīdil signals Ibn 'Arabī's idea that "there is no repetition in [God's] self-disclosure" (*lā tikrār fi'l tajallī*).

To resume our interpretation of the *tarjī'-band*, the speaker's passage into "bewilderment" signals what, in Bīdil's *masnavī 'Irfān* as in this poem, is the psychological beginning of a gradually deepening gnostic introspection into the true Self at the origin of and within the phenomenal one. Moreover, the personification of Love articulates the passage from this stanza to the next one in which Love, a familiar Akbarian cosmogonic principle, partitions a Beginningless silence into the utterances of creatures. Noteworthy here is the function of Bīdil's textual metaphor for cosmogony. Verbal formulation, regardless of whether it is oral or written, entails a fixing and delimiting of the limitless Real and is, as such, coeval with the human. Love utters the couplet refrain as the beginning of an answer to the intellect's bewilderment. But this utterance, as the third stanza observes at the beginning, is already the partitioning of Beginningless silence into creaturely speech. Ibn 'Arabī's "Love" that serves as a model here exhales beings into actuality by carving them in its breath, the word *kalama* or "utterance" significantly also being cognate with the word for "cutting."[32] In keeping with the ontologically defective valence Bīdil assigns color, a valence at the center of Chapter 1, the cosmogonic passage of the Real from unity to multiplicity is a passage from colorlessness and silence into color and sound.

If color and visuality were at the center of Chapter 1 sound, silence and language are at the thematic center of this chapter. Apophasis, the ineffability of the most Real is, as remarked above, a feature of such emanationist ontologies. It is thus a *condition* of representation. It is a condition in the double sense of this word as *limit* and *possibility*: the Real cannot, because of its beginningless (*azalī*) character, be formulated in the inevitably sequential and therefore temporal character of language. But this limit therefore also makes possible linguistic sequences and partitions asymptotic approximations. This is why Bīdil's *Dīvān* abounds in *ghazal* formulations of the topos (*mazmūn*) of the apophatic defeat of language:

> *sharar-i tamhīd sāzad maṭlab-i mā dāstān'hā rā*
> *dahad parvāz-i bismil mud'ā-i mā bayān'hā rā*[33]

> A sparking dispersal does my purpose make of stories.
> My object grants words the flight of a beheaded/sacrificed bird.

We will here consider two aspects of the uses in his *tarji'-band* of this topos in stanzas seven and twenty-seven. Both stanzas could be interpreted as synecdoches for Bīdil's formulations of the nature and functions of language throughout his oeuvre. Central to these formulations is the aforementioned monosemy underlying all superficially distinct nouns as ultimately signifying one of God's attributes and all superficially distinct verbs as ultimately signifying God's acts of self-disclosure (*tajallī*). It is by this implication of radical monosemy that he appropriates the *ghazal* technique of "observing the similar" (*murāʻāt al-naẓīr*, also called *tanāsub*), a trope entailing the extended use of lexemes from the same semantic field. Let us pause to consider his uses of this trope in stanza seven as a case of his appropriation of the otherwise mystically unmarked heritage of tropes for Sufi authorship.

In stanza seven the already needless divine gaze looks backward, as it were, upon the creaturely world that is made up of possible or contingent manifestations of the necessary One. In doing so, it observes how each creature's actions are limited to the practices it is known for and so how each fails to comprehend the totality expressed in the concluding strophe. Consider how Bīdil formulates this cluster of ideas in the following selection of couplets from this stanza:

> Everyone is destined to dwell upon himself.
> The knee holds the brow's mirror.
> The dust rests its feet in pride's skirt
> Thinking – this is where divine Mercy's spring is.
> The water laughs at how the sea from here
> Sets out riding in a hot sweat.
> The wind rides confident that the phoenix
> Unfolds its wings in this very nest.
> The flame is unveiled, saying "O spectators!
> There's not a garment here, here's nude self-disclosure!" [...]
> Despite all the awareness if the sense of this secret
> Isn't understood it is foolishness:
> The world is nothing but a self-disclosure of the Friend.
> This talk of "I" and "us" is a self-same addition to Him.[34]

The opening couplet states the destined self-absorption of each creature by using the phrase *sar-nivisht*, meaning "destiny" but containing the word for head – *sar*. The second hemistich of this couplet exploits this in its illustration of this assertion by using a metaphor for introspection that is at least as old as the poet Niẓāmī Ganjavī (d. 1209): the hunched and seated posture with the forehead rested so long on the bent knee that it is burnished to mirror brightness. This play on a lexemic overlap between the two hemistichs of the couplet anticipates the trope of "observing the similar" that dominates the rest of the stanza: the dust from which the world's garden grows takes pride in being the origin of "divine Mercy's spring"; the water or dew is pleased with being the origin of the busy sea; the wind is confident that the fabulous phoenix that symbolizes God takes flight in it; and the flame invites its spectators to gaze upon what it thinks is divine self-disclosure itself. But in its egotism none of the four elements that together symbolically make up the entire sublunary world has grasped the secret of the strophe: that they are all the Friend's self-disclosure and each is a phenomenal modulation of His oneness. We remarked in Chapter 1 that it was because Bīdil aimed to submit the particularity of every event to the generality of a myth that he drew, at the level of the sentence, on semantic fields already known in Persian literature. The monosemy we have discussed above is a semantic equivalent of such mythicizing. No *ghazal* trope served this end of monosemy better than "observing the similar" because it allowed him, as we see above, to innovate within the bounds of a known semantic field by teasing elements out of it or adding them to it. But unlike in a *ghazal*, the strophe of the *tarjī'-band* allows him to negate each of the compound metaphors in this series in favor of the divine oneness they have each missed.

To turn now to stanza twenty-seven of the *tarjī'-band*, when confronted with a realization of its deep monosemy, speakers grow conscious of the partitions of language and fall silent. They recognize that gnostic awareness equalizes speech and silence, rendering them equally futile. At this stage knowledgeable silence imitates the Beginningless silence at the origin of creation, a single and singular silence that was partitioned into the utterances of creatures. But this futility is not only a function of the excess of the limitless Real in relation to limited language. It is also a function of the futility of the agential nature of speech. To the extent that the speaker even breathes to speak he is complicit in the vanity of action. And the phenomenal self, not the true one, ideally undertakes action. This is why Bīdil's *ghazal*s typically identify breathing with sin or a turbulence of the disposition and the holding of the breath with the virtuous calm of Neo-Platonic asceticism:

> *ghazāl-i amn kih ulfat khiyāl-i mubham-i ūst*
> *ba har kujā nafasī gard mīkunad ram-i ūst*[35]
>
> The gazelle of repose – intimacy its dim specter –
> Starts wherever the breath blooms in dust.

Four of the opening couplets of stanza twenty-seven call for a relinquishing of action and the raising of lament instead. The imagery of lamentation or crying out signifies despair over the impossibility of representation as well as a kenotic negation of language in favor of ventriloquism for the One. The opening couplet of this stanza therefore reads: "What could anyone say in this charmed world of images [*ṭilism-i khiyāl*]/For bewilderment has waylaid speech?" This call to lament articulates the transition in the poem to the next major topic – namely that of *incapacity-as-empowerment*. But before I explain this term, we must note that this transition emphasizes that "the charmed world" in which bewilderment "waylays speech" is one of "images" or *khiyāls*. This word means "mental image" but also refers by abbreviation to the poetic practice of *tarz-i khiyāl* or "the [*ghazal*] technique of the imaginary" to which I will return at length in Chapter 5. For now, I will observe that this was a technique by which the poet so encrypted the topos (*maẓmūn*) or topoi (*maẓāmīn*) in a *ghazal* distich that the reader was only able to recognize it after much effort and time. It was a technique of hermeneutic arrest at which Bīdil excelled, a resistance to immediate comprehension on account of which he was, and continues to be, variously admired and denounced.

In this stanza he presents an implicit justification for this technique. The stanza opens by implying that bewildered silence accompanies "the charmed world of images." We must recall from Chapter 1 that the key Akbarian term *barzakh* signified "isthmus" as well as "the World of Imagination" and, as such, covered all corporeality.[36] For Bīdil, then, poetry's field of reference was coextensive with the sensory world itself. I will not repeat Chapter 1's exposition of this term here and instead note that Bīdil adds a crucial dimension to the ontological inevitability and ubiquity of "the imaginal world of the body," namely the call for a relinquishing of willing that would transform such corporeality into a locus for the manifestation of the Real or the One. So, having named submission or passion Khiẕr or the guiding prophet in Sufi quests in the immediately previous couplets, the fourteenth couplet of the stanza reads:

avval a̱sbāt-i hastī-i khvud kun
ba'd az ān bar khiyāl-i khvīsh bebāl[37]

First, prove your own being.
Then, swell with pride at your images.

Proving one's own being entails relinquishing the vanity of conversation itself to the point where, as Bīdil puts it in a koan-like paradox, "Gnosis [*ma'rifat*] is ignorance, take heed!/Awareness is complacency, rub your eyes!" That is, even the words "gnosis" and "awareness" are ideally, at this stage, voided of meaning. And it is in this silence that Bīdil urges the reader to contemplate yet again the thought of the couplet refrain "That the world's nothing but a self-disclosure of the Friend…"

Bīdil's justification for his controversial uses of the "technique of the imaginary" may thus be described as a solution to a kenotic problematic central to Sufi discourses on language. This is the problematic of how to speak of the limitless and ultimately ineffable One who is the only real Actor by the gross materiality and egotism of even the slightest gesture or utterance. In Ibn 'Arabī and his inheritors this problematic was posed in terms of the possible forms prayer could take. In this tradition, as Ian Netton has remarked, prayer was no longer just praise or petition but God's act of imagining Himself through His creature; or His creature's exercise of the imagination to manifest Him to himself.[38] By this logic, corporeality or the world of the imaginary was to be scrutinized, rather than looked past, for God's immanence to its iridescent signs. So, in the twentieth stanza, Bīdil asks his reader to attend carefully to the world's ambient signs since even the phenomenal has its gnostic uses: "that which is hierophanous do not consider empty/Whatever is in conversation do not take lightly" for "The world is nothing but a self-disclosure of the Friend […]."[39] The time-taking "technique of the imaginary" was a spiritual exercise by which the reader was compelled to dwell at length on the world's corporeal manifold through the mimesis of Bīdil's "wrought words." To direct such an arrested hermeneutic gaze at creatures demands that all willing be given a quietus. This is arguably why Bīdil chose his pen-name: "Bī-dil" literally means "heart-less" in the sense of a lover who has withdrawn his heart's investments in objects of this world for the Beloved. Such passion, in turn, leads kenotically to empowerment when the Real comes to inhabit the inner theater of the poet-ascetic's heart. It is to this subject of passion-as-empowerment that we will now turn.

Bīdil addresses this theme in ten stanzas in the *tarjī'-band* and returns to it recurrently throughout his *ghazal* corpus. We may grasp the centrality of this theme, following Bīdil's poem, in two steps. The first of these is the privilege accorded the human. The second is the call addressed to the human to empower itself by submitting in all its willing to the Real. With respect to the first, the tenth stanza announces the human as the most privileged of creatures because, as we have already noted, it is capable of gnosis (*'irfān*) or the self-transforming knowledge of the primordial One whence the Many of creation issued. What is noteworthy from the perspective of literary history is that the following stanza textualizes the human as a *ghazal* text signifying the One: "To set in order the order/verse of possibility [*naẓm-i imkānī*]/We are like the refrain and rhyme of a ghazal." The human-as-*ghazal* is a neutral resource that could be used well or badly:

> Life's the guiding thread of our attention
> If ignorant of ourselves we are death.
> The eye is somewhat like a trap for hierophany
> If the vial shatters we are like fairies.

Humans were brought into being to "set in order the order/verse of possibility," *imkān* being also translatable as "contingency." Humans, in this iteration of an ethic familiar from Ibn 'Arabī, thus bear an ability and responsibility to know themselves within their allotted lifetimes and always risk failing to do so. This responsibility includes the obligation to know the world. Bīdil invokes this double responsibility in the eighteenth stanza by employing the word *'ālam* punningly in both its senses – "world" and "state." This word is also cognate with *'ilm*, the word for "knowledge." He calls for an avoidance of "imitation" (*taqlīd*) because it is a form of action. Originality or the untrodden path is relinquishing the self itself and "following the untrodden path" under the effects of "yearning" (*shawq*) that can transform stone into sparks. Bīdil's image for such empowering relinquishment or kenosis that transforms self and world at once is, as already noted, wailing or lamenting (*nālah*). Cautioning humans against the error of failing to do so is "this point" – namely, the couplet refrain "That the world's nothing but a self-disclosure of the Friend…"

What bears attention here is the centrality of the *ghazal* as an analogy for the human and the specification of the correlated affect of "yearning" (*shawq*) with which a *ghazal* is uttered. At the basis of this textualization of the human is the doctrine invoked by Ibn 'Arabī of the mimetic correspondence between the three books of creation, revelation and the soul, a correspondence justifying itself by reference to the Qur'ān 41:53: "We shall show them Our signs on the horizons [*al-āfāq*] and in their souls [*anfusihim*] until it becomes clear to them that He is the Real."[40] The *ghazal*, on this apotheosis of it, would be nothing less than the text of the soul. And if each individual soul is bewildered at why the "colorless" Real took on the creaturely form of written letters "gnosis-seeking yearning" (*shawq-i ma'rifat-āhang*) eventually picks up a melody alerting it to the Real.[41]

One of Bīdil's *ghazal* distiches comprises a complex iteration of this notion of yearning as a hermeneutic attitude towards the *ghazal*-world's signs. A brief excursus on it will let us recognize the amplificatory relations indicated in Chapter 1 between his prose, long verse and verse in the *ghazal* genre:

> *shawq dar bī-dast u pā'yī nīst ma'yūs- ṭalab*
> *chun qalam sa'ī-i qadam mībālad az muzhgān-i mā*[42]
>
> Yearning, in its helplessness, seeks no despair.
> Quill-like do effortful steps arise from our eyelashes.

He discovers in the image, long conventional in Persian poetry, of a quill as lacking in all but one organ (variously imagined to be the mouth or an eye or leg) an analogy for "yearning" in its "helplessness." The word "helplessness" here translates the idiom that literally means "without hands and feet" (*bī-dast u pā*). Yearning, seeking mystical intuition, does not yield to despair because effort takes steps forward, swelling like ink from a quill's brush, here analogized to eyelashes. What swell from eyelashes are tears but here, by the logic of the metaphor, could also be ink. This ambivalence condenses two topoi (*maẕāmīn*), both frequent in Bīdil's *ghazal*s, into an image: the topos of "yearning" (*shawq*) or the ardent mystical imperative to read and write the phenomenal world's signs of the most Real; and the contrary topos of apophasis or the ultimate inadequacy of human discourse to the most Real.

Resuming our attention to the *tarjī'-band*, we left off where "gnosis-seeking yearning" detected a melody that alerted it to the Real. This melody, differently framed again, is the couplet refrain. This is why Bīdil calls on his reader in the thirty-first stanza to abandon his false self and recognize himself as a "clear verse" of "the text of Power" (*musḥaf-i qudrat*) that is the true Self in himself. This apotheosis of the *ghazal* also accounts for why he excerpted some of the couplets of the *tarjī'-band* as free-standing *ghazal* distiches.[43]

Two passing observations: first, it is easy to imagine how this apotheosis of the poetic genre that Bīdil was – and remains – best known for strengthened his position in the literary debates his reputation was entangled in. It would potentially have invoked on those who criticized him for the apparent obscurities of his *ghazal* style the charge of denying the ethical priority of the human shared by all Islamic cosmogeneses. Second, it also alerts us, as Chapter 1 did, to an ontology of the literary that is disparate to ours today. The first of these observations concerns Bīdil's place in the literary politics of his milieu. This is a topic I will not develop here but will indirectly address in Chapter 4 that comprises a study of Bīdil's student Ārzū whose oeuvre can be interpreted as an elaborate defense of his teacher's *ghazal* "technique of the imaginary." The second observation should already be obvious from the discussion in Chapter 1 of Bīdil's apologia for *sukhan*. But I make it here to recall that debates over poetic style were invested with stakes beyond or other than what we consider "literary" today, bearing ontological and ethical import only obscurely part of most contemporary consciousness of the literary.

The second of these two stages is, as I observe above, the call to the human to absolutely submit in its willing to the Real. Figured in terms of the logic of Bīdil's imagery, such submission is yearning's wailing. The yearning with which the *ghazal*-text of the human is uttered transforms the human into what his heart already is: "Don't be negligent of your own state for in the heart/You have the 'Preserved Tablet' in your side."[44] The "Preserved Tablet" (*lawḥ-i maḥfūẓ*) is a reference to the Qur'ānic notion that all future events were already inscribed in the Beginningless tablet preserved by God. The human is thus a temporal condensation whose nature the human himself must discover by punishing asceticism (*khvūn-khwārī*). Herein lies an explanation for why Bīdil's *ghazal*s abound in distiches that are characterized by topoi of spiritual despair and failure:

za sa'ī-i ṭāla'-i nā-sāz agar rasam ba kamālī
hamān palang ba daryā'īm u nahang ba saḥrā[45]

If, ill-starred, I struggle to perfection
I'd still be a leopard in the ocean, a whale in the jungle.

By reading such distiches the assumed disciple-reader, whether courtly nobleman or scribe or hospice-based Sufi, would mimetically rehearse Bīdil's own gestures of an ascetic abandonment of willing. Such asceticism is seeing the Real by paring away its attributes till the quotidian reality of each attribute is magnified into a sign of the Real.

This is the point, in the twenty-first stanza, at which Bīdil uses a Qur'ānic metaphor which he uses in his *ghazal*s, too – that of Solomon and the ant. As this metaphor condenses his ideal of kenosis into an image-cluster or topos and thus serves us, like his student-readers, as a didactic mnemonic, let us reflect on it. The following consideration will let us appreciate the senses in which this *tarjī'-band* may be read as a condensed key to the rest of Bīdil's oeuvre. Here he says:

Strive so that in the manifestation of the Attributes
You see the self-disclosure of the signless Divine Essence [...]
So that you witness in the frail ant's heart
The power of Solomon's magnificence.[46]

The topos occurs in the course of a sequence of topoi formulating variations on the same injunction: to witness the most Real in its slightest phenomenal manifestations. Its embeddedness in this explanatory context lets us explain its free-standing appearances in his *ghazal*s. These free-standing uses of the same topos are arguably harder to comprehend for a reader not acquainted with the rest of Bīdil's oeuvre. Compounding this hermeneutic resistance is the articulation of such *ghazal* distiches with extended hypotaxis – typically taking the form of extended uses of the *iẕāfah* or unmarked but vocalized adjectival or possessive particle – and compound words. Chapter 3 includes an excursus on these related stylistic features. Here, we will confine ourselves to observing that a certain isomorphy relates syntactical and worldly complexity in Bīdil. Hypotaxis corresponded to his vision of the coruscating complexity of the created world in which God was immanent. Here is one of Bīdil's most syntactically elaborate *ghazal* iterations of this topos with the *iẕāfah*s and caesurae between clauses marked in bold:

> *ishārah-**i** dastgāh-**i** khāqān 'iyān **za** muzhgān-**i** mūyī chīnī*
> *gushād o bast-**i** dar-**i** sulaymān **za** pardah-**i** chishm-**i** mūr paydā*[47]
>
> Signaled by his barber's eyelashes is the might of the Chinese emperor.
> Manifest in the ant's batting eyes are the opening and closing of Solomon's doors.

The reader or listener coming to this distich with little or no prior familiarity with Bīdil and only a familiarity with the prior tradition of the Persian *ghazal* would, arguably, find it perplexing. The most immediately perplexing feature is the extended *iẕāfah*-construction in each hemistich. Each hemistich opens with a chain of *iẕāfah*s – here transcribed by *i* – that ends with *za*, here meaning "by" or "through." The caesura of this *za* is followed in both hemistiches by another *iẕāfah* chain. Each hemistich's unconventionally extended clause, then, stands qualified by the equally extended clause separated from it by the caesura. Compounding the unconventionality of such hypotaxis is the relatively strange imagery of the metaphors. While the second hemistich's imagery of Solomon and the ant recognizably draws from the Qur'ān 27:18, the metaphor it is preceded by – that of the barber and the Chinese emperor – would appear strange to our presumed reader.

A hermeneutically sympathetic eighteenth-century reader acquainted with the treatises on "Speaking Anew" syntax and metaphor that Bīdil's student Ārzū had authored would recognize both hemistiches as instances of what Ārzū terms a "compound simile" (*tashbīh-i murakkab*).[48] That is, both compare terms under multiple aspects. He would also recognize that Bīdil had invented such compound similes by adding attributes to the Qur'ānic topos of Solomon and the ant, giving the ant eyelashes and Solomon palace doors. Recognizing this, he would acknowledge that this distich was an instance of what the literary treatises of the period called *maẕmūn-āfrīnī* – "topos-creation" or "topos-elaboration." Were this reader further acquainted with the Speaking Anew *ghazal* of the eighteenth century, he would not be surprised on recognizing in *dast* (literally "hand") which is the first part of the word for "might" – *dastgāh* – an embedded semantic echo of "signaled." Nor would he find remarkable the pun on the proper noun "Chinese" in the suffix *chīnī* of the compound word *mūyī chīnī* that I translate here as "barber" but which literally means "hair-plucker." Further, he would recognize that both hemistiches were employing instances of the trope (*badī‘*) of "hyperbole" or *mubālighah.* But having arrived at such recognitions, he might well ask what these images are metaphors for? What, in other words, do these metaphors mean? This is where he would likely fall silent. Unless, of course, he was already familiar with Bīdil's poetic oeuvre that, by the hermeneutic criterion of interpreting the part in consonance with the whole, relates to this distich as context for its text.

What is this textual context? The first hemistich hyperbolically echoes the import of the second's hemistich's imagery of Solomon and the ant. The humble barber corresponds to the humble ant while the mighty Chinese emperor corresponds to mighty Solomon. Bīdil's use of the Solomon-and-the-ant pair here concurs with his use of it in two other instances in his oeuvre. One is his aforementioned use of it his *tarjī‘-band.* The other occurs in the *ghazal* distich discussed below. Both instances serve to convey the Sufi topos (*maẕmūn*) of meekness as might, incapacity (*‘ajz*) as power (*bī-niyāzī*), submission as dominion. The second instance is the following *ghazal* distich:

bī-niyāzī baskih mushtāq-i laqā-i ‘ajz būd
kard khāl-i rū-yi dast-i khvud sulaymān mūr rā[49]

So ardent was self-sufficiency for frailty's face
Solomon adorned his palm with the mole of an ant.

This topos of triumphal frailty has precedents in Manṣūr Hallāj's famous "ecstatic proclamation" (*shaṭḥ*) "I am the Truth/God" (*an'al-ḥaq*), ‘Aṭṭār's *Muṣībat-nāmah*, Rūmī's quatrains (*rubā‘iyāt*) and ‘Irāqī's *tarjī‘-band* among other texts: the topos of the speaker's kenotic apotheosis. Here, the ant wins an audience with Solomon – who is implicitly divinized by the descriptor "self-sufficiency" (*bī-niyāzī*) – by the littleness or virtual invisibility of its ego. And the divine Solomon, in turn, beautifies the face of his palm with the frailty of the mole of the ant.

The twenty-fifth stanza opens a new and final movement in Bīdil's *tarjī‘-band.* It identifies Bīdil himself in his choral voice as the embodiment of such empowered passion and so as the teacher others need to discover their true selves. Bīdil explicitly implicates himself in this choral group whose protean forms derive from their perfect submission by calling them *bī-dilānī* or "those who have lost their hearts," a pluralization of his own pen-name. This appropriation then culminates in the twenty-sixth stanza in a series of appropriations by this Sufi elect, the second hemistich of each distich ending with "are we/is us" (*mā'īm*). This return of the "us" analeptically modifies its first appearance in the *tarjī'-band* because it now explicitly includes Bīdil and now refers to the elect who can teach the rest. This stanza thus also discloses the pedagogical aims of this poem and ends by Bīdil taking possession of the couplet refrain in the collective first person as a now passionately empowered collective author.

The penultimate stanza of the poem hails man as the highest potentiality for the realization or actualization of the true Self in the false self. Here, in the fourteenth couplet, Bīdil gives us an instance of his Sufi adaptation of a technique characteristic of Speaking Anew: literalizing a metaphor to build another metaphor on it.[50] Bīdil conveys his call to submit oneself passionately to the Real by literalizing the infinitive *shikastan,* "to break," in the compound verb *kār shikastan* or "the defeat of an undertaking." He matches the "breaking" in this verb with that in the second hemistich's idiom *kulāh shikastan* or "to doff a cap" to say: "Don't count worldly defeat as incapacity [*'ajz*]./Self-sufficiency has doffed its cap." That is, being shattered in one's worldly undertakings is in fact divine Self-sufficiency's rakish doffing of its hat, at once a gesture of grace and power.

The thirty-fourth and final stanza is addressed to Bīdil himself, as I noted towards the beginning of this chapter, as an elemental and therefore inevitably frail mixture and, yet, as such, the protean or "colorful" hierophany of the Friend:

> This is self-sufficiency, not the shape of incapacity,
> That self-disclosure adorns you in a hundred colors.

Here, Bīdil presents a genesis of poetic craft:

> From you have arisen the crafts of the universe [*ṣanā'i'-i āfāq*]
> Even if, in fact, you are alone.
> Your craft has emerged without limit
> So that you may adorn the world by yourself.

But here, to grasp the ontological meanings of adornment, we must read him here in conjunction with the passage from his autobiography discussed in Chapter 1. Adornment burgeons out of his kenotically discovered, singular, transpersonal and all-encompassing Self as an aesthetic resource with which to signify this Self. Such a resource should not be taken in the sense of mere rhetorical device. Rather, as he formulates it in his autobiography in the passage interpreted more comprehensively in Chapter 1, the word "with" (*ma'*) in the Prophetic dictum "I have with God an appointed hour" signals the unavoidable necessity for the duality of representation in creation.[51] But for such representation general unity (*aḥadiyyat*) – that is, the unity of creatures with God that retains their servanthood in relation to Him – would be inconceivable to humans. Verbal artifice is only as contrived as the ritual practices of fasting and praying. All of these are the human creature's necessary compromises with the duality of representations in order that he be granted an intuition of the most real. They are all therefore necessarily bound to rules of comportment, to *adab*. In this sense, as I have explicated in the Chapter 1, Bīdil presents poetic craft as a verbal confirmation of Islamic orthopraxis.

This is why he concludes his poem by quoting in part, standing by convention for the whole, a *Hadīs̱* guiding all Sufi *askesis* – "He who knows his self knows his Lord":

> *He who knows his self* is your adequate guide
> So you may know that you are the singular Divine Essence [*z̲āt-i yek-tā'yī*].

The "I and us" (*man u mā*) of the couplet refrain is exposed in its final instance as the effect of Bīdil's own momentary creaturely negligence while the "Friend" of the refrain now appears as his true Self.

Notes

1 As, for example, Harold Bloom's use of it as a category central to a chapter in his book in which he writes "I take *kenosis* from St. Paul's account of Christ as 'humbling' himself from God to man." Harold Bloom, *The Anxiety of Influence: A Theory of Poetry* (New York: Oxford University Press, 1997), 87.
2 Of the twenty topics Aḥsan al-Ẓafar lists as being Bīdil's major themes throughout his oeuvre only four – "oneness of being" (*vaḥdat al-vujūd*), "bewilderment" (*ḥayrat*), *sukhan* and "the renewal of similars" (*tajaddud-i ams̱āl*) – could be said to designate technical terms whose meanings he modifies. The rest are topics and terms he inherits from Sufi traditions without modification. Sayyad Aḥsan al-Ẓafar, *Mirzā 'Abd al-Qādir Bedil: ḥayāt aur kārname: jild-i duvvum* (Rāmpūr: Rāmpūr Raẓ̈ā Library, 2009), 6.
3 'Abd al-Qādir Khān Bīdil, *Kulliyāt-i Bīdil: jild-i avval* (Tehrān: intishārāt-i Ilhām, 1386/2007), 437.
4 Bahram Jassemi, "Dimensions of the Mystical Journey," *Journal of the Muhyiddin Ibn 'Arabi Society* 38 (2005), 91–104.
5 'Abd al-Raḥmān Jāmī, *The Precious Pearl: al-Jāmi's "Al-Durrah al-Fākhirah" together with its Glosses and the Commentary of 'Abd al-Ghafur al-Lārī*, Translated with an Introduction, Notes and Glossary by Nicholas Heer (Albany, NY: State University of New York Press, 1979), 67.
6 Jāmī, *The Precious Pearl*, 67.
7 Bīdil, *Kulliyāt-i Bīdil*, 475.
8 http://dsalsrv02.uchicago.edu/cgi-bin/philologic/getobject.pl?c.1:1:5632.steingass
9 Bīdil, *Kulliyāt-i Bīdil*, 254.
10 Ibid., 253.
11 Chittick translates *tanzīh* and *tashbīh* as "incomparability" and "similarity," respectively. William C. Chittick, *Ibn 'Arabi: Heir to the Prophets* (Oxford: Oneworld, 2005), 19. Ian Richard Netton, *Allah Transcendent: Studies in the Structure and Semiotics of Islamic Philosophy, Theology and Cosmology* (London: Routledge, 1994), 276.
12 Netton, *Allah Transcendent*, 280.
13 Mullāh Tāhir Ghanī Kashmīrī, *Dīvān-i Ghanī* (Srinagar: Jammu and Kashmir Academy of Arts, Culture and Languages, 1984), 257–59.
14 'Abd al-Qādir Badāyūnī, *Tārīkh-i Badāyūnī* (also well-known as *Muntakhab al-tavārīkh*) (Osnabrück: Biblio Verlag, 1983).

15 Paul Ricoeur, "Structure, Word, Event," in Charles E. Reagan and David Stewart (eds), *The Philosophy of Paul Ricoeur: An Anthology of his Work* (Boston, MA: Beacon Press, 1978), 109–19.
16 William C. Chittick, "'Eraqi, Fakr-al-Din Ebrahim," at: www.iranicaonline.org/articles/eraqi (last updated December 15, 1998).
17 Mehdī Derakhshān, "In tarjī'-band az kīst?" *Gawhar* (Mehr: 1352/1973: 9), 860–68.
18 Erich Auerbach, *Mimesis: The Representation of Reality in Western Literature* (Princeton, NJ: Princeton University Press, 2003), 70–71, 166–67, 212 and 241.
19 Shams al-Dīn Ḥāfiẓ, *Dīvān-i Ḥāfiẓ* (Tehrān: Anjuman-i khvushnavisān-i Irān, 1368/1989), 50.
20 Farīd al-Dīn 'Aṭṭār, *Dīvān-i ghazaliyāt va tarjī'āt va qaṣā'id* (Tehrān: kitāb-khānah-i Sanā'i, 1335/1957), 18.
21 Denis. E. McCauley, "'See Him in a tree, and see Him in a stone': Ibn 'Arabi's Ultra-monorhyme in Comparative Perspective," *Journal of the Muhyiddin Ibn 'Arabi Society* 47 (2010), 63–86.
22 Ibid.
23 Michael A. Sells (ed.), *Early Islamic Mysticism: Sufi, Qur'an, Mi'raj, Poetic and Theological Writings* (New York: Paulist Press, 1996), 244–50.
24 Sells, *Early Islamic Mysticism*, 243.
25 Hans Blumenberg, "Light as a Metaphor for Truth: At the Preliminary Stage of Philosophical Concept Formation," in David Michael Levin (ed.), *Modernity and the Hegemony of Vision* (Berkeley, CA: University of California Press, 1993), 30–62.
26 http://quran.com/24/35
27 Netton, *Allah Transcendent*, 270.
28 Maḥmūd Shabistarī, *Gulshan-i rāz* (Islamābād: Markaz-i taḥqīqāt-i Fārsī-i Irān va Pākistān, 1978), 18. I translate Shabistarī's *ẕāt* in keeping with Chittick who translates Ibn 'Arabī's *al-dhāt* as "Divine Essence." William C. Chittick, *The Sufi Path of Knowledge: Ibn 'Arabi's Metaphysics of the Imagination* (Albany, NY: State University of New York Press, 1989), 135.
29 Bīdil, *Kulliyāt-i Bīdil*, 254.
30 http://dsal.uchicago.edu/cgi-bin/philologic/getobject.pl?c.5:1:1668.steingass
31 "Qur'anic *saj'* has a much greater tendency to mono-rhyme than does later *saj'*. A small number of rhymes … are predominant in the Qur'ān whereas rhyme in later *saj'* shows greater variation." Devin J. Stewart, "Saj' in the Qur'ān: Prosody and Structure," *Journal of Arabic Literature* 21: 2 (1990), 102.
32 Chittick, *Ibn 'Arabi: Heir to the Prophets*, 59.
33 Bīdil, *Kulliyāt-i Bīdil*, 430.
34 Ibid., 258.
35 Ibid., 701.
36 For an explication of this point and the source of my translation of the term, see Chittick, *The Sufi Path of Knowledge*, 14.
37 Bīdil, *Kulliyāt-i Bīdil*, 274.
38 Netton, *Allah Transcendent*, 287.
39 Bīdil, *Kulliyāt-i Bīdil*, 268.
40 http://quran.com/41/53
41 Bīdil, *Kulliyāt-i Bīdil*, 268.
42 Ibid., 440.
43 One of these excerpted distiches is the following: "A lock on the heart's treasury is silence./Ask the oyster about this riddle." (*qufl-i ganj-i dil ast khamūshī/az ṣadaf purs īn mu'ammā rā*). Bīdil, *Kulliyāt-i Bīdil*, 254.
44 Bīdil, *Kulliyāt-i Bīdil*, 262.
45 Ibid., 442.
46 Ibid., 269.

47 Ibid., 379.
48 Sirāj al-Dīn ‘Alī Khān Ārzū, *‘Aṭiyah-i kubrā va Mawhibat-i ‘uẓmā* (Tehrān: Firdaws, 1381/2003), 59–60.
49 Bīdil, *Kulliyāt-i Bīdil*, 435.
50 Shamsur Rahman Faruqi first made this observation in Shamsur Rahman Faruqi, "A Stranger in the City: The Poetics of *Sabk-e Hindi*," *Annual of Urdu Studies* 19 (2004), 1–94.
51 ‘Abd al-Qādir Khān Bīdil, *Chahār ‘unṣur*, in *Āvāz'hā-i Bīdil* (Tehrān: mu'assasah-i intishārāt-i Nigāh, 1386/2007), 365.

Bibliography

Aḥsan al-Ẓafar, Sayyad. *Mirzā ‘Abd al-Qādir Bedil: ḥayāt aur kārname: jild-i duvvum.* Rāmpūr: Rāmpūr Raẓā Library, 2009.

Ārzū, Sirāj al-Dīn ‘Alī Khān. *‘Aṭiyah-i kubrā va Mawhibat-i uẓmā.* Tehrān: Firdaws, 1381/2002.

‘Aṭṭār, Farīd al-Dīn. *Dīvān-i ghazaliyāt va tarjī‘āt va qaṣā'id.* Tehrān: kitāb-khānah-i Sanā'i, 1335/1957.

Auerbach, Erich. *Mimesis: The Representation of Reality in Western Literature.* Princeton, NJ: Princeton University Press, 2003.

Badāyūnī, ‘Abd al-Qādir. *Tārīkh-i Badāyūnī/Muntakhab al-tavārīkh.* Osnabrück: Biblio Verlag, 1983.

Bīdil, ‘Abd al-Qādir Khān. *Kulliyāt-i Bīdil: jild-i avval.* Tehrān: intishārāt-i Ilhām, 1386/2007.

Bīdil, ‘Abd al-Qādir Khān. *Chahār ‘unṣur*, in *Āvāz'hā-i Bīdil*, 335–676. Tehrān: mu'assasah-i intishārāt-i Nigāh, 1386/2007.

Bloom, Harold. *The Anxiety of Influence: A Theory of Poetry.* New York: Oxford University Press, 1997.

Blumenberg, Hans. "Light as a Metaphor for Truth: At the Preliminary Stage of Philosophical Concept Formation," in *Modernity and the Hegemony of Vision.* Berkeley, CA: University of California Press, 1993, 30–62.

Chittick, William C. *The Sufi Path of Knowledge: Ibn ‘Arabi's Metaphysics of the Imagination.* Albany, NY: State University of New York Press, 1989.

Chittick, William C. "‘Eraqi, Fakr-al-Din Ebrahim": www.iranicaonline.org/articles/eraqi (last updated December 15, 1998).

Chittick, William C. *Ibn ‘Arabi: Heir to the Prophets.* Oxford: Oneworld, 2005.

Derakhshān, Mehdī. "In tarjī‘-band az kīst?." *Gawhar.* Mehr: 1352/1973: 9, 860–68.

Faruqi, Shamsur Rahman. "Stranger in the City: The Poetics of Sabk-i Hindi," *Annual of Urdu Studies* 19 (2004), 1–94.

Ghanī Kashmīrī, Mullāh Tāhir. *Dīvān-i Ghanī.* Srinagar: Jammu and Kashmir Academy of Arts, Culture and Languages, 1984.

Jāmī, Nūr al-Dīn ‘Abd al-Raḥmān bin Aḥmad. *The Precious Pearl: al-Jāmi's "Al-Durrah al-Fākhirah" together with its Glosses and the Commentary of ‘Abd al-Ghafur al-Lārī.* Albany, NY: State University of New York Press, 1979.

Jassemi, Bahram. "Dimensions of the Mystical Journey," *Journal of the Muhyiddin Ibn ‘Arabi Society* 38 (2005), 91–104.

McCauley, Denis. E. ‘"See Him in a tree, and see Him in a stone": Ibn ‘Arabi's Ultramonorhyme in Comparative Perspective," *Journal of the Muhyiddin Ibn ‘Arabi Society* 47 (2010), 63–86.

Netton, Ian Richard. *Allah Transcendent: Studies in the Structure and Semiotics of Islamic Philosophy, Theology and Cosmology*. London: Routledge, 1994.

Ricoeur, Paul. "Structure, Word, Event," in Charles E. Reagan and David Stewart (eds), *The Philosophy of Paul Ricoeur: an Anthology of his Work*. Boston, MA: Beacon Press, 1978, 109–19.

Sells, Michael A. (ed.), *Early Islamic Mysticism: Sufi, Qur'an, Mi'raj, Poetic and Theological Writings*. New York: Paulist Press, 1996.

Shabistarī, Maḥmūd. *Gulshan-i rāz*. Islamābād: markaz-i taḥqīqāt-i Fārsī-i Irān va Pākistān, 1978.

Stewart, Devin J. "Saj' in the Qur'ān: Prosody and Structure," *Journal of Arabic Literature* 21: 2 (1990), 101–39.

3 A Hindu allegory of the Islamic philosopher-king

The tale of Madan and Kāmdī in Bīdil's *masnavī 'Irfān*

In 1712 in Delhi, having begun composing it thirty or thirty-four years before in Mathura, 'Abd al-Qādir Bīdil completed his *masnavī* titled *'Irfān* (Gnosis).[1] This narrative poem comprising 11,000 rhyming couplets is the longest of his *masnavīs* and is his most extended interpretation of the theistic monism of the Andalusian Sufi Ibn 'Arabī (d. 1240) whose thought pervaded North India during the period. As the latest of his *masnavīs*, it has been considered by some scholars to be the summation of his oeuvre.[2] Like the rest of his multi-generic oeuvre this *masnavī*, too, is motivated by the pedagogical aim of alerting his disciple-reader to the phenomenality of his individual self, guiding this self's preoccupations with the iridescent manifold of the created world and orienting it towards the transpersonal true Self within itself, namely the divine One whence the ambient Many had emanated.

Having narrated the descent of the One into "entifications" (*ta'ayyunāt*) or the various levels of reality before the creation of the human, Bīdil commences his narration of human's (*ādam*) career in the world.[3] The human who is the teleological fulfillment of creation and the manifestation of the most comprehensive of God's names, knows he is the culmination of God's hierarchy of creatures and thus the highest bearer of God's nature himself. Moreover, he knows that he is the best able of all creatures to heed the divine imperative to ponder the origin of all beings in God. But when he tries to contemplate God's nature by contemplating his own, he is bewildered. His "bewilderment" (*ḥayrat*, *taḥayyur*, *ḥayrānī*) – the affect in Bīdil's oeuvre accompanying frustrated desire for ontological ascent – arises on being unable to the comprehend the most Real for which his own form, like that of other creatures, is a metaphor (*isti'ārah*).[4] Such metaphors of God's similarity (*tashbīh*) to His creation remain partially illegible to the human because God, in this as in other Islamic theologies, remains ultimately incomparable (*tanzīh*) to His creation. The human thus struggles to see what exceeds visibility (*ghayb*) in the defective mirrors of the imagination (*takhyīl*, *khiyāl*) and finds himself incapable.[5] Throughout Bīdil's oeuvre human "incapacity" (*'ajz*) signifies the end of the egotism of willing and thus the beginning of what I have conceptualized in the previous chapters as kenosis. Here, the lesson in kenosis begins when the human turns to the sun for an answer.[6] The sun directs the human to look within himself for an answer, relating an allegory in ten sub-chapters, this allegory comprising the greater part of *'Irfān* which concludes with it.

The longest of the tales contained within the allegory is that of the lovers Madan and Kāmdī. Bīdil's version of this tale transforms an intertext made up of several earlier versions in Persian and other languages. The most authoritative of these intertexts and thus the most probable hypotext for Bīdil's tale is an Avadhi version of it composed in 1582–83 by a poet called 'Ālam. 'Ālam was in the entourage of the Mughal emperor Akbar's finance minister, Raja Todar Mal, and dedicated his poem to both the minister and the emperor. I offer a synopsis and interpretation of 'Ālam's tale in a later section of this chapter. For now, I will confine myself to observing in brief that Bīdil's plot, a variation on 'Ālam's, relates the separation of the lovers by a king, another king's just war on behalf of the lovers with the king who keeps them apart, the just king's mistaken decision to test the parted lovers' love for each other by telling each that the other is dead, the apparent deaths of the lovers in shock at the news of the other's death, the just king's remorse and, finally, the revival of the lovers when their bodies are brought together, this joyful erotic union concluding the tale.

The orienting question of this chapter is: why did Bīdil adapt the tale in question in the way he did? My answer will work towards demonstrating the thesis that Bīdil transformed a canonical Avadhi-mediated Sanskrit topos to teach his disciple-reader by an exemplum of Sufi self-governance at a time when political kingship in late Mughal Delhi was in crisis; and to thereby amplify his own authorial authority by variously identifying himself with this exemplum. After a brief account of the political crisis to which this *masnavī* was a response, I will argue that the tale of Madan and Kāmdī circulated as part of a larger and famous tale-cycle. This cycle's overarching theme and entropic temporality of royal justice account for the wide appeal of the tale and thus for its transmission, mediated by Mughal receptions, from its probable origins in Gujarat to the northern and eastern regions of Mughal India. I will then argue that Bīdil who was, as I have stated in Chapter 1, patronized by the threatened ruling elites of Mughal Delhi discovered in this tale a timely resource. The tale served him as a resource by which to imagine the remote promise of royal power as an allegory for the equally remote end of Sufi asceticism in union with God. By such an appropriation, I argue, Bīdil distinguished his Sufi authorship by mixing poetic codes. Specifically, he overlaid the dominant topos of Persianate literatures, that of "erotic separation" (*firāq*), with the Avadhi-mediated Sanskrit topos of "tragic separation leading to erotic union" (*karuṇavipralambhaśṛṅgāra*), using the Persian *ghazal* poetics of "the imaginary" (*khiyāl*) to mediate between these codes. His characterization of human existence in terms of the *ghazal* poetics of the imaginary was a poetic interpretation of Ibn 'Arabī's notion, discussed in Chapter 1, of *barzakh*. Such a mixing of codes was anticipated by the Mughal prince Dārā Shikūh's *Majma' al-baḥrayn* (The Meeting Place of the Two Oceans, 1655) which asserted terminological parallels between Sufi and Upanishadic thought. However, Dārā Shikūh's translation projects were distinguished by their aim to disclose a theological unity underlying superficial differences in terminology between Muslim and Hindu scripture.[7] By contrast, as this chapter will show, Bīdil's translation recognized, retained – and depended for its ethical and aesthetic power on retaining – a difference between Persian and Indic poetics. As such, his translation constitutes a distinctive instance in his oeuvre of his self-authorization by an appropriation of a canon and aesthetic local to India and thus partly explains the aesthetic locality that his student Sirāj al-Dīn 'Alī Khān Ārzū (1688–1756), who forms the subject of Chapter 4, came to defend.

The political crisis to which Bīdil responded

When Bīdil began to compose *'Irfān* in around 1682 a crisis beset both the land-revenue (*jāgīrdārī*) system of the empire as well as the system of Mughal princely power. A *jāgīr* was a landholding assigned by the emperor to its holder – a *jāgīrdār* – to be taxed by him. The *jāgīrdār* was expected in turn to defray the costs of own lifestyle from these tax revenues as well as raise an armed contingent to be placed in the service of the emperor. Some historians have argued that, beginning in the late seventeenth century, the emperor Aurangzeb's invasion of the Deccan simultaneously drained the state's revenues and swelled the number of high-ranking noblemen who expected *jāgīr*s commensurate with their ranks.[8] The Mughal state was increasingly unable to defray its administrative costs while the lack of profitable *jāgīr*s led to intensifying competition among the nobility who were hard put to financing their lavish lifestyles.[9] Certain noblemen responded by distributing patronage to form factions in their own support, this factionalism leading to incoherence in imperial policy.[10] Other historians have argued that what precipitated the crisis was Aurangzeb's expansion of his powers, beginning in this period, by increasing the size of directly administered revenue lands and his oversight and control of his sons' households. This increasingly curtailed the princes' ability to project Mughal imperial power across the regions of the vast empire which they jointly commanded.[11]

Patronized by the Mughal court, Bīdil was witness to such factional infighting at the highest military-administrative levels of the Mughal state and the political impasses it induced. He began to compose his *maṡnavī* around twenty-five years before Aurangzeb's death in 1707 and completed it in 1712, the year of the death of the next emperor, Bahādur Shāh I. Before his own death in 1720 Bīdil witnessed the diminishing authority of the Mughal emperor who, though retained as a symbolic figurehead, was victim to contests among the nobility over his person. There followed a quick succession of emperors after Bahādur Shāh I: Jahāndār Shāh (1712–13), Farrukh Siyar (1713–19), Rafī al-Darajāt (1719), Rafī al-Dawlat (1719) and Muḥammad Shāh (1719–48). Before he died in the second year of Muḥammad Shāh's reign, Bīdil would have known of Jahāndār Shāh's shocking break with imperial precedent on becoming emperor. Instead of ensuring that his brothers and nephew whom he had executed for challenging his claim to the throne received proper burials he let their bodies "rot under the open sun for a number of days before ordering their interment."[12] Bīdil would also have known of the blinding and execution of the next emperor, Farrukh Siyar, by the Sayyad brothers, powerful noblemen who dominated imperial politics during the last two decades of the poet's life. His successors, Rafī al-Darajāt and Rafī al-Dawlat, both appointed by the Sayyad brothers, died within the same year of tuberculosis. Munis Faruqui writes that "The year 1719" – that is, the year before Bīdil's death – "marked the final collapse of the Mughals as an effective ruling dynasty as well."[13] In the decades after the poet's death the emperor Muḥammad Shāh's failed early attempts to reform the *jāgirdārī* system were followed by a further de-sacralization of the emperor's body whose person then became no more than a legitimating symbol to be manipulated by regionally ensconced noblemen.[14] It was possibly this long-drawn exacerbation of the crisis of royal authority that maintained elite esteem for Bīdil's *'Irfān* in the remaining 137 years of increasingly nominal Mughal rule.

A brief interpretation of the circulation of the tale of Madan and Kāmdī

A brief reflection on the transmission of the tale of Madan and Kāmdī's love for each other reveals that its popularity was bound up with its overarching theme of just kingship. The earliest known written version of this tale dates to around 1300 when a Sanskrit poet named Ānandadhara told it under the title of *Mādhavānala ākhyānām.*[15] Already in this version, the king who successfully undertakes to reunite the parted lovers, Mādhavānala and Kāmakandalā, is the legendary Vikramāditya who, in keeping with the literal Sanskrit meaning of his name – "the sun of valor" – was exemplary for his valor and justice. The more popular early reception of the tale, however, seems to have occurred in Western India. In around 1528 in Amod in the region of Broach in Gujarat a poet called Gaṇapatī composed a version in Old Gujarati or Old Western Rajasthani titled *Mādhavānala-kāmakandalā-prabandha.*[16] This version, too, included an account of Vikramāditya's just war on behalf of the lovers followed by his moral lapse and then restoration. So, too, did another Old Gujarati version completed around 1559 in Jaisalmer by a Jain monk called Kushalābha.[17]

That these and other early Western Indian versions of the tale were all told as accounts of royal justice on behalf of the lovers suggests that the tale circulated as part of the larger cycle of tales relating the deeds of Vikramāditya.[18] This cycle of tales of unknown authorship, narrated throughout India, was known in its earliest Sanskrit versions under a few titles that were variations on the currently accepted one – *Simhāsana dvātrīmshikā* (Thirty-Two Tales of the Throne) – and has been dated in its written forms to between the late thirteenth and early fourteenth centuries.[19] This dating significantly places the written recensions of the tale squarely within the periods of Islamic rule over large regions of North India. It later circulated more widely in vernacular adaptations, typically known in North India under the title *Singhāsan-battīsī* or a close variation on this name. A brief summary of the frame story of this tale cycle lets us infer a certain understanding of the temporality of ideal kingship and will orient us towards Bīdil's eventual interest in it.

A synopsis and interpretation of the frame story of "Thirty-Two Tales of the Throne"

Raja Bhoj hears of an illiterate shepherd in his own kingdom who is reputed for his justice and skill at resolving disputes on a hillock top and, seeking him out, asks him how he came to possess such skills. The shepherd replies that he only comes to possess such skills when he sits on top of the hillock in question. Convinced the hillock contains a magical object, Raja Bhoj has it dug and discovers a jewel-studded throne of gold hung with thirty-two female statuettes. As soon as he tries to sit on it one of the statuettes shakes with laughter and says that the throne was once the property of Raja Vikramāditya and must only be occupied by a king who equals Vikramāditya in one of his royal virtues. She then tells him a story illustrating this virtue.

Each of the thirty-two statuettes – each given a feminine name that varies according to the tale's recension – thus goes on to arrest his attempts to mount the throne by telling him a didactic tale of Vikramāditya's virtues, beginning with how he came into possession of the throne. The last statuette asks Raja Bhoj why he no longer seems enthusiastic to occupy the throne. Bhoj replies that the tales of Vikramāditya's great virtues have led him to despair of ever being so virtuous and that he has decided to bury the throne again where he had found it. At this the statuettes rejoice, the queen statuette telling him they would no longer adorn the throne and that he came to encounter the throne because he already possessed part of Vikramāditya's virtues. She also adds that the throne would go on to lose its powers and luster, decaying like all creations. Then, all the statuettes fly into the sky and Bhoj reburies the throne. Here the frame story in some recensions comes to an end but some others contain an epilogue that relates how robbers dig a tunnel and steal the buried throne to sell it to a distant king in the south. When word spreads of the southern king's wondrous throne Raja Bhoj grows curious and has the hillock checked. When he finds it empty, he visits the southern king to find out whether he was indeed so virtuous as to sit on the throne. He narrates the tale of his discovery of the throne to the southern king who says he never had a problem sitting on it. But he has his jewelers and goldsmiths reassess the throne and this time finds that its gold has deteriorated to brass and its jewels to glass. The southern king has it ritually sunk in the river Kaveri. For centuries hence kings have divers search the Kaveri for the throne but do not find it. People say that if a king worthy of the throne were to reappear the throne would be rediscovered.

The tale cycle assumes the entropic temporality and the asymptotic nature of ideal kingship. By the time Raja Bhoj discovers the throne its ideal occupant, Raja Vikramāditya, already belongs to a legendary past only available in stories. Didactic stories of kingship are thus here self-consciously second-order representations of a lost ideal. Furthermore, Raja Bhoj's discovery begins the end of the throne's powers as it enters the time of human history and thus of decay. Raja Bhoj is himself never able to rightfully occupy the throne as he only ever possesses a part of Vikramāditya's royal virtues. Nor does the southern king who occupies it do so rightfully as he sits on a diminished version of the throne. The southern king, like Raja Bhoj, "reburies" the throne by ritually sinking it in the Kaveri when he, too, discovers his unworthiness of the throne. The throne is thus not a magical object that ensures ideal kingship by itself. It has to be matched by a king bearing the ideal virtues. The time of history is thus filled with defective approximations of Vikramāditya, the primordial and mythic archetype of the ideal king. The throne's discovery, burial, recovery, reburial and possible future recovery describe and prescribe a mythic cycle of approximations towards and defections from the ideally just kingship of Vikramāditya.

No wonder the Mughals – to whose ruling elites Bīdil was affiliated – showed much interest in this tale cycle. Inheriting a Late Ancient and then Islamic interest in India as a source of wisdom and royal advice literature, the Mughals commissioned numerous Persian and Hindavī translations of this cycle of tales prescribing royal virtue, beginning with Akbar's commission of 'Abdul Qādir Badāyūnī and Chaturbhuj bin Mehrchand's Persian translations and followed by the emperors Jahāngīr and Shāhjahān's commissions of its translation as well as one perhaps by the emperor Aurangzeb.[20] What, however, explains Bīdil's interest in this framing conception of the remoteness of ideal royal virtue?

The circulation of 'Ālam's hypertext for Bīdil's tale

Part of the answer lies in the political geography of 'Ālam's hypertext for Bīdil's tale. The poet 'Ālam, about whom nothing is known except what he says of himself in his *Mādhavānal-kāmakandalā*, composed the work a decade after Akbar's conquest in 1572–73 of Gujarat where, as I noted above, its tale seems to have had its earliest vernacular circulation.[21] It does not appear from 'Ālam's dedication of the tale to Akbar or his description of the circumstances in which he came to compose it that he drew on Gaṇapatī's Old Gujarati version or on some other version in circulation in Gujarat. However, the modern scholarly consensus on the Western Indian provenance of the tale as well as its eastward spread subsequent to Akbar's conquest of Gujarat strongly suggest that 'Ālam's motivations for composing it in Avadhi and Raja Todar Mal's possible commission of it were bound up with Akbar's well-known imperial investment in Sanskrit and Sanskrit-informed vernacular literatures. That 'Ālam aimed to convey norms of kingship by his work is arguably already implicit in the genre unit of his poem: a narrative or descriptive quatrain (*chaupai*) followed by a typically homiletic couplet (*dohā*). This genre format was already current in the Sufi genre of the Hindavī or Avadhi *premākhyān*. But it was associated in its didactic applications with early modern Apabhramsha poetry by Digambar Jains in Gujarat and Western India, a didactic tradition 'Ālam arguably evoked by his choice of a didactic tale of known Gujarati provenance.[22] It is worth noting in this connection that it was only a year after Akbar's conquest of Gujarat – that is in 1574/75 – that 'Abdul Qādir Badāyūnī completed the translation the emperor had commissioned him to make of the Sanskrit *Simhāsana dvātrīmshikā*.[23]

'Ālam's quatrain and couplet describing how he came to compose the tale and his aesthetic aims in composing it are worthy of attention:

> Some of it's my own work, some I've appropriated from that of others.
> To the best of my abilities I fitted letters together,
> Adorned in the established manner of *viraha* [*sakal singār viraha kī rīti*]
> The tale of the love of Mādhau and Kāmakandalā.
> Having listened to a little of the Sanskrit tale,
> I bound it in Avadhi [*bhāshā*] by conjoining quatrains [*chaupahī*].[24]

Noteworthy is the poet's declaration of partial originality and his suggestion of the plurality of his sources, itself a sign of the tale's availability to him in multiple versions. Even the Sanskrit version – possibly Ānandadhara's – he only claims to have heard "a little of," thus signaling his independence of the Sanskrit, an independence underscored by his foregrounding of the vernacular Avadhi and its distinctive genre-feature of the quatrain or *chaupai*. This self-conscious distance from Sanskrit qualifies his use of the word *rīti* in: *sakal singār viraha kī rīti*. I have translated this half-line as "adorned in the established manner of *viraha*." The term *rīti* also designated "Brajbhasha renditions of Sanskrit treatises on literary topics," one of the earliest such renditions or *rītigranth*s being composed by Keshavdās in the same courtly milieu as 'Ālam in 1591.[25] However, Keshavdās hewed closely to Sanskrit taxonomies in his rendition of Braj poetic topics. By contrast, 'Ālam's use of the term does not signal his close conformity in tropes and topoi to Braj or Sanskrit poetics. It must be understood only as an authorizing appeal to prestigious Sanskrit poetics rather than a detailed use of its taxonomies.[26] It also signals his affiliation to the then incipient rise to courtly prestige of literature in Braj although Avadhi, the language of his poem, had already attained such prestige in the Afghan and Rajput courts of pre-Mughal North India.

The other noteworthy feature of the half-line and its ambient prefatory verses is the poet's emphasis on the affect of *viraha* that he aims to evoke in his listener-reader. I have left the word *viraha* untranslated in the above quotation because it designates a key Indian literary-theological concept. The term literally means "erotic separation" and seems to have first appeared in the famous dramaturgical treatise dated to between the first century BCE and second century CE and attributed to the sage Bharata, *Nātyaśāstra*. It also came, from the turn of the first millennium CE, to designate the predominant affect of *bhakti* or the popular practices of devotion to one or more of the Hindu deities.[27] The very distance between the divine beloved and human lover incited the human's desire for the deity, leading to a regionally varied and long developing aestheticization of this eroticized separation, the most famous image of this being the pining of the cowherd women for the god Krishna. Among 'Ālam's most conspicuous rhetorical accomplishments in the main body of the poem, therefore, are the hyperbolic descriptive embellishments of the two lovers in separation from each other, the terms *viraha* or *biraha* and *viyog* or *biyog* (also meaning separation) appearing with leitmotif frequency in the symmetrical sections thematizing the plight of the lovers.[28]

However, 'Ālam's appropriation of the term and its literary conventions in this particular work are of a recognizably profane rather than devotional character. Nowhere are there indications of an allegorical framing of the erotic separation of the lovers that might lead us to impute theological identities to the characters or metaphysical meanings to their actions. Partly accounting for this is the courtly context of his composition.[29] Partly, too, it must be explained by its continuity with "the secular poetic tradition," dating to as early as 235 BCE, in Prakrit, Apabhramsha and Sanskrit.[30] The courtly origins of the poem also account for 'Ālam's emphasis on Raja Vikramāditya's assistance to Madhavānala. Not only is this episode of royal assistance assigned a separate chapter in 'Ālam's poem, it also contains an extended and artfully alliterative description of the war Vikramāditya fights on the lovers' behalf.[31]

'Ālam's prestigious proximity to Akbar and his dedication of the poem to the emperor, suggesting that the poem implicitly described and prescribed Akbar's justice on Vikramāditya's model, seem to have inaugurated the tale's circulation among Mughal ruling elites. It then came to be told in various vernacular and similarly profane versions, spreading to Mughal Bengal where, in 1660–63, a Persian version titled *Ma̱snavī Mādhavānal-Kāmakandalā mawsūm ba Maḥẕ-i i'jāz* was composed by Ḥaqīrī Kāshānī who was employed by Mīr Jumlah, the Mughal governor of Bengal.[32] Ḥaqīrī's *ma̱snavī* which does not seem to have circulated as widely in manuscript as 'Ālam's version presents itself explicitly in its concluding chapter as an "ornamentation" in Persian (*darī*) of 'Ālam's Avadhi (*hindavī*) version.[33] It conforms closely to its Avadhi predecessor in its profane mode of reference, key characters and plot. But this is where what A.K. Ramanujan conceptualized in the context of *Rāmāyaṇa* translations as "iconicity" – the geometrical mapping of every feature of a text onto those of its translation – ends.[34] In all other aspects Ḥaqīrī's translation is an instance of Ramanujan's "indexical" translation: "the text is embedded in a locale, a context, refers to it, even signifies it, and would not make much sense without it." So, it depends at the level of the distich – the largest textual unit of Persian rhetorical analysis – for part of its aesthetic pleasure on the reader's recognition of 'Ālam's Avadhi tropes and metaphors as they are replicated, elided or transformed by Persian ones. It is embedded in the locale of the Persian *ma̱snavī* and "would not make much sense without it."

Given the prestige and paradigmatic status of 'Ālam's version in Mughal North India as well as its descriptive similarities with Bīdil's, we would not be mistaken in regarding 'Ālam's version as the most probable hypotext for Bīdil's version. I now offer an interpretation of 'Ālam's version that may be taken as a template for subsequent versions.

An interpretation of 'Ālam's hypotext for Bīdil's hypertext

Every narrative, like every semiotics, possesses two simultaneous aspects: one or more *sequences* and one or more *states of being*. Any narrative may thus be analyzed under these two simultaneous aspects, that of the plot or action and that of description. The abstraction and generality of this analytical distinction also lets us compare two or more narratives with respect to their sequences and states. In what follows, I offer a brief interpretation of the sequences and states that make up 'Ālam's tale. I thus arrive at a formalization from which Bīdil may be understood to depart. My focus on certain passages in this interpretation will be oriented by the overriding aim of this chapter, which is to understand Bīdil's innovations on this hypotext.

'Ālam's plot opens with the kingdom of Pushpāvatī where a virtuous Brahmin polymath called Mādhavānal attends the court of the just king Gopīchand, performing his ritual duties. He plays the *bīn* (i.e., the *vīnā* or a stringed instrument) so incomparably well that the city's women abandon their duties to gather around him, swooning from desire. Despairing at the collapse of social order, the city's residents send the king a deputation requesting him to banish Mādhavānal lest they quit the kingdom themselves. The king decides to verify the charge against the musician and assembles twenty young women to witness Mādhavānal play his *bīn*. When he observes their growing discomposure at his music he pleads with Mādhavānal to leave the kingdom.

The hero departs with his *bīn* and comes upon a kingdom called Kāmavatī where he decides to rest. In that city lives a courtesan called Kāmakandalā who is unmatched in beauty and the arts of song and dance. She is to dance at the king's court that evening and guests throng to the event. Eager to see her dance, too, Mādhavānal arrives at the court with his *bīn* but, being a stranger, is obliged by the chamberlain to listen to the performance standing outside at the door. Within, Kāmakandalā dances to the rhythm of twelve percussionists. But one of these twelve, seated next to the fourth, lacks a finger on one of his hands and so beats out a slightly defective rhythm. A discerning listener, Mādhavānal detects the fault and declares his disappointment in the assembly's aesthetic discrimination to the chamberlain, telling him to inform the king that a Brahmin at the door has divined such and such a fault. The king is astonished, has the percussionist in question checked and, on recognizing the correctness of the criticism, invites Mādhavānal in to be seated next to him. He rewards the musician with money, a crown and his signet ring. Mādhavānal then enthralls the court, especially Kāmakandalā, by playing on his *bīn*. Kāmakandalā then begins to dance, balancing a water-filled cup on her head. As she displays a certain expressive gesture (*bhāv*) a bee settles on her, beginning to sting her. Rather than brushing it away with her hand and thus deforming the gesture, she quickens her pace, twirling so swiftly that the resulting breeze drives the bee away. Only Mādhavānal catches sight of this. Praising her openly, he casts at her feet all the gifts the king had presented to him. On being questioned for this action by the king, he replies by declaring the courtly assembly to be aesthetically unworthy of Kāmakandalā whose virtuoso presence of mind they altogether missed. Insulted, the king banishes him from the kingdom.

But Kāmakandalā, who recognizes Mādhavānal's artistic accomplishments and now loves him as he loves her, persuades him to stay on hidden in her house where, at her request to teach her the arts of lovemaking, he remains with her for days. After days steeped in pleasure Mādhavānal resolves to leave, finding it too risky to linger. She begs him to stay another night, asking him to somehow prolong the night. He so plays on his *bīn* that the moon halts in its course and the night grows long.

But the night eventually comes to an end with his music and he departs, leaving behind Kāmakandalā who grows more dead than alive with "the pain of erotic separation" (*viraha*). Similarly afflicted, Mādhavānal decides to seek out the king Vikramāditya, fabled for his justice, in his kingdom of Ujjain. (Here, it is worth noting that the near-death state of the lovers invokes the tenth of the classical "ten stages of love" – the *daśadaśā* – taxonomized by rhetoricians, dramaturgists and eroticians in Sanskrit.)[35] Lacking the means to enter Vikramāditya's court, he places a couplet (*dohā*) describing his condition at a temple frequented by the king. On discovering the couplet the king recognizes Mādhavānal as afflicted by *viraha* and summons him to court. There the lover persuades the king and his assembly of the pathos (*karuṇā*) of his condition, leading Vikramāditya to mount an expedition on the kingdom of Kāmavatī where Kāmakandalā is held.

Once at Kāmavatī Vikramāditya decides to test the sincerity of the heroine's love and enters her home in disguise. Despite finding her equally afflicted by *viraha* he announces to her, by way of a test, that Mādhavānal did not survive the pain of separation. On hearing of her lover's death she cries out his name and dies. Remorseful, the king returns to his camp to announce her death at which news Mādhavānal dies too. Consumed by guilt, Vikramāditya prepares to take his own life by mounting a funeral pyre.

Word spreads of the king's decision and even the gods gather to witness this sight. However, the king's friend Vetāl stays the king by bringing him a life-restoring nectar (*amrit*) that is then administered to Mādhavānal who revives, uttering Kāmakandalā's name. The king returns to Kāmakandalā's home disguised as a physician and revives her with the nectar too. (Worth recalling here is the conception of the king, of long currency in the Persianate world, as a physician to the kingdom's body).[36] After reassuring her of his help he returns to his kingdom and dispatches a messenger to the king of Kāmavatī, demanding the release of Kāmakandalā. Insulted at the demand, the king refuses to comply. The kings go to war, waging a bloody battle into the fourth watch (*pahar*) of the day. Finally accepting defeat, the king of Kāmavatī surrenders Kāmakandalā to Vikramāditya who returns to Ujjain with the two happily reunited lovers.

Stated formally, 'Ālam's plot alternates between states of disequilibrium and equilibrium. The pervasive incitement to this alternation and transition from one state to the next is the socially destabilizing character of the artistic virtuosity of the lovers, virtuosity only the king Vikramāditya recognizes and defends. Here is an early quatrain and its concluding couplet introducing the first state of equilibrium in the kingdom of Pushpāvatī and Mādhavānal's virtuosity:

> *pushpāvatī nagr ik sunau – gopīchand rāj vah gunau*
> *dharmpañthu din prati pagu dharai – pahumi pavitra pāpu nahiñ karai*
> *tihipur basai sadāñ sukh tyāgī – mādahu vipra nām vairāgī*
> *rājā pās prāt uṭhi jāvai – lai tulsī dal dev pujāvai*
> *dev pujāi vipr phiri āvai – prāt bhayeñ puni daras dikhāvai*
> *bāñchai bed purān nau byākaran bakhānai*
> *jotik āgam jāni sāmudrik sāñgīt sab*[37]

Before I offer a translation we should note that the end-rhymes of the half-lines (*ardhālī*) phonemically underscore their semantic and prosodic symmetry. The rhymes thus frame two symmetrical units of sound and sense, marking each couplet off as a discrete unit of narration even if embedded within a semantically coherent quatrain. In this sense, each line of the Avadhi quatrain corresponds to the end-rhymed couplet that forms the narrative unit of the Persianate *maṣnavī*, surely an interlingual and intergeneric similarity known to many Indo-Persian literati. Here is a translation that inevitably misses such rhythmic and phonemic components of meaning:

> In a city called Pushpāvatī, I hear – Was a virtuous king called Gopīchand.
> Daily he strode on the path of righteousness – Considering the earth holy, he never sinned.
> In his city lived an ever-happy renunciant – a Brahman ascetic named Mādhau.
> Every dawn he'd go to the king – Taking a basil-leaf [*tulsī*], he'd perform ritual worship [*pūjā*] before the sacred idols.
> Having performed ritual worship the Brahman would return – The next dawn he'd appear to present the gods again.
> He had studied the Vedās, Purānas and the nine grammarians.
> He knew astrology, the sciences of prediction, physiognomy, music-and-dance and all the rest.

This account of a fusion of artistic skill and ethical stature also corresponds to the Perso-Arabic notion of *faẕl*, a word that translates both as "virtue" and "scholarship." That Mādhavānal, a bearer of Indic *faẕl*, distinguished the court of the virtuous king Gopīchand may well have appealed to the emperor Akbar who prided himself on the musicians, poets and painters who attended his court. The ensemble of linguistic, poetic, music-and-dance related (*sangīt*), physiognomic (*sāmudrik*) and erotological (*sringār*, *singār*) skills that Mādhavānal excels at and later teaches Kāmakandalā correspond to those explicated in the second part of the fourth book of *Āyīn-i Akbarī* (The Institutes of Akbar, 1589–98), part of the court-sponsored history of the emperor's reign.[38] They also correspond to the courtly practices of pleasure explicated in around 1675 in Mirzā Khān ibn Fakhr al-Dīn's encyclopedia of "the current Indian sciences," *Tuḥfat al-Hind* (Gift from/to India).[39] Mirzā Khān dedicated his work to the emperor Aurangzeb's son, the prince Muḥammad A'ẓam who patronized Bīdil and prided himself on his expertise in, among other arts (*fann*), "the knowledge of music and dance."[40] Bīdil's membership in these courtly circles that cultivated such "Indian sciences" would have put him in proximity with the aesthetics of 'Ālam's tale and the kind of artistic accomplishment it exalted.

To return to my observation of the alternating states of 'Ālam's tale, its opening and state of equilibrium yields to a state of disequilibrium (Mādhavānal's banishment from Pushpāvatī) brought about by his artistic virtuosity. This yields again to a state of equilibrium (Mādhavānal's elevation to the king's companionship in Kāmavatī). This results in another state of disequilibrium (Mādhavānal's banishment from Kāmavatī) on account of his virtuosity that then passes into a state of equilibrium (his secret union with Kāmakandalā) in which both lovers exult in the ensemble of the performative arts that include that of lovemaking. But this yields again to a state of disequilibrium (the symmetrically described *viraha* of the parted lovers) that is only reversed after prolonged waiting and war that culminates in Vikramāditya's victory.

The plot's consistent emphasis is thus on the tension between the pervasively disordering effects on society of artistic accomplishment and the rarity in the same society of aesthetic discernment equal to such accomplishment. A possessor of such discernment would, it is implied, know how to contain the instability resulting from such virtuosity. Just how he would achieve this containment we are not shown. But Vikramāditya's just war on behalf of such virtuosity lets us infer the possibility that all of his kingdom's subjects would imitate his discernment and thus master themselves as he could when they see and hear such artistry. But we cannot know this with certainty because the tale's final equilibrium lies in a future located after its conclusion. It is an equilibrium that is only projected into the future by the departure of the lover-artists with the victorious Vikramāditya for Ujjain and thus for a kingdom as rare as its storied king. It is in this deeper sense that this tale belongs to the cycle of *Thirty-Two Tales of the Throne*, ending like each tale without closure. Here, as in the other tales of the cycle, the end of the narrative sequence is not the same as the proleptically final state of being.

An interpretation of Bīdil's hypertext: a beginning

For the purposes of this chapter's focus on Bīdil's appropriation of this Indic canon of stories what is remarkable is the following: the utopian future under Vikramāditya was amenable to an explanation in terms of the Islamic-Neo-Platonic ideal of a state ruled by a philosopher-king. This ideal was variously transmitted through *akhlāq*, the principle discourse of royal ethics, to the Persianate world Bīdil inhabited. The founding philosopher of Islamic Neo-Platonism, Abū Naṣr al-Fārābī (*c.*878–950), had argued that:

> The ruler of the best state must be the best of its citizens, endowed to the highest degree with natural, moral and intellectual qualities, an object of imitation for other citizens, a perfect philosopher who has become intellect in act. As such the ruler has attained a high degree of human happiness or felicity, a proximity to the life of the transcendent Agent Intellect which we can compare to the "assimilation to the divine" sought by the Neoplatonic philosopher.[41]

To be sure, nothing of this metaphysical significance is already evident or even implicit in the Avadhi tale or its Indic and Persianate intertexts. All Bīdil had to hand was a popular, prestigious and profane intertext relating the union, parting and reunion through the efforts of a just king of two lovers of symmetrically described artistic skills and mutually reciprocated desire. Indeed, a bare summary of Bīdil's plot would not suggest otherwise: Kāmdī who is a supremely skilled dancer at court hears of Madan's skills as a singer in another kingdom's court. She falls in love with him – or more precisely grows besotted with his mental image (*khiyāl*) – and seeks him out in his courtly setting. In one of many modifications of 'Ālam's plot it is Kāmdī rather than Madan who is unable to gain entrance to the court for want of social connections. However, her fame as a dancer precedes her and the king's cultured courtiers persuade him to arrange a joint performance by the two artists. Beside himself at the skill of Kāmdī's dance, Madan flings at her feet the necklace which the king had previously gifted him in appreciation for his singing. Incensed at this impropriety, the king banishes him from his kingdom. However, Kāmdī persuades him to remain a night and visits him in solitude. At night's end the lovers are parted and pine away in separation.

Madan lies dying in a desert when a king – not named Vikramāditya but his equivalent in the plot – catches sight of him while hunting. Observing the birds near him repeating Kāmdī's name he infers that they have learned the name by his passionate repetition of it and that he is dying of separation from Kāmdī. Informed by Madan of how he came to this pass, the king resolves to reunite the lovers and writes to the king who holds Kāmdi, asking him to free her. (The hypotext here is Niẓāmī Ganjavī's *Laylī u Majnūn*, completed in 1188, in which a Bedouin warrior undertakes to nobly defend unjustly parted lovers. But Bīdil also had for an intertext Ḥaqīrī Kāshānī's aforementioned translation which is in the same meter as Niẓāmī's *masnavī* and also cites Majnūn's desert desolation in describing Mādhavānal's desolation). Insulted at the request to free Kāmdī, the king refuses and both kings go to war with each other. The war ends with the victory of the king who defends the lovers. The victorious king decides to test the lovers' steadfastness in mutual love and has told each that the other is dead. Each appears to die of grief at the news of the other's death. But when the king repents of his deceit and resolves to commit suicide his physicians declare on reflection that the lovers are not dead but paralyzed. They place the lovers in each other's arms and soon life, kindled by love's latent heat, returns to their bodies. The tale thus ends with the reunification of the lovers.

But such a plot summary barely conveys the pleasure and significance of Bīdil's version. It does little more than alert us to how he edited the plot of the Indic intertext he inherited for his purposes. What were his purposes? We may answer this by observing that the theme of a royally defended symmetry of artistic virtuosity and desire that was central to all prior versions of the tale as well as to 'Ālam's hypotext served Bīdil in two analytically separable ways. I will state these in brief and then expand on them in the next section of this chapter. First, the theme allowed him, by his narrative location of the tale at a certain point in his *masnavī*, to re-semanticize the tale into a politico-theologico allegory absent in the profane intertexts of the tale he inherited. This was a technique he had already used in his early *masnavī* of 1667, *Muḥīt-i a'ẓam* (The Greatest Ocean). There, he rearranged the relations of story and commentary in a tale of a king from the *Yoga Vāsiṣṭha* so his reader would be taken in by the tale's aim to convey the created world's illusoriness. The effect of the succeeding explanation was thus not only to instruct the reader, but also to shock him.[42] By specific poetic procedures that I will discuss, he refashioned the tale into a Neo-Platonic-Sufi allegory of ideal kingship as the defense of the universal sympathy of kindred souls for each other; and of the philosopher-king who, by ascetically ascending to the divine One, sets his subjects an example and thus drags them up with himself. Such an allegory would have appealed to his elite Mughal readers who were beset with the crisis of royal authority and political power.

Second, by this allegorization of the tale he was able to estrange or make foreign the conventional Persian Sufi semiotic of "erotic separation" (*firāq*) by overlaying it with the Avadhi-mediated Sanskrit poetic topos of "tragic separation leading to erotic union" (*karuṇavipralambhaśṛṅgāra*). By this estrangement Bīdil spoke the Sufi poetic anew, a renewal he was canonically associated with as the most authoritative stylistic threshold in the Persian *ghazal* after Sā'ib Tabrīzī (d. 1676). I now turn to the first of Bīdil's uses of the tale, beginning with an account of a heresy and then analyzing his intervention in it. I will then conclude with a discussion of the second of his uses.

Metempsychosis

Bīdil set his narration of the tale within the sun's multi-part allegorical answer to the human, a conversational situation drawn from a section of the Hindu (specifically Advaita Vedanta) philosophical allegory *Yoga Vāsiṣṭha*, as we will observe. By this setting, as well as his silence on such immediate Hindu models for the tale, he was able to appropriate the authority of his profane and sacred hypotexts while recalling to his reader the sacral or devotional origins and allegorical poetics of *viraha*.[43] We may begin to explicate the central allegorical meaning he assigns the tale by recalling my suggestion in Chapter 1 that by describing an iconic relation between himself or "the Bīdilian nature" and his portrait, Bīdil was raising the heretical possibility of metempsychosis (*tanāsukh*). More precisely, the episode of the portrait that faded and flared in keeping with his health presented an instance of a single soul simultaneously animating two discrete bodies. I suggested that this was part of the reason he tore up his own portrait. By this episode, significantly composed in approximately the same years as *'Irfān,* he implicitly presented a version of metempsychosis but with cautious brevity and without naming it thus or advocating it himself. Rather, as we saw, Bīdil put the phenomenon down to an unintentional effect of the preparedness (*isti'dād*) of his kenotically transformed soul to make the Real manifest. It is in *'Irfān* that he presented this doctrine extensively if poetically, appropriating it for his purposes while mostly displacing ultimate responsibility for it onto Hindu traditions.

Metempsychosis was considered a heresy in most Sunni and Shi'i sects throughout Islamic history because it disassociated the human soul from its particular corporeal locus. By this it denied the Qur'ānic idea of the Day of Resurrection when, at the end of time, the dead would be raised from their graves and all humans would be assembled before God in the particular bodies they were born with. To espouse metempsychosis would thus have been tantamount to denying the tenet of bodily resurrection that was central to Islamic eschatology. However, because of Plato and Plotinus's open advocacy of the transmigration of the soul all Islamic thinkers knew of the doctrine as a Greek idea. Moreover, the long enduring authority of both thinkers in the Islamic world kept constant in various forms the risk of lapsing into metempsychosis.[44] But this was a risk that was only rarely actualized to the degree of receiving full theological and philosophical justification by Muslim thinkers.[45] Rather than philosophers or theologians, it was radical Sufi groups (*ghulāt*) and politically powerful individuals who were publicly known as advocates of the doctrine. The best-known instances of the latter were the Safavid emperor Shāh Ismail (1487–1524), who rose to power with the assistance of his Qizilbash devotees who were "famous for their messianic fervor, belief in metempsychosis and red iconic headgear"; and Akbar, the emperor of Mughal India (1542–1605).[46] In both cases the espousal of metempsychosis formed an element of these emperors' imperial self-fashioning as messiahs at the end of the first millennium of the Islamic calendar. All these instances must thus be regarded as exceptions to the norm by which metempsychosis was a heresy. Significantly for the purposes of this chapter,

> most writers saw the idea of the transmigration of the soul as a characteristic of Hindu religious thought. In such a system the soul of an individual human being passes at death into the body of another human or that of a lower animal according to the merit earned or sins committed in the life just ended. After cycles of death and rebirth, some souls rise in station to a point where they escape the physical world altogether. Others, however, remain forever drifting from one to another form of corporeal existence.[47]

Bīdil put this Hindu association of metempsychosis to specific symbolic use. But it must be noted that he also kept this Hindu intertext, like 'Ālam's intertext, at a certain distance. That is, similarly to his appropriation of the history of the *tarjī'-band* studied in Chapter 2, he avoided a direct citation of any one intertext.

By this distance he was able to creatively manipulate such intertexts for his distinct purposes. Here, he drew at once on Muslim and Hindu intertexts for the symbolism of the sun. The sun was central to Niẓāmī Ganjavī's poetic symbolism in his *masnavīs* as well as to Rūmī's *Dīvān-i Shams* whose very title literally means "The Dīvān of the Sun," an allusion to his teacher Shams of Tabriz. But the more exact of these canonical Islamic precedents for the human's apostrophe to the sun that inaugurates the allegory was Khāqānī Shīrvānī's (d. 1187–99, Tabriz) *masnavī*, *Tuḥfat al-'Irāqayn* (The Gift of the Two Iraqs), over three-quarters of which he addresses to the sun.[48] Unable to leave Shīrvān himself, the poet asks the sun to undertake the Hajj on his behalf. Bīdil's citation of Khāqānī's *masnavī* may have fortified his *masnavī* against the potential charge of heresy. But also at play is Hindu prayer to the sun, a practice the Mughal elite would also have associated with the emperor Akbar's adoption of it in courtly ritual.

To understand the concrete uses Bīdil made of Hindu metempsychosis we must attend to his expositions of it as well as their location in his long cosmogony. They appear after the emanation of the "three kingdoms" or stages (*mavālīd-i sih-gānah*) of the mineral, vegetal and animal souls culminate in the emanation of the human. The souls at each level desire ascent to the level of the human but remain arrested at their particular levels because of a weakness that distinguishes each level. This cosmogonic sequence is Islamic-Neo-Platonic and Hindu at once for it alludes to a chapter of the *Yoga Vāsiṣṭha* that had come to be accepted since the ninth century as a teaching text for Advaita or non-dualist Vedānta. In Chapter 99 of Book 6, Part 2, of this text that was available to Bīdil in multiple Persian translations we read:

> All the various kinds of animals are endowed with all other animal faculties and inclinations like those of mankind. The drowsy plant kingdom, the dormant mountain, and other unconscious natures are fully conscious within of an empty intellectual power on which they exist.[49]

Since the human includes something of each level within himself this permits Bīdil a rudimentary anthropology. He thus distinguishes between humans who retain the "stony nature" (*fasurdah-aṭvār*) of the mineral level, the weakness of resolve of the vegetal level (*faskh*) and the incapacity for self-knowledge and thus gnosis of the animal level (*maskh*). He observes that nothing but metempsychosis comes to the assistance of the three pre-human levels. At this stage in the cosmogony, then, Hindu metempsychosis signifies a particular soul's means to ontological ascent along a long familiar Aristotelian-Islamic creaturely hierarchy towards the human and, through the human, towards the divine. Already in the thirteenth century Rūmī, who presented the tradition of the Sufi *masnavī* with some of its most enduring paradigms, had traced this very ascent from the mineral to the vegetal, the vegetal to the animal, the animal to the human and the human to the trans-human or angelic in his *Masnavī-i ma'anvī*.[50] This is why Bīdil titles the sub-section narrating the emanation of the human: "A description of the human whose form, when it swelled,/Became the final seal on the book of wisdom."[51]

It is immediately after this that Bīdil undertakes "A description of the relation of soul and body [*jān u jasad*]/That cannot be snapped till Post-Eternity [*abad*]."[52] Given the foregoing exposition of the heretical status of metempsychosis in most Islamic traditions, the title of this sub-section appears to conform to the standard Islamic eschatological stipulation of the inseparability of the soul and body. But this proves to be a deceptive conformity when we pay attention to Bīdil's exposition of this inseparability.

His argument in this sub-section may be formalized thus: the body is the soul's perfection and the soul is God's breathing of His names (*asmā*) into the dust of the body.[53] In this *general* sense, soul and body are therefore inseparable. Moreover, the human body is the supreme manifestation of God's self-disclosure and thus the perfection of "the three kingdoms" (*mavālīd*) of minerals, plants and animals. All three are immature versions of what, when it grows "gnostically aware" (*āgāh*), becomes the human. In the concluding lines of this section, Bīdil says: "Thus from the complex to the elemental world/Is the body and knowledge of one comprehensive human."[54] That is, the entire embodied-and-ensouled world is, in reality, *one* human. This one, all-encompassing human is arguably the highest self-disclosure of the God of Bīdil's Akbarian monism. But what this also implies is the generality rather than the specificity of the relation between body and soul. That is, it now becomes apparent that, in terms of this exposition, there is no necessary relation between a particular body and a particular soul. The only necessary relation – the one implicit in the sub-section's title – is that between the general body and its general soul. Although Bīdil does not say it, nothing now disallows the cohabitation by a particular soul of two or more particular bodies because all such particular souls and bodies are members of the one general and enveloping (*muḥīt*) God-shaped human.

Bīdil's narrative prefiguration of the tale of Madan and Kāmdī and its genre

The royally defended lovers Madan and Kāmdī, long imagined in Bīdil's inherited intertext of their story as symmetrical in their artistic virtuosity and love for each other, served him as an exemplary case of such a double-bodied soul. To be sure, this notion is not quite the same as Hindu metempsychosis that, even in terms of Bīdil's exposition of it, is the migration of a soul at death from one body to another. What Bīdil presents as Hindu metempsychosis is in fact the projection of an Islamic-Neo-Platonic idea of love as the action of the double-bodied soul onto this "Hindu" tale.[55] It is a case of what, with reference to *Rāmāyaṇa* translations, A.K. Ramanujan called "symbolic translation": "Text 2 uses the plot and characters and names of Text 1 minimally and uses them to say entirely new things, often in an effort to subvert the predecessor by producing a counter-text."[56] Let us consider how he accomplishes such a projection and translation.

Although he does not term the love of Madan and Kāmdī for each other an instance of Hindu metempsychosis, he does relate two tales of what he explicitly denominates metempsychosis immediately before this one, thus letting us arrive at such an interpretation by prefigurations. The brief but remarkable section that prefaces Bīdil's narration of the tale is titled "If awareness listens to the mystery of truth/It won't deny the lute of metempsychosis."[57] It is the only passage in *'Irfān* where Bīdil speaks in his own voice when validating the reality of metempsychosis. Rather than displacing responsibility for this validation onto supposed Hindu sources and informants, he urges his normatively Muslim reader in his own voice to heed the lessons of popular Hindu belief in and manifestations of metempsychosis. However, after a brief exposition of the Hindu doctrine of the soul's transmigration at death into another human or animal body according to its merit in its just completed life, he says:

> I, too, from the novelties of this situation,
> Have seen spectacles in dreams and the imagination.
> Were I to state them at length
> I'd acknowledge my debts to a world.
> I'll clarify it as needed with a summary [*mujmalī*]
> So hidden prodigies come to light.[58]

The "summary" or "compendium" that follows is an anecdote the subsection titles a *ḥikāyat* (pl. *ḥikāyāt*). This was a genre label with a long history in Persian Sufi and ethical-didactic literature. The paradigmatic collection of ethical-didactic *ḥikāyāt* was Sa'dī's *Gulistān* (The Rose Garden, 1258, Shiraz) while Rūmī made exemplary Sufi use of this genre in his *Masnavī-i ma'navī* (The *Masnavī* of Inner Meaning, completed shortly before 1273 in Konya). This is not the place to offer an extended explication of this term as Sa'dī or Rūmī use it. It will suffice to note that for both thinkers the *ḥikāyat* comprised a narrative that facilitated the reception by an ideally disposed reader of an ethical or ontological insight. They thus framed such anecdotes in ways that solicited an interpretation on two levels, the salient and superficially enjoyable level on the one hand and the non-salient, edifying and privileged one on the other.[59] However, Bīdil's use of the genre descriptor *ḥikāyat* does more than signal such a parabolic or double function of the tales of Hindu metempsychosis that follow. It also permits him to validate metempsychosis through a non-expository and thus cautiously non-explicit and yet imaginative and emotionally affecting use of language. Hence the full verse title of the section: "From this tale [*ḥikāyat*] that is affecting/The people's lesson [*'ibrat*] draws sights." The word *'ibrat*, too, signals a long Perso-Arabic history of invoking a kind of gaze that draws lessons of worldly transience from ambient material remains. By this innovative invocation of discourses traditionally invested with truth-values in Persian literary culture, then, Bīdil implicitly signals the material reality and validates the ethical-ontological worth of the events of Hindu metempsychosis he then narrates.

The tale, in brief, is that of the father of a Hindu acquaintance of Bīdil – this personal relation implicitly underscoring the tale's veracity – who was bothered by a crow. On consulting "scripturally informed ascetics" (*faqīrān-i shāstar-āgāh*), the father learned that the crow was a soul who, in his previous life, had owed the father a debt but had died without repaying it.[60] This failure to repay the debt had led him to be reborn as a crow and that crow was seeking the father's forgiveness. The father forgives the crow and is thus rid of it.

Following the tale is a meditative section observing that Gnostic knowledge among the Hindus mainly takes the form of breath in the human body. This section thus expounds what is implicitly the Sanskrit-Vedantic ontological idea of the self as *ātman* or "breath" in terms of what is implicitly Ibn 'Arabī and Jāmī's ontological notion of "the Breath of the All-Merciful" (*nafas-i raḥmānī*).[61] That Bīdil does not mention either the Sanskrit or Perso-Arabic term only heightens the resemblance and enables his translation of one philosophical idea in terms of another. This reflection on the single breath that swells multiple beings into their creaturely reality frames our interpretation of the tale of sati that follows as the action of this single merciful breath. This is a somewhat longer tale from Bihar, where Bīdil grew up, of a seven-year-old girl called Rājvantī. Unbeknownst to the girl, her child-husband dies. Despite being uninformed by her relatives of her husband's death Rājvantī walks into her family's shrine room and sets herself on fire, forbidding her watching family from intervening. This, Bīdil remarks, is because Hindu teaching maintains:

> That women are the inner nature of men
> They draw upon themselves the actions of the indivisible person
>
> *kih zanān khulq-i bāṭin-i mardand*
> *jāẕib-i fi'l-i jawhar-i fardand.*[62]

The end-rhymes imply a semantic relation between "men" (*mard*) and "the indivisible person" (*fard*), the latter being the indivisible soul of the all-enveloping human. By this logic, widowed women only find release (*najāt*) in their husbands' funeral pyres. The widowed Rājvantī was only acting out the command of "the indivisible person" when she set herself on fire.

Both of these tales establish an allegorical frame of reference for the tale of Madan and Kāmdī. The first tale of the crow and the man presents, on what Bīdil presents as credible authority, a case of a moral transaction left incomplete in human life. The result is the metempsychosis of the soul of one of the two humans into the body of a crow in his next life, a punishment relieved only when the human partner in the transaction forgives him. The second tale presents a case, from the poet's home region of Bihar and thus implicitly on the poet's own authority, of two bodies unconsciously subject to the same soul. When one of the bodies dies the other one acts out the soul's command to achieve release by immolating itself. By narrative prefiguration, then, the characters of Madan and

Kāmdī inherit a moral imperative to consummate the primordial sympathy by which their souls incline towards each other.[63]

However, the scholar Aḥsan al-Ẓafar refutes the interpretation I present by pointing to Bīdil's own explicit attribution of Hindu belief in metempsychosis to "fantasy-worship" (*vaḥm-parastī*).[64] But this is a hasty interpretation for more than one reason. First, and obviously, if Bīdil were only describing Hindu beliefs to refute them, then why did he bother describing them at all? Furthermore, why would he have described them at such length and with such an evident expenditure of poetic effort?

Here, it is worthwhile pausing briefly to reflect on Bīdil's debts to the Hindu philosophical text mentioned earlier in this chapter as being well known in Persian translation in his Islamicate milieu. The sun's response to the first human, a response that takes up most of *'Irfān*, is modeled on a certain section of the *Yoga Vāsiṣṭha*, a vast compendium of Sanskrit allegories that had been accepted, as observed earlier in this chapter, since the ninth century CE as a teaching text for the Advaita or non-dualist Vedanta philosophical tradition. Of this relation between *'Irfān* and the *Yoga Vāsiṣṭha* Wagesh Shukla writes:

> The global plan of the narrative in *'irfān* follows the *aindavopākhyāna*, comprising the chapters 85 to 103 in *utpattiprakaraṇa*, the third section of the *Yoga Vāsiṣṭha*. Briefly, the *aindavopākhyāna* starts with the story of ten children of a Brahmin who become creators of ten different worlds. Each one of these worlds of course has a Sun and one Sun narrates the story. Bedil also has this story of ten children of a Brahmin, ten worlds, and the Sun. This global plan is too complex to compare and analyze the similarities and dis-similarities between Bedil's narrative and the narrative in *Yoga Vāsiṣṭha*. Bedil is a poet, not a plagiarist. The central theme remains the Many-Worlds Theory, a shocking innovation in the universe of discourse within which Bedil was working.[65]

Such plot resemblances should not surprise us for the Persian *masnavī* tradition had always been receptive, on the model of Firdawsī's *Shāhnāmah*, to non-Islamic plots, variously appropriating them for Islamic purposes. But Shukla goes further than pointing to such structural debts, observing that certain of Bīdil's key ideas are at odds with Islamic philosophical theology because he derived them in an unmodified form from Hindu textual traditions. His conception of *sukhan*, for example, is one that Shukla explains as "purely the Indian thesis that the world is created by *vāk* (=Language) as agent. The idea has been expanded upon in great detail in tantric texts."[66] And his understanding of metempsychosis (*tanāsukh*) "is quite simply *punarjanma*, the closed circuit of life and birth."[67] However, the notion of language as agent is equally a commonplace of Qur'ānic cosmogony as also of Ibn 'Arabī's. And Bīdil's presentation of metempsychosis, though explicitly attributed in *'Irfān* to Hindu sources, is framed by a narrative of creation that rehearses an Islamic-Ptolemaic cosmology and Islamic-Aristotelian psychology. The more plausible explanation of the presence of such Hindu models, then, is that Bīdil did not passively receive these Hindu ideas and plots. Instead, he appropriated them by invoking only those elements of Hindu thought that corresponded to already authoritative Islamic equivalents. By this he permitted his readers a bivalent understanding of some of his central notions, *sukhan* and metempsychosis among them. This bivalence, as I will amplify in my conclusion to this chapter, was key to his popularity in Mughal India.

To return to Bīdil's invocation of Hindu belief in metempsychosis, we must recall that he invokes these beliefs in continuity with his immediately prior account and validation of metempsychosis. This validation, as I argued above, took the form of arguing that the three pre-human levels of souls – mineral, vegetal and animal – struggled to rise to the level of the human through metempsychosis. The account of Hindu metempsychosis, though distinct from this vision of ontological and moral ascent, appears immediately after this exposition as a local or distinctively Indian and Hindu belief. Contrary to what Aḥsan al-Ẓafar argues, its locality does not disqualify it for Bīdil for, if it did, he need not have addressed it all. Nor would he have explicitly celebrated Krishna – whose worship was local to India – in *The Four Elements* as the long-departed and still-lamented manifestation of the cosmogonic principle of Love (*'ishq*).[68] Rather, Hindu metempsychosis served him as a local tradition which he could appropriate for the trans-local idiom of the Sufi *masnavī*. Indeed, it was such appropriations of Hindu – and specifically Vaishnava – theologies and mythologies that found stylized expression in Khvushgū's reverential report that Bīdil had memorized the *Mahābhārata* – "than which, amongst Indians [*hindīyān*], there is no more esteemed book.".[69] The story of Madan and Kāmdī would thus appear as a local validation of Bīdil's conception of metempsychosis. Rather than invalidating it, as Aḥsan al-Ẓafar argues, the locality in the Islamic world of Hindu metempsychosis would have corroborated his conception. Indeed, as I have noted, Hindu metempsychosis receives Bīdil's explicit validation in a brief passage. However, since metempsychosis was heretical in Islamic traditions Bīdil resorted to ambiguity. His main means to such cautiously ambiguous validation of Hindu metempsychosis was to relate reports he had heard from reliable Hindu informants or to relate tales from places he had been in or was known to have been in such as Bihar. He thus displaced responsibility for these reports onto his sources or onto the irrefutable if inexplicable prodigies he had witnessed. Having thus related these reports in a poetic idiom he was renowned for, he struck a self-consciously conventional and thus intentionally weak posture of dismissal by terming such beliefs "fantasy-worship."

Second, as Aḥsan al-Ẓafar himself notes, Bīdil speaks in more than one voice on Hindu metempsychosis. Immediately after narrating Rājvantī's tale, Bīdil – or rather the sun – says:

> Whether certainty or speculation, it is knowledge.
> In every direction the guide is that very knowledge.

And:

> The origin of every truth and falsity is one.
> The roads are many and the destination one.

That is, even Hindu metempsychosis is one of several worldly and phenomenal manifestations of knowledge (*'ilm*). Despite quoting these verses, Aḥsan al-Ẓafar concludes "that there were no influences of Vedānta on his [i.e., Bīdil's] Islamic thoughts and ideas; rather, he conclusively presented Islamic truths in even clearer words."[70] That Bīdil said Hindu metempsychosis was "fantasy-worship" is correct. But to infer Bīdil's doctrinal positions by what he thus *says* is to forget that literature does not always simply mean what it says; and that what it *means* is often at odds with what it *says*.

To resume my interpretation of Bīdil's tale, then, the symmetry of desire between Madan and Kāmdī corresponds to a symmetry in their descriptions. Bīdil opens his tale by describing Kāmdī's prowess as a dancer in her courtly setting and follows it only nineteen couplets later with a description of Madan's skills as a singer in another kingdom. By eliminating the inaugural motif of socially destabilizing artistic virtuosity that incited the transitions of 'Ālam's tale as well as those of others, Bīdil signaled the greater and theological importance of the mutuality of their love. He implied that if 'Ālam and the profane Indic intertext he inherited presented the love of Madan and Kāmdī at all it was because souls of the same kind already leaned towards each other. He signals the theological import of the tale in the very opening couplet:

> The musician on the lute sounding the melody of power
> Plucks again on the harp
>
> *muṭrib-i sāz-i iqtidār-āhang*
> *mīzanad zakhmah'ī digar bar chang.*[71]

The musician, God, plays "a melody of power." But the compound *iqtidār-āhang* is also translatable as "aiming for power," thus suggesting that the tale to be related will be a parable of power.

An excursus on two related stylistic features

The compound *iqtidār-āhang* also gives us an occasion to reflect briefly on two much-noted features of Bīdil's style throughout his verse and prose: the invention of compound words and the use of the unwritten but vocalized genitive or adjectival marker (*iẓāfah*) for unusually extended lexemic sequences (e.g., *muṭrib-i sāz-i iqtidār-āhang*). The former was a linguistic resource of Persian already exploited by such old masters as Niẓāmī Ganjavī (d. 1209) but later especially associated with the poetics of Speaking Anew. The latter, too, characterizes Speaking Anew and forms the immediate semantic challenge to comprehending Bīdil's texts. Scholarship on Bīdil concurs on his participation in and extension of Speaking Anew poetics. However, what has not been explained is precisely how his use of these two stylistic features, rather than simply being elements of his stylistic morphology, relates to his metaphysics. I argue that the most noteworthy effect in this context of both features is the elimination of prepositions. In any natural language prepositions specify the articulation of thought and its object and of objects with objects. That is, they capture the mode in which a thinking subject relates to the object of her or his thought as well as the mode in which objects relate to each other. Persian has fewer prepositions than certain other languages. In addition, its grammar is not a case grammar whereby a word's ending would already indicate its grammatical relation with the other parts of a sentence. It is thus characterized by a semantic ambiguity that its littérateurs have exploited over its history. Bīdil radicalized this ambiguity by eliminating as many prepositions as the meter of a hemistich would allow. His two main means to such elimination were the invention of compound words and the extension of the genitive or adjectival marker. Since both features resulted in relatively large lexemes, he preferred to use longer meters in his *ghazal*s than his contemporaries.[72] Within the bounds of such long meters that could be partitioned into two, three or four syllabic units he extended his use of compound words and genitive or adjectival markers, thus minimizing his use of prepositions. By this extreme reduction of prepositions he signaled the *identity of* – rather than the *relation between* – thought and its object or object and object. This is why his oeuvre abounds in compound words: *ṭūfān-nafas* (storm-breathed), *kudūrat-khīz-i awhām* (raising the dust of fantasy), *hasrat-khānah-i asbāb* (secondary causality's house of sorrow), *qalam-rav-i barq-i jamāl* (jurisdiction of beauty's lightning). At the heart of any reading experience of Bīdil is this grammatically signaled compound unity of beings: "The musician on the lute sounding the melody of power" is, despite the English translation's grammatical specifications of "on" and "of" that are absent in the original, in fact a single ambiguously compounded entity, a cluster of images or *khiyāl*s: *muṭrib-i sāz-i iqtidār-āhang*. This grammatical ambiguity of the interrelations of beings corresponded to the ontological ambiguity of Bīdil's creaturely world. This world, as I have observed in Chapter 1 with respect to Ibn 'Arabī's ontology and as Bīdil himself observes in an early passage in *'Irfān*, was the *barzakh* or the interstitial world comprising bodies or *khiyāl*s bridging God who is the necessary (*vujūb*) reality and His unseen (*ghayb*) self-disclosures.[73] The powerful and wide impression Bīdil's poetry made on Mughal India's Persian readership was thus bound up with this inscription of Ibn 'Arabī's theistic monism into the very morphology of its style.

The *ghazal* poetics of "*khiyāl*" as mediating between the Indic hypotext and Ibn 'Arabī's "*barzakh*"

In this sub-section I want to refine this observation by arguing that this inscription – taking the form of the poetics of *khiyāl* – was also a specifically Persian poetic interpretation of Ibn 'Arabī's concept of *barzakh*. I have already explicated *barzakh* in Chapter 1 and will not do so again here. I will focus instead on the significations of *khiyāl* as they accrue through Bīdil's descriptions of the states the lovers traverse.

In keeping with the double sense of the etymologically cognate *takhyīl* or "the imaginary" in classical Arabic poetics, *khiyāl* in Bīdil's poetics designates both the ability to generate mental images and such images themselves.[74] However, he assigns the word ontological significations not already implicit in classical Arabic rhetoric. As an ability in Bīdil, it mainly characterizes God who, more powerfully than His human approximations, imagines the world into being. As the result of this ability, it equally characterizes God who discloses Himself in images as well as His human approximations who are such images and create them in turn. It is "the [divine] musician on the lute sounding the melody of power" who narrates the tale of Madan and Kāmdī. Both characters are thus self-disclosures of God. In turn, they manifest God in their artistic practices. They are *khiyāl*s and create *khiyāl*s in turn. This, as always in Bīdil's oeuvre, means that they are polysemic and many-splendored signs who, in turn, create polysemic and many-splendored signs. But it also means that these signs, like their human creators, are clouded mirrors of the divine Creator. Being thus only partially legible, these signs induce desire in those who read them for their ultimate and divine referent. Kāmdī reads the signs of Madan's soul – that is, she hears of Madan's artistic prowess and falls in love with him because her soul, equally matched with a power to make God manifest in dance, desires union with his:

> At such artistry in him at everything
> Kāmdī was tormented by *khiyāl*s
>
> *bā chunīn jawharīsh dar hamah ḥāl*
> *kāmdī būd khār khār-i khiyāl*[75]

Bīdil works variations on his Indic intertext to signal this ontological symmetry. By these variations he transforms for his Mughal readers the memory of the particular Indic version they may have read. His Persian Sufi hypertext thus casts a backward light, as it were, on the profane Indic and Persian hypotexts, leading the reader to reread them as mystical allegories, as *khiyāl*s. Central to this allegorization of the Indic intertext is the resonance between the poetics and erotics of *viraha*, expounded earlier in this chapter, and the Persianate – in particular *ghazal*-related – aesthetic mood of "erotic separation" (*firāq*) and its poetics of *khiyāl*.

Khiyāl is what the lovers Madan and Kāmdī must settle for while they are parted from each other: "In the place of distinctions between erotic separation and union [*firāq u viṣāl*]/He [i.e., Madan] lost sense of distinction through an overabundance of *khiyāl*."[76] Various personifications of their psychophysical capacities – such as their "broken hearts" or "hope" – urge each lover to strive in his or her attachment to no more than the imagination (*khiyāl*) of the other.[77]

Here, remarkably, Bīdil returns to the Arabic origins of *khiyāl* whose earliest uses in pre-Islamic or *jāhiliyya* poetry refer to the image of the beloved as it appears to the lover in the small and tortured hours of their night of separation.[78] So, at the end of Madan and Kāmdī's secret night of union their "broken heart" cries out:

> If you seek the night of union from fate
> Ask that it be dawnless like the night of separation.
> At such an opportunity, as brief as a glance,
> You won't suffer regret over union.
> If you've grown intimate with clasping
> Like eyelids have you parted from each other.
> Forbid hope with patience.
> Of union content yourself with no more than a *khiyāl*.[79]

At various points Bīdil subtly inserts himself into the tale by identifying himself with Madan. Describing Madan's love-lorn madness in the desert, he writes punning on his own pen-name, "O those who have lost your hearts [*bīdilān*], love tends to intoxication/The speech of the mad is of this sort."[80] He also invokes a leitmotif of his *ghazal*s, that of "egotism" (*mā-u-man*), to universalize Madan's condition as well as his own: "That which is in the intimacy and distance of egotism [*mā-u-man ast*]/Is the form of Madan's helplessness [*madan ast*]."[81]

Such descriptions of the lovers' states of being in "erotic separation" (*firāq*) from each other – corresponding to the Indic poetics of "erotic separation" (*viraha*) – invoke "the technique of the imaginary" (*ṭarz-i khiyāl*) that Bīdil's *ghazal*s were famously associated with. This was a technique of "abstruseness and subtlety," as Bīdil's student Ārzū glossed it, by which the topos (*maẕmūn*) of a *ghazal* distich was so encrypted that the reader recognized it only "after much contemplation and endless thought, the meaning being one unknown to those who know poetry."[82] Although this *masnavī*'s descriptions do not cultivate such abstruseness to the same degree they do, as I have observed, employ the same compound words and extended uses of the genitive or adjectival marker (*iẕāfah*) as his *ghazal*s, displaying a similarly novel lexemic density.

Let us consider another instance of such lexemic density as it translates 'Ālam's Avadhi text. Bīdil's extended description of the war between the kings implicitly solicits a comparison with the corresponding war-tableaux in 'Ālam and Ḥaqīrī's texts by the ingenuity of its metaphors and acoustics. First, here is a quatrain from 'Ālam's poem describing the kings at war:

> *rāvat par rāvat chaḍhi dhāye – dhānash par dhānash chaḍhi āye*
> *pāik sauñ pāik bhaye jorā – larat vār yau mush nahiñ morā*
> *gaj sauñ gaj kīnhe chau dantā – chikraiñ kuñjar maimat mañtā*
> *bājai loh uṭhai ṭañkārā – tāpar phiraiñ khaḍañg kī dhārā*
> *phūṭaiñ phūṭ muñḍ kaṭi jāhīñ – bājai sār sār chhan jāhīñ*[83]

Warrior rushes upon warrior – Bow after bow arches in waves.
Spearhead joins with spearhead – Charge upon charge with unwavering face.
Elephant locks tusks with elephant – Each elephant trumpets drunkenly.
Iron resounds, a clanging arises – Upon which again a flying of sword-edges.
Burst and blast, heads lie severed – Steel on steel, a ringing is heard.

Here is the corresponding passage from Bīdil's *maṯnavī*:

sāz-i āhang-i fitnah shūr andākht
du qiyāmat muqābil-i ham tākht
ghalghal-i kaws u kurnā u nafīr
ṣūr rā kard nā-umīd-i safīr
kīnah bast az tazalzul-i tak-u-tāz
kūh rā dar falākhan-i āvāz
zān khurūshī kih dāsht tūp u tufang
mīparīd az rukh-i qiyāmat rang
pīlbān-i 'ammārī-i gardūn
chūn kajak mīshud az ḥarās nigūn[84]

The lute of tumult's melody raised an uproar.
Two Days of Judgment rushed at each other.
The boom of drum, trumpet and fife's dinning
Led Isrāfīl's horn to despair of trilling.[85]
By a cascade of charges had malice bound
The mountain in a slingshot of sound.
By the blast of gun and cannonade
Did the face of the Day of Judgment fade.
The driver in the sky's elephant-litter
Like his elephant-hook hung upside down in terror.

Despite the preponderance in 'Ālam's passage of retroflex phonemes absent in Persian phonology, the assonantal end-rhymes of the Avadhi half-lines find an echo in the long assonantal end-rhymes of the Persian. Equally resonant with the corresponding Persian passage are the various Avadhi doublet terms, signaling the symmetrically matched armies. We should note, however, that such translations or trans-codings from an Indic language into Persian were submitted to an unwritten rule: only such imagery was translated or trans-coded as corresponded to a prior Persian descriptive convention. This was an effect of assumption by Perso-Arabic poetics that the largest unit of verse text for metaphorical and syntactic prescriptions was the distich (*shi'r*). This implied that whereas poets were subject to the heritage of models at the level of the distich, they were relatively free to organize sequences of distiches – that is, narratives – more or less idiosyncratically. Moreover, this also implied that where such a correspondence between metaphorical and syntactic conventions was absent the Persian-language poet took the liberty to elaborate the description in terms consistent with Persian descriptive conventions. Since war description forms a traditional topos of the genre of the *mas̱navī* from its very beginnings Bīdil innovates on the *mas̱navī* heritage of metaphors associated with "the war topos" (*razm*) to present a partial if equally imagistically and phonically dense replication of ʻĀlam's onomatopoeia and lexemic doubling.

So, where ʻĀlam says "Elephant locks tusks with elephant – Each elephant trumpets drunkenly" Bīdil matches this with an ingenious comparison (*tashbīh*) characteristic of his poetry – especially his *ghazal*s – that revels in identifying emotional states with physical features: "The driver in the sky's elephant-litter/ Like his elephant-hook hung upside down in terror." However, the preceding and subsequent metaphors bear no relation to ʻĀlam's text, drawing instead on Bīdil's *ghazal* innovations on older Persian metaphors. So, later in the same passage he invokes ʻĀlam's half-line description of severed heads ("Burst and blast, heads lie severed") by trans-coding it into Persian descriptive conventions that are in quantitative and metaphorical excess of ʻĀlam's half-line:

zīr-i mū gum shud az hujūm-i kharāsh
sar-i mardān chū khāmah-i naqqāsh
hamah jā mīkishīd tīgh-i ajal
nīm-rukh shakl'ha-i mustaqbal
chūn ḥabāb az talāṭum-i sar'hā
dāsht daryā-i khūn kadū-i shinā[86]

Lost under hair from scratching overmuch
Were men's heads like a painter's brush.
Everywhere did Death's sword draw
In profile the front-facing faces it saw.
Bubble-like from a buffeting of heads
Did the sea of blood show bobbing gourds.

The first couplet invokes a metaphor drawn from the kind of courtly drawing and painting traditions discussed in Chapter 1. By likening the soldiers' disheveled heads to a painter's upside-down and splayed brush Bīdil did more than simply invent an ingenious metaphor. He also invoked the poetics of "the imaginary" or *khiyāl* that was, it must be recalled, the pre-eminently visual mode of being of creatures in their interstitial state of *barzakh*. The second couplet amplifies this painting metaphor by likening death to a draughtsman who with his sword cleaves front-facing faces (*mustaqbal*) into profile portraits (*nīm-rukh*). Both metaphors echo his uses of them in *The Four Elements* as well as his *ghazal*s. The third couplet uses a metaphor he was particularly attached to in his *ghazal*s, that of heads as gourds afloat in the ocean of mystical knowledge. The inability of these empty heads to sink any deeper than the ocean's surface was a manifestation of their spiritual failure even if it appeared as if they had saved themselves by staying afloat. This is its sarcastic sense in one of his *ghazal* distiches: "This ocean isn't without the bobbing of bubbles./Even the empty head has a buoy."[87] His use of this metaphor in this *mas̱navī* translation of 'Ālam's poem thus invokes this dominant signification of the metaphor in the rest of his oeuvre to impute a deficient or phenomenal degree of reality to these bloody war scenes. Here, as in the rest of his oeuvre, the colorful coruscation of the world of the senses stands in inverse proportion to its degree of reality. Recognizing this demanded, not negligence of such a world, but an iconoclastic refusal to grant ultimate ontological primacy to it and thus an ascetic distance from and mastery over it. A model for this lay in Bīdil's mastery over his body double in his portrait that, as we saw in Chapter 1, he tore up and then mastered by replicating it verbally in "the faintly traced outline" of his autobiography. In this sense, such rhizomic interconnections between his *mas̱navī*s, autobiography and vast corpus of *ghazal*s let us argue that all of his oeuvre makes up a single work whose parts variously expound the single Sufi thesis of theistic monism. On the larger scale of the tale of Madan and Kāmdī, taken as a whole, such resonances with Bīdil's *ghazal* poetics of *khiyāl* form the strategy at the largest level of rhetorical analysis – that of the distich – by which he sacralized his profane Indic intertexts, transforming them by thus soliciting the Sufi anagogy by which his *ghazal*s demanded to be interpreted.

Conclusion: the strange novelty of the plot's ending

This novel lexemic density corresponded at the level of the distich to the novelty of the plot that, exceptionally for a Persianate *mas̱navī*, ended with the joyous union of the lovers rather than their deaths. The Sanskrit poetics of *rasa* or "aesthetic mood" and the vernacular poetic traditions indebted to it like Avadhi and Braj theorized "the erotic aesthetic mood" (*śṛṅgāra*) as *always* mutual.[88] Unrequited, one-sided love was pejoratively categorized as "counterfeit *rasa*" (*śṛṅgārasābhāsa*), not "genuine" *rasa*, but a mere "semblance" thereof. Moreover, Sanskrit poetry or *kāvya*, a profane and "this-worldly" (*laukika*) poetic, celebrated the aesthetic mood of the erotic (*śṛṅgāra*) as its dominant *rasa*, its "master flavor" (*rasarāja*).[89] This was in direct contrast to Persianate poetics that elevated "erotic separation" (*firāq*) to the status of dominant aesthetic mood. The vernacular – in this case Avadhi or Hindavī – poetics of *viraha* or "erotic separation" mediated between the Sanskrit and Persian poetic traditions by celebrating the separation of lovers who desired each other equally. By modeling Madan on Niẓāmī's (d. 1209) paradigmatic lover Majnūn as addressing birds and animals in his *firāq* or separation from Kāmdī and by leading Madan and Kāmdī to their grief-stricken deaths in separation, Bīdil confirmed generic expectations of a Persian Sufi tale. Indeed, he was anticipated in this by Ḥaqīrī Kāshānī who, as I have observed already, composed his *mas̱navī* version of the tale in the same meter as Niẓāmī's *Laylī u Majnūn*. However, the final reunification of the lovers by a just king, here an allegorical conduit of divine action, invoked a topos foreign to Persianate poetics but known in Sanskrit poetics and vernacular adaptations of it, namely "tragic separation leading to erotic union" (*karuṇavipralambhaśṛṅgāra*).[90] This sudden concluding disclosure of the counterfeit character of their deaths and the narration of their happy reunion renewed the dominant Sufi topoi of "the Beloved's cruel heedlessness and the lover's abject supplication" (*nāz-u-niyāz*) and "erotic separation" (*firāq*) by analeptically assigning them the significance of "tragic separation leading to erotic union."

Rather than making familiar the foreignness of the Indic semiotic of the hypotexts that he transformed by translation, Bīdil rendered the familiar Persianate semiotic foreign.[91] By this he insisted through his very aesthetic on "the internal distance" between his text and the political "ideology" it appeared to support.[92] If Bīdil's *masnavī* cannot be read only as a social document it is because the strange density of its metaphors and syntax as well as the novelty of its plot ending defamiliarized the imperial ideology of his patrons. He insisted that it was not the external instruments of power that truly secured the polity but a deepened self-knowledge and self-transformation. Irreducible to an instrumental logic of flattery and patronage, his text presented his elite reader in politically threatened late Mughal Delhi with an admonitory Sufi paradigm of ascetic self-government. Identifying himself by a pun with Madan at the victory of the king who went to war for him, he writes:

> Whoever helps those who have lost their hearts [*bīdilān*]
> Is protected from the waning of his star.
> Wherever the castle of fortune arises
> Its rope-ladder is the aid of the weak.
> O you whose head is affected by the smoke of vanity,
> Ignorant of the vengeance of the proud sky,
> You turned away from the sighs of the incapable [*'ājizān*]
> And fell a target to the arrow of despair.
> The shield to this arrow is not armour,
> The dam to this lightning is not an iron mountain.[93]

Rather than reading this passage instrumentally as a bid for patronage by his royal and noblemen readers, we should understand it, as the more sophisticated of Bīdil's readers arguably understood it, as a call to a kind of *askesis*, to a care of the soul by transforming it ascetically on Bīdil's own model into an object worthy of divine defence.

Any accounting for Bīdil's popularity in Mughal India in his own lifetime and later, and for the readerships he continues to have in Central Asia must include more than a discussion of such ethico-political import. For he combined it with the two elements that equally pervaded his oeuvre: the elimination of prepositions to signal by compound words and extended lexemes an Akbarian unity of beings; and an amenability to being read bivalently in terms of simultaneously Hindu and Islamic frames of reference. The former feature invoked what was perhaps the most authoritative Sufi metaphysics ever since Muslim kingship and Sufi authority had entered, in the wake of the Mongol invasions of the thirteenth century, into a mimetic relationship. In this context, Sufi parables of ascetic power were implicitly parables of royal power too. The latter feature, namely the Hindu-Islamic bivalence of his works, offered Mughal bureaucrats, a large number of whom were pious Hindus, an aesthetic by which to make their investment in Islamic political power theologically meaningful to themselves. Key to this bivalence was the distance Bīdil kept from his Sanskrit and Hindavī intertexts, never mentioning by name the Hindavī sources or the *Yoga Vāsiṣṭha* from which he drew his plots while presenting such appropriations at the level of the distich in terms of a radicalization of the already familiar poetics of the Speaking Anew *ghazal*. Indeed, this is what accounts for his popularity, then and now, among Central Asian and Iranian readers who, judging by modern Persian language literary criticism on Bīdil, barely even suspect the existence of Sanskrit or Hindavī models for his works.

Notes

1 "Gnosis" is an inevitably provisional translation of a term that has not been translated with consistency among English-language scholars. However, I hope the remainder of this chapter will justify this translation. Gerhard Böwering translates it as "Islamic theosophy," a term I avoid because the English-language term "theosophy" designates a discipline whose genealogy in India is bound up with English colonialism. See Gerhard Böwering, " *'Erfān*" at www.iranicaonline.org/articles/erfan-1 (last updated January 19, 2012). Bindrāban Dās "Khvushgū" says Bīdil completed *'Irfān* over thirty years while the modern scholar Aḥsan al-Ẓafar checks Khvushgū's claim by citing a letter by Bīdil as evidence of his having begun it thirty-four years previously in Mathura. Sayyad Aḥsan al-Ẓafar, *Mirzā 'Abd al-Qādir Bedil: ḥayāt aur kārname: jild-i duvvum* (Rāmpūr: Rāmpūr Raẕā Library, 2009), 275.

2 Nūr al-Ḥasan Anṣārī writes: " *'Irfān* is the compact essence of Bīdil's lifetime of imagination, thought, affects, experiences and feelings and, after [Rūmī's] *Masnavī-i ma'navī* in Persian literature, is the most important treasury of metaphysical knowledge and gnosis [*'ilm o 'irfān*]." This is an internal quote from Aḥsan al-Ẓafar, *Mirzā 'Abd al-Qādir Bedil: jild-i duvvum*, 276. Jan Rypka: "This work most tellingly bears witness to the philosophical, social and ethical views of its author." This, too, is an internal quote from Aḥsan al-Ẓafar, *Mirzā 'Abd al-Qādir Bedil*, 277. Aḥsan al-Ẓafar himself concurs with both these views.

3 'Abd al-Qādir Khān Bīdil, *Kulliyāt-i Bīdil: jild-i sivvum* (Tehrān: mu'assasah-i intishārāt-i Ilhām, 1386/2007), 84. For *'Irfān* itself, see 9–395.

4 Bīdil, *Kulliyāt-i Bīdil: jild-i sivvum*, 91. The term *isti'ārah* is a meta-category in Bīdil's semiotics that includes all beings that have issued from "the divine speech-act" (*ḥarf-i qudrat*) because they are all signs – or "formulations" (*'ibārāt*) and "gestures" (*ishārāt*) – that are properly interpretable only by the human. Bīdil here exploits the Arabic etymology of *isti'ārah* whose trilateral root means "to borrow."

5 Bīdil, *Kulliyāt-i Bīdil: jild-i sivvum*, 93.

6 Ibid., 100.

7 Jonardon Ganeri, "Dārā Shukoh and the Transmission of the Upaniṣads to Islam", in William Sweet (ed.), *Migrating Texts and Traditions*, (Ottawa: University of Ottawa Press, 2009). This aim is already implicit in the title *Majma' al-baḥrayn*, a Qur'ānic phrase alluding to a cosmological idea current in the Late Ancient Near East of the meeting place of primordial rivers and their association with the rivers of paradise. Tommaso Tesei, "Some Cosmological Notions from Late Antiquity in Q 18:60–65: the Quran in Light of its Cultural Context," *Journal of the American Oriental Society* 135: 1 (2015), 19–32.

8 Satish Chandra, *Parties and Politics at the Mughal Court: 1707–1740* (New Delhi: Oxford University Press, 2002), 7.
9 Chandra, *Parties and Politics*, xii–xvi.
10 Chandra, *Parties and Politics*, 281.
11 Munis D. Faruqui, *Princes of the Mughal Empire, 1504–1719* (New York: Cambridge University Press, 2012), 279–80.
12 Ibid., 318.
13 Ibid., 321.
14 Chandra, *Parties and Politics*, 296–97.
15 M.R. Majumdar (ed.), "Mādhavānala ākhyānām," in *Mādhavānala-kāmakandalā-prabandha: prathama khanda* (Baroda: Oriental Institute, 1942), 341–79.
16 M.R. Majumdar (ed.), "Mādhavānala-kāmakandalā-prabandha," in *Mādhavānala-kāmakandalā*, 1–340.
17 M.R. Majumdar (ed.), "Mādhavānala-kāmakandalā chaupai," in *Mādhavānala-kāmakandalā*, 381–442.
18 The four recensions in which the tale cycles relating Vikramāditya's deeds have survived do not contain the tale of Mādhavānala and Kāmakandalā. However, the centrality of Vikramāditya to the plot of the tale of these lovers indicates that the tale was, in certain regions of India and in certain periods, absorbed into this cycle.
19 A.N.D. Haksar, *Simhāsana dvātrīmshikā: Thirty-Two Tales of the Throne of Vikramāditya* (New Delhi: Penguin India, 1998), xv. This edition freely combines stories from the four recensions that were edited and translated in 1917 by Franklin Edgerton who prepared a critical edition that places all four versions side by side. Franklin Edgerton, *Vikrama's Adventures or the Thirty-Two Tales of the Throne* (Cambridge, MA: Harvard University Press, 1926).
20 For a list of Persian, Braj and Urdu manuscripts of these translations of the tale cycle, see Ed Sachau *et al.* (eds), *Catalogue of the Persian, Turkish, Hindustani and Pushtu Manuscripts in the Bodleian Library* (Oxford: Clarendon Press, 1889), 815–16. For an entry on Badāuni's no longer extant translation, see http://perso-indica.net/work.faces?idsec=16&idw=77
21 'Ālam, *Mādhavānal-kāmakandalā*, in Gaṇesh Prasād Dwivedī (ed.), *Hindī Premgāthā Kāvya Sangraha* (Allāhābād: Hindustān Akademi, 1953), 175–231.
22 Thomas de Bruijn, *The Ruby in the Dust: Poetry and History in Padmāvat by the South Asian Sufi Poet Muḥammad Jāyāsi* (Leiden: Leiden University Press, 2012), 150.
23 http://perso-indica.net/work.faces?idsec=16&idw=77
24 'Ālam, *Mādhavānal-kāmakandalā*, 187. I thank Imre Bangha of the University of Oxford for proposing that *rīti* be translated as "established manner" and for alerting me to the contrast between 'Ālam and Keshavdās's relations to Sanskrit poetics.
25 Allison Busch, "The Anxiety of Innovation: the Practice of Literary Science in the Hindi/Riti Tradition," *Comparative Studies of South Asia, Africa and the Middle East* 24: 2 (2004), 45–59.
26 I thank Thomas de Bruijn of the University of Leiden for this observation.
27 For a detailed discussion of the chronology, philology and theological poetics of *bhakti* as it formed the pre-history of the *Bhāgvata Purāna*, see Friedhelm Hardy, *Viraha-bhakti: the Early History of Kṛṣṇa Devotion in South India* (Delhi: Oxford University Press, 1983).
28 'Ālam, *Mādhavānal-kāmakandalā*, 203–06.
29 Eugenia Vanina remarks on this absence of allegorical framing, too, in Eugenia Vanina, "*Mādhavānal-kāmakandalā*: a Hindi Poem of Akbar's Epoch," *The Indian Historical Review*, Vol. XX, Nos. 1, 2 (1996): 66–77.
30 Friedhelm Hardy, *Viraha-bhakti: the Early History of Kṛṣṇa Devotion in South India*, 51–115.
31 'Ālam, *Mādhavānal-kāmakandalā*, 225–30.

32 Ḥaqīrī Kāshānī, *Masnavī Mādhavānal-Kāmakandalā Mawsūm ba Maḥẕ-i I'jāz*, ed. Yog Dhyān Ahuja (New Delhi: dānishgāh-i Dehlī), 1965.
33 Kāshānī, *Masnavī Mādhavānal-Kāmakandalā*, 126.
34 A.K. Ramanujan, "Three Hundred *Rāmāyanas*: Five Examples and Three Thoughts on Translation," in *The Collected Essays of A.K. Ramanujan* (New Delhi: Oxford University Press), 156–57.
35 R.S. Nagar and K.L. Joshi, *The Nātyaśāstra of Bharatamuni: Volume Three* (Delhi: Parimal Publications, 2005), 193–94. Later taxonomies, such as Vātsyāyana's *Kāmasūtra*, included similar versions of these ten stages. Notably, even Bīdil's elder contemporary and member of the same social circles, Pandit Jagannātha, the great Sanskrit literary theoretician and poet patronized by the emperors Shāhjahān and Aurangzeb, included such a list in his Panditarāja Jagannātha, *Rasagangādhara = Stream of Bliss* (Chandigarh: Mithila Prakashan, 1998).
36 One of many canonical literary formulations of this conception appears in a *qaṣīdah* by the medieval master of the wine-panegyric, Manūchhirī Dāmghānī (d. 1040), *Dīvān-i Manūcchirī Dāmghānī* (Tehrān: intishārāt-i Zavvār, 1370/1992), 13–16.
37 'Ālam, *Mādhavānal-kāmakandalā*, 185.
38 'Abul Faẕl Mubārak Allāmi, *Āyīn-i Akbarī* (Calcutta: The Baptist Mission Press, 1869), 6–183.
39 Prashant Keshavmurthy, http://perso-indica.net/work.faces?idsec=15&idw=84 (accessed October 26, 2013).
40 Bindrāban Dās Khvushgū, *Safīnah-i Khvushgū: daftar-i thālith* (Patna: idārah-i taḥqīqāt-i 'Arabī va Fārsī, 1959), 42.
41 Dominic J. O'Meara, *Platonopolis: Platonic Political Philosophy in Late Antiquity* (Oxford: Clarendon, 2005), 191–92. I thank my colleague in McGill University, Robert Wisnovsky, for alerting me to the philosophical genealogy of Bīdil's idea.
42 Hajnalka Kovacs, "The Tavern of the Manifestation of Realities: The Masnavi Muhit-i Azam by Mirza Abd al-Qadir Bedil (1644–1720)," (PhD diss., University of Chicago, 2013), 121.
43 Bīdil also speaks explicitly of the affect of erotic separation, central to Krishna *bhakti*, in his rhapsodically rhyming description of Mathura and the long-departed but still-lamented Krishna as a manifestation of the Sufi cosmogonic principle of Love (*'ishq*) in 'Abd al-Qādir Khān Bīdil, *Chahār 'Unṣur*, in *Āvāz'hā-i Bīdil* (Tehrān: mu'assasah-i intishārāt-i Nigāh, 1386/2007), 482.
44 Paul E. Walker, "Metempsychosis in Islam," in Wael B. Hallaq *et al.* (eds), *Islamic Studies Presented to Charles J. Adams* (Leiden: E.J. Brill, 1991), 219–38. This essay summarizes the positions on metempsychosis of Islamic thinkers of the Perso-Arab world until the eleventh century CE, concluding by touching on later inheritors.
45 The justification by early Mu'tazilite theologians of their advocacy of metempsychosis was exceptional in Islamic history and disparate to Hindu-Buddhist-Jain conceptions of it. Walker, "Metempsychosis in Islam," 226–27.
46 A. Azfar Moin, *The Millennial Sovereign: Sacred Kingship and Sainthood in Islam* (New York: Columbia University Press, 2012), 161. Also see Colin Mitchell, *The Practice of Politics in Safavid Iran: Power, Religion and Rhetoric* (London: Tauris Academic Studies, 2009), 22.
47 Walker, "Metempsychosis in Islam," 220.
48 Afẕal al-Dīn Khāqānī Shīrvānī, *Tuḥfat al-'Irāqayn* (Tehrān: markaz-i pizhūhishī-i Mīrāṯ-i Maktūb, 2006).
49 *Yoga Vāsiṣṭha, Volume 2*, trans. Vihari Lala Mitra (Tuscon, AZ: Handloom Publishing, 2013), 240. This is the only complete English translation yet of the *Yoga Vāsiṣṭha.* Among the Persian translations that may have been available to Bīdil is the one commissioned by the Emperor Jahāngīr when he was still a prince, a translation made by Niẕām Pānipatī, *Jog bāsisht: dar falsafah va 'irfān-i Hind*, Sayyad Muhammad Riẕā Jalālī Nā'inī and N.C. Shukla (eds) (Tehrān: Iqbāl, 1340/1961).

50 Jalāl al-Dīn Rūmī, *Kulliyāt-i Masnavī-i ma'navī: daftar-i chahārum* (Tehrān: chāp-khānah-i 'Ilmī, 1342/1963), 173–74.

51 Bīdil, *Kulliyāt-i Bīdil: jild-i sivvum*, 255.

52 Ibid., 257.

53 Bīdil here calls God "the image-binder of air" (*naqsh-band-i havā*). Though he attributes this image to the Hindus, it is also in keeping with Ibn 'Arabī's idea that God created bodies by breathing their names into being, an idea Bīdil probably received through Jāmī's exposition of Ibn 'Arabī's cosmogonic image of "the Breath of the Merciful" (*nafas-i raḥmānī*), Bīdil, *Kulliyāt-i Bīdil: jild-i sivvum*, 257.

54 *pas za tarkīb tā jahān-i basīṭ/jism u 'ilm-i yek ādam ast muḥīṭ*. Bīdil, *Kulliyāt-i Bīdil: jild-i sivvum*, 260.

55 Arguably the most famous image in the world today of love as the action of the double-bodied soul appears in Plato's *Symposium*. Members of the circle of translators in ninth-century Baghdad, a circle presided over by the philosopher Al-Kindī (*c.*800–70 CE), translated parts of the Platonic corpus into Arabic. For one such translation, see Franz Rosenthal, *The Classical Heritage in Islam* (Berkeley, CA: University of California, 1965), 106–07. It is also well known that Plato's legacy in the Islamic world was shaped by certain books of Plotinus's *Enneads* – another source of such theistic monism – that were misattributed to Aristotle and thus translated under the title of *The Theology of Aristotle*. For a study of this translation as an Islamic philosophical adaptation, see Peter S. Adamson, *The Arabic Plotinus: A Philosophical Study of the Theology of Aristotle* (London: Duckworth, 2002). The circulation of this idea in the Persianate world through its formulations in one of the main genres of ethical writing, *akhlāq*, as well as the vast metaphysical authority of Ibn 'Arabī's theistic monism, itself an adaptation of Neo-Platonic ideas, would also have authorized this conception.

56 Ramanujan, "Three Hundred *Rāmāyanas*," 157.

57 Bīdil, *Kulliyāt-i Bīdil: jild-i sivvum*, 265.

58 Ibid., 256.

59 It is also worth noting that Bīdil's Sufi use of "Hindu" *ḥikāyāt* had authoritative Islamic precedents in, among others, Rūmī's innovative use of the originally Hindu-Jain-Buddhist parable of the men blind from birth who were shown an elephant by a king and asked to describe it. Each of the men reaches a different conclusion after grasping only a part of the elephant's body. In the Buddhist version from the Pali canon dating to the second century BCE, the Buddha compares the blind men to the disputing monks and scholars of his time who only ever grasped a part of reality. It was very likely this version that al-Ghazālī, Sanā'ī, Rūmī, Amīr Khusraw and other Islamic thinkers appropriated as a parable on the partiality of dialectical knowledge of the One. Rūmī's innovation was to locate the elephant in a dark room and present sighted men entering it to be eventually shown the elephant by a candle-bearing teacher. The authority of this innovation set a precedent for Bīdil. Ben-Ami Scharfstein, *A Comparative History of World Philosophy: From the Upanishads to Kant* (Albany, NY: State University of New York Press, 1998), 33. For a translation of the Buddhist parable, see *The Minor Anthologies of the Pali Canon*, Pt. 2, *Udāna: Verses of Uplift and Itivuttaka: As It Was Said*, trans. F.L. Woodward (London: Oxford University Press, 1948), 81–83 (*Udāna*, 68–69).

60 Bīdil, *Kulliyāt-i Bīdil: jild-i sivvum*, 265.

61 For a study of Jāmī's interpretation of Ibn 'Arabī, see Sajjad Rizvi, "The Existential Breath of *al-raḥmān* and the Munificent Grace of *al-raḥīm*: the *Tafsir Surat al-Fātiḥa* of Jāmī and the School of Ibn 'Arabi," *Journal of Qur'anic Studies* 8: 1 (2006), 58–87. As a result of his methodological commitment to doing little more than paraphrasing the plot and topics of Bīdil's *'Irfān*, as well as his tendency to take Bīdil at his word, Aḥsan al-Ẓafar fails to notice this act of philosophical translation. Aḥsan al-Ẓafar, *Mirzā 'Abd al-Qādir Bedil*, 360.

62 Bīdil, *Kulliyāt-i Bīdil: jild-i sivvum*, 268.
63 It is worth noting that another manuscript of 'Ālam's poem, dating to 1542–43, contains an account of Kāmakandalā's previous births. Vanina, "*Mādhavānal-kāmakandalā*," 67.
64 Aḥsan al-Ẓafar, *Mirzā 'Abd al-Qādir Bedil*, 362.
65 Wagesh Shukla, "Bedil's '*Irfān* and *Yoga Vāsiṣṭha*," unpublished paper presented at the International Conference on Bedil, March 17–21, 2003.
66 Shukla, "Bedil's '*Irfān* and *Yoga Vāsiṣṭha*," 9.
67 Ibid., 5.
68 Bīdil, *Chahār 'unṣur*, 482.
69 Khvushgū, *Safīnah-i Khvushgū*, 118.
70 Aḥsan al-Ẓafar, *Mirzā 'Abd al-Qādir Bedil*, 364.
71 Bīdil, *Kulliyāt-i Bīdil: jild-i sivvum*, 282.
72 The authors of a study of Bīdil's prosody note: "Length, heaviness and being capable of division into two are among the characteristics of Bīdil's preferred meters." Mehdī Kamālī, Muḥammad Kāẓim-Kahdū'ī, Sayyad Maḥmūd Ilhāmbakhsh, "Bar-rasī-yi āmārī-yi awzān-i ghazal'hā-i Bīdil-i Dihalvī va muqāyasah-i ān bā vazn-i ghazal-i Fārsī va sabk-i Hindī," *Funūn-i adabī*, Year 1, No. 1 (1388/2010), 119.
73 "Now it sought the *barzakh*/Like the unity between the unmanifest and the Necessary Existent" (*shud kunūn barzakhīsh maṭlūb/hamchū vaḥdat miyān-i ghayb u vujūb*). Bīdil, *Kulliyāt-i Bīdil: jild-i sivvum*, 46.
74 Wolfhart Heinrichs, "Introduction," in Geert Jan Van Gelder and Marle Hammond (eds), *Takhyil: the Imaginary in Classical Arabic Poetics* (Oxford: Gibb Memorial Trust, 2008), 1–14.
75 Bīdil, *Kulliyāt-i Bīdil: jild-i sivvum*, 283.
76 Ibid., 300.
77 Ibid., 293–94.
78 Renate Jacobi, "The *Khayāl* Motif in Early Arabic Poetry," *Oriens* 32 (1990), 50–64.
79 Bīdil, *Kulliyāt-i Bīdil: jild-i sivvum*, 293.
80 Ibid., 302.
81 Ibid., 299.
82 Sirāj al-Dīn 'Alī Khān Ārzū, *'Aṭiyah-i kubrā*, in *'Aṭiyah-i kubrā va Mawhibat-i 'uẓmā* (Tehrān: Firdaws, 1381/2002), 67.
83 'Ālam, *Mādhavānal-kāmakandalā*, 229.
84 Bīdil, *Kulliyāt-i Bīdil: jild-i sivvum*, 307.
85 Isrāfīl is identified by convention as the archangel in the Qur'ān whose horn blast heralds the Day of Judgment.
86 Bīdil, *Kulliyāt-i Bīdil: jild-i sivvum*, 307.
87 *nīst īn baḥr bī-shina-i ḥabāb/sar-i bi-maghz ham kadū dārad*. Bīdil, *Kulliyāt-i Bīdil: jild-i duvvum*, 30.
88 For this and its related observations involving Sanskrit poetics, I am grateful to Satyanarayana Hegde.
89 Sheldon Pollock, *The Language of the Gods in the World of Men: Sanskrit, Culture and Power in Premodern India* (Berkeley, CA: University of California Press, 2006), 13.
90 Rudraṭa, the ninth-century Sanskrit literary theorist, formulates it thus: "The tragic-erotic-in-separation is the erotic itself" (*karuṇavipralambhastu śṛṅgāra eva*). Rudraṭa, *Kāvyālaṅkāra (A Treatise on Rhetoric) of Rudraṭa with the Sanskrit Commentary of Namisādhu*. Edited with the *Prakāsha* Hindi Commentary by Pandit Rāmadeva Shukla (The Vidyabhawan Rastrabhasha Granthamala 136). (The Chowkhamba Vidyabhawan: Varanasi, 1989), 394.
91 Making the foreign familiar by translation was the procedure adopted in translating the Upanishads into Persian by the Mughal prince and fellow Qādirī intellectual, Dārā Shukūh who, it is worth noting, moved in the same circles as Bīdil. Ganeri, "Dārā Shukoh and the Transmission of the Upaniṣads to Islam," in *Migrating Texts*.

92 Louis Althusser, "A Letter on Art in Reply to Andre Daspre," in *Lenin and Philosophy* (London: New Left Books, 1971), 222–23.
93 Bīdil, *Kulliyāt-i Bīdil: jild-i sivvum*, 309.

Bibliography

'Abul Faẕl Mubārak, Allāmi. *Āyīn-i Akbarī*, H. Blochmann (ed.). Calcutta: The Baptist Mission Press, 1869.

Adamson, Peter S. *The Arabic Plotinus: A Philosophical Study of the Theology of Aristotle*. London: Duckworth, 2002.

Aḥsan al-Ẓafar, Sayyad. *Mirzā 'Abd al-Qādir Bedil: ḥayāt aur kārname: jild-i duvvum*. Rāmpūr: Rāmpūr Raẓā Library, 2009.

'Ālam, *Mādhavānal-kāmakandalā*, in Gaṇesh Prasād Dwivedī (ed.), *Hindī Premgāthā Kāvya Sangraha*. Allāhābād: Hindūstān Akademi, 1953,175–231.

Althusser, Louis. "A Letter on Art in Reply to Andre Daspre," in *Lenin and Philosophy*. London: New Left Books, 1971, 222–23.

Ārzū, Sirāj al-Dīn 'Alī Khān. *'Aṭiyah-i kubrā va Mawhibat-i uẓmā*. Tehrān: Firdaws, 1381/2002.

Bīdil, 'Abd al-Qādir Khān. *Kullliyāt-i Bīdil: jild-i duvvum*. Tehrān: mu'assasah-i intishārāt-i Ilhām, 1386/2007.

Bīdil, 'Abd al-Qādir Khān. *Kulliyāt-i Bīdil: jild-i sivvum*. Tehrān: mu'assasah-i intishārāt-i Ilhām, 1386/2007.

Bīdil, 'Abd al-Qādir Khān. *Chahār 'unṣur*, in *Āvāz'hā-i Bīdil*, Tehrān: mu'assasah-i intishārāt-i Nigāh, 1386/2007, 335–676.

Böwering, Gerhard. "*'Erfān*" at www.iranicaonline.org/articles/erfan-1 (last updated January 19, 2012).

Bruijn, Thomas de. *The Ruby in the Dust: Poetry and History in Padmāvat by the South Asian Sufi Poet Muḥammad Jāyasī*. Leiden: Leiden University Press, 2012.

Busch, Allison. "The Anxiety of Innovation: the Practice of Literary Science in the Hindi/Riti Tradition," *Comparative Studies of South Asia, Africa and the Middle East* 24: 2 (2004), 45–59.

Chandra, Satish. *Parties and Politics at the Mughal Court: 1707–1740*. Delhi: Oxford University Press, 2002.

Edgerton, Franklin. *Vikrama's Adventures or the Thirty-Two Tales of the Throne*. Cambridge, MA: Harvard University Press, 1926.

Faruqui, Munis D. *Princes of the Mughal Empire, 1504–1719*. New York: Cambridge University Press, 2012.

Ganeri, Jonardon. "Dārā Shukoh and the Transmission of the Upaniṣads to Islam," in William Sweet (ed.), *Migrating Texts and Traditions*. Ottawa: University of Ottawa Press, 2009.

Haksar, A.N.D. *Simhāsana dvātrīmshikā: Thirty-Two Tales of the Throne of Vikramāditya*. New Delhi: Penguin India, 1998.

Hardy, Friedhelm. *Viraha-bhakti: the Early History of Kṛṣṇa Devotion in South India*. Delhi: Oxford University Press, 1983.

Heinrichs, Wolfhart. "Introduction," in Geert Jan Van Gelder and Marle Hammond (eds), *Takhyil: the Imaginary in Classical Arabic Poetics*. Oxford: Gibb Memorial Trust, 2008, 1–14.

Jacobi, Renate. "The *Khayāl* Motif in Early Arabic Poetry." *Oriens* 32 (1990), 50–64.

Jagannātha, Panditarāja. *Rasagangādhara = Stream of Bliss*. Chandigarh: Mithila Prakashan, 1998.

Kamālī, Mehdī, Muḥammad Kāẕim-Kahdū'ī, Sayyad Maḥmūd Ilhāmbakhsh. "Bar-rasī-yi āmārī-yi awzān-i ghazal'hā-i Bīdil-i Dihalvī va muqāyasah-i ān bā vazn-i ghazal-i Fārsī va sabk-i hindī." *Funūn-i adabī*, Year 1, No. 1 (1388/2010), 86–87.

Kāshānī, Ḥaqīrī. *Masnavī Mādhavānal-Kāmakandalā Mawsūm ba Maḥẕ-i I'jāz*. New Delhi: dānishgāh-i Dehlī, 1965.

Khāqānī Shīrvānī, Afẓal al-Dīn. *Tuḥfat al-'Irāqayn*. Tehrān: markaz-i pizhūhishī-i Mīrās̱-i Maktūb, 2006.

Khvushgū, Bindrāban Dās. *Safīnah-i Khvushgū: daftar-i thālith*. Patnā: idārah-i taḥqīqat-i 'Arabī va Fārsī, 1959.

Kovacs, Hajnalka. "The Tavern of the Manifestation of Realities: The Masnavi Muhit-i Azam by Mirza Abd al-Qadir Bedil (1644–1720)." PhD diss., University of Chicago, 2013.

Majumdar, M.R. (ed.), "Mādhavānala ākhyānām," in *Mādhavānala-kāmakandalā-prabandha: prathama khaṇḍa*. Baroda: Oriental Institute, 1942, 341–79.

Manūchhirī Dāmghānī. *Dīvān-i Manūcchirī Dāmghānī*. Tehrān: intishārāt-i zavvār, 1370/1992.

O'Meara, Dominic J. *Platonopolis: Platonic Political Philosophy in Late Antiquity*. Oxford: Clarendon, 2005.

Mitchell, Colin. *The Practice of Politics in Safavid Iran: Power, Religion and Rhetoric*. London: Tauris Academic Studies, 2009.

Mitra, Vihari Lala (trans.). *Yogavāshishṭa, Volume 2*. Tuscon, AZ: Handloom Publishing, 2013.

Moin, A. Azfar. *The Millennial Sovereign: Sacred Kingship and Sainthood in Islam*. New York: Columbia University Press, 2012.

Nagar, R.S. and K.L. Joshi, eds. *The Nātyaśāstra of Bharatamuni: Volume Three*. Delhi: Parimal Publications, 2005.

Pānipatī, Niẓām (trans.). *Jog bāsisht: dar falsafah va 'irfān-i Hind*, Sayyad Muhammad Riẓā Jalālī Nā'inī and N.C. Shukla (eds). Tehrān: Iqbāl, 1340/1961.

Pollock, Sheldon. *The Language of the Gods in the World of Men: Sanskrit, Culture and Power in Premodern India*. Berkeley, CA: University of California Press, 2007.

Ramanujan, A.K. "Three Hundred *Rāmāyanas*: Five Examples and Three Thoughts on Translation". In *The Collected Essays of A.K. Ramanujan*. New Delhi: Oxford University Press.

Rizvi, Sajjad. "The Existential Breath of *al-raḥmān* and the Munificent Grace of *al-raḥīm*: the *Tafsir Surat al-Fāṭiḥa* of Jāmi and the School of Ibn 'Arabi," *Journal of Qur'anic Studies* 8: 1 (2006), 58–87.

Rosenthal, Franz. *The Classical Heritage in Islam*. Berkeley, CA: University of California, 1965.

Rudraṭa. *Kāvyālaṅkāra (A Treatise on Rhetoric) of Rudraṭa with the Sanskrit Commentary of Namisādhu*. Edited with the *Prakāsha* Hindi Commentary by Pandit Rāmadeva Shukla (The Vidyabhawan Rastrabhasha Granthamala 136). Varanasi: The Chowkhamba Vidyabhawan, 1989.

Rūmī, Jalāl al-Dīn. *Kulliyāt-i Masnavī-i ma'navī: daftar-i chahārum*. Tehrān: chāpkhānah-i 'ilmī, 1342/1963.

Sachau, ed. *Catalogue of the Persian, Turkish, Hindustani and Pushtu Manuscripts in the Bodleian Library*. Oxford: Clarendon Press, 1889.

Scharfstein, Ben-Ami. *A Comparative History of World Philosophy: From the Upanishads to Kant*. Albany, NY: State University of New York Press, 1998.

Shukla, Wagesh. "Bedil's *'Irfān* and *Yoga Vāsiṣṭha.*" Unpublished paper presented at the International Conference on Bedil, March 17–21, 2003.

Tesei, Tommaso. "Some Cosmological Notions from Late Antiquity in Q 18: 60–65: the Quran in Light of its Cultural Context". *Journal of the American Oriental Society* 135: 1 (2015), 19–32.

Vanina, Eugenia. "*Mādhavānal-kāmakandalā*: a Hindi Poem of Akbar's Epoch," *The Indian Historical Review*, Vol. XX, Nos. 1, 2 (1996): 66–77.

Walker, Paul E. "Metempsychosis in Islam," in Wael B. Hallaq and Donald P. Little (eds), *Islamic Studies Presented to Charles J. Adams*. Leiden: E.J. Brill, 1991, 219–38.

Woodward, F.L. (trans.). *The Minor Anthologies of the Pali Canon*, Pt. 2, *Udāna: Verses of Uplift and Itivuttaka: As It Was Said*. London: Oxford University Press, 1948.

4 The local universality of poetic pleasure

Sirāj al-Dīn ʻAlī Khān "Ārzū" and the speaking subject

Among the remarkable aspects of the Persianate literary culture of late Mughal India is the widely divergent character of the responses to the crises of sovereignty.[1] Poetry and polity were twinned here as they arguably had been throughout Persian literary history. But in eighteenth-century North India they were related in ways perhaps more diverse than ever before. The last three chapters studied the mystical appropriations of Persian and Indic literary history by which ʻAbd al-Qādir Bīdil, responding to the crisis in the Mughal polity of his time, fashioned his authorial authority. This chapter studies the historicist and philological uses of Persian literary history by one of Bīdil's students, Sirāj al-Dīn ʻAlī Khān "Ārzū" (1687–1756), showing how his project of self-fashioning was distinct to that of his teacher.

Chapter 3 concluded by observing how Ārzū authorized his teacher Bīdil's "technique of the imaginary" by assigning it a place in his taxonomy of metaphors. His poetics, like all poetics, was thus a formalization of already current poetic practices that authorized them by classificatory recognition. However, Ārzū's oeuvre was more complex than – and more interesting than – a mere defense of Bīdil's poetic practices. What fundamentally distinguished his oeuvre from Bīdil's was its historicist ontology of poetic language. Bīdil insisted, as Chapter 5 will demonstrate in passing, on his contemporaneousness with the primordial origin of *ghazal* topoi. This appropriation of a Neo-Platonic idea of creativity implied that his poetry could be read alongside that of some of the earliest masters without a sense of historical differences in style. Any stylistic differences were results of his willful difficulty rather than changes in Persian stylistic criteria over the passage of time. For Ārzū, by contrast, as this chapter aims to demonstrate, the trans-temporal and trans-spatial concept and criterion of "linguistic purity" (*faṣāḥat*) had always had local content specific to pedagogically trained peoples within a period and across periods. Bīdil and Ārzū thus took opposite attitudes towards the temporality of the Persian poetic tradition. And yet, Ārzū's historicism, like Bīdil's ahistorical mysticism explicated in Chapter 1, was equally a self-authorizing response to the crisis of political authority and its concomitant crisis in Persian canonicity. Moreover, it was related to Bīdil's mystically inflected poetic style, not by a validation of its indifference to the historicity of language, but by a validation of its well-known strangeness as an instance of the temporal locality of all poetic language. It is this complex distance between Ārzū's historicist philology and Bīdil's mysticism that the following chapter aims to explicate.

Ārzū adapted for his conception of *sukhan*, not the influential cosmogonic and Qur'ānic significations deriving from Niẓāmī Ganjavī's (1141–1209, Ganja in present-day Azerbaijan) famously influential chapter on "the virtue of *sukhan*" in his *Makhzan al-asrār* (The Treasury of Secrets, *c.*1166), but a more profane set of values and meanings. Such profane significations are not absent in Niẓāmī's oeuvre. But the more proximate or probable model for Ārzū's conception of *sukhan* was Sa'dī's *Gulistān* (The Rose Garden, 1258). Completed in Shiraz in the year in which the Mongols sacked Abbasid Baghdad and dedicated to the Salghurid Atabeg ruler of Fārs and his son, *The Rose Garden* was marked by and responded to the exigencies of its political context. Here is a tale (*ḥikāyat*) from its fourth chapter, "On the benefits of silence":

> A merchant suffered a loss of a thousand dinars. To his son he said, "You must not speak [*sukhan*] of this to anyone."
>
> "Father," he said, "I will obey you and not speak of it, but I would like you to explain to me what the benefit is in keeping it secret."
>
> "Lest calamity strike twice," he said, "once with the loss of capital, and second with the gloating of neighbors."
>
> Do not disclose your sorrows to enemies, for they will rejoice while saying, "How terrible."[2]

Immediately noticeable is the fundamental difference in overt and covert meanings between Bīdil's image of mystical silence – in the verse on the silent underwater pearl quoted in Chapter 1 – and Sa'dī's image of it here. Sa'dī's is unambiguously an everyday, non-mystical conception of silence as a judicious keeping of one's counsel. In this sense, such silence is of a piece with the rest of *The Rose Garden* that prescribes a worldly ethics of cautious moderation in all practices and advises the cultivation of virtues and skills it considers inalienable by the vagaries of historical circumstance. As I observe in Chapter 5, *The Rose Garden* acquired a new salience and legibility in late Mughal Delhi whose ruling elite felt their grip on affairs of state similarly loosened by accident and misfortune.[3] But by then it had already long been a standard element of a child's education throughout the Persianate world. When he invoked *The Rose Garden* for his purposes, then, Ārzū was staking out his literary-intellectual positions on *sukhan* within a frame that was already culturally prestigious and politically timely.

The most conspicuous form this invocation took was his commentary *Khiyābān* (Garden Pathway) on *The Rose Garden.* In his preface to his commentary, Ārzū says he began to compose it in his childhood but then put it away and resumed it only after thirty years, supplementing or correcting two earlier Mughal commentaries on it. That he explicitly associated *The Rose Garden* with his childhood is more than merely an autobiographical fact. It signals his pride in his early character formation on long canonical models. This is why he repeated this detail in his entry on himself in his student Bindrāban Dās Khvushgū's biographical compendium of poets, *Safīnah-i Khvushgū*. The canonical model of character formation in question here was that of *adab*. Often inadequately glossed as "refinement and cultivation," the term *adab* covers a complex of ethico-aesthetic norms in Perso-Arabic cultural contexts. We might gloss it by quoting Lālā Tek Chand "Bahār," Ārzū's friend, from his gloss of the term in his dictionary of Persian poetic idioms completed in 1752 under Ārzū's supervision, *Bahār-i 'Ajam* (The Springtime of Persia):

> *Adab* – to keep in view or bear in mind the limit [*ḥadd*] of each thing and is a figurative usage [*majāz*] that means "a desirable method or mode" and is used with the words "to do" [*kardan*], "to give" and "to receive" [*khvurdan*], the latter with the sense of "to receive a reprimand."[4]

Since this gloss includes a reference to another key term – *ḥadd* – here is Bahār's gloss on it:

> *Ḥadd*: Direction and side, plural *ḥudūd*; a kind of legal-moral punishment [*siyāsat-i shar'ī*] in which sense it is used with the words "to strike" and "to receive," and with the word 'to acquire" was a reference [*kināyah*] to "reaching perfection."[5]

By reading these two mutually implicated glosses together we might gloss *adab* as a proceeding towards perfection with a continually corrected sense of limit, whether such correction was self-applied or received from another.

Ārzū interpreted this legacy of profane ethical self-fashioning through discipline and punishment in terms of a historicist philology. That is, he construed this norm of ethical delimitation as a historicist correction of *sukhan*. To grasp the historicism of his interpretation and pedagogy of this norm here is his gloss from his commentary on Sa'dī's *The Rose Garden* on the Persian word for God, *khudā*:

> God [*khudā*] … and so forth till the end of the passage: This word is one of the names for the Almighty Creator [*bārī ta'ālā*], in point of fact [*ḥaqīqatan*] meaning "the self-originating" [*khvud āyandah*] which is an implicit reference [*kināyat*] to the Necessary Existent [*vājib al-vujūd*], as scholars [*ahl-i taḥqīq*] have said, and figuratively [*majāzan*] meaning "one who has ownership/is the owner" [*ṣāḥib*] and "master" [*mālik*], having become current in this sense [i.e., "master"] while the first meaning [i.e., "owner"] fell out of use [*mahjūr*]. Some say this is incorrect because the phrases "the house of god" [*khānah-i khudā*] and "the kingdom of god" [*dawlat-i khudā*] and suchlike indicate that it means "owner" [*ṣāḥib*]. They also say "the master of the world" [*khudā-i jahān*] and *khudāvand* and "master of its properties" while *khudāyagan* means "owner" [*ṣāḥib*]. I say that the detailed answer to this is written in other texts such as [my] *Sirāj al-lughāt*. Know that they do

> not apply [*iṭlāq*] this word to any other than the Almighty Creator [*ẕāt-i bārī*] unless in conjunction with a thing such as "master of the village" [*dih khudā*] and "master of the house" [*kad khudā*]. Just as they do not apply the word *rabb* in Arabic without predication [*iẕāfat*] to any other than Him the Almighty, such as in "the master of the country" [*rabb al-dār*] and "master of the throne" [*rabb al-'arsh*]. However, since the names of God [*asmā' allāh*] are descriptive and it is incorrect, without a commentator's permission, to apply them to Him the Almighty, is calling the Almighty by this name absolutely [*muṭlaqan*] difficult? It might be answered that its application depends on a person's juridical disposition [*bar maẕhab-i kasī'st*]. That is, on whether he does not regard the names of God to be descriptive at all or whether he applies these names to avoid committing any impropriety. Thus in his *Fiqh akbar* did Abū Hanīfa, upon whom be peace, regard as permissible the application of the word "God" [*khudā*] and other Persian names, the details of which I have written in [my] commentary on [Niẓāmī Ganjavī's] *Sikandarnāmah.*[6]

Why would Ārzū have chosen to gloss – that too at such length and in such scholarly detail – a word as unproblematic as the Persian word for God? The answer lies implicit in the very question. It was precisely the undisputed significations of this word that led him to single it out for his purposes. Among his historically proximate purposes was to defend against the charges of Shaykh 'Alī Ḥazīn (who was mentioned in the Introduction) the temporal locality of Speaking Anew, the *ghazal* style that he, Bīdil and a group of other poets across Mughal India and Safavid Iran practiced. In the passage above he did so by demonstrating that even Sa'dī, a master littérateur of undisputed canonicity, used literary Persian in ways that were accepted only on dialectical or consensual grounds by the educated elites of his age. That is, these ways were not independent of the historically contingent norms of a linguistic community: the letter *vāv* in the Persian word *khud* had, "through frequent usage, been dropped, thus being a synonym for the Necessary Existent."[7] Nor were they free of acts of inter-lingual translation comparable to ones in multilingual India. They were also not free of their own historical shifts that had rendered certain senses of a word archaic, and of juridical perspectivalism and philological disputes that necessitated the marshaling of authoritative precedents. Sa'dī's exemplum was a time-bound authority, not a historically transcendent one or one that issued somehow naturally from his Iranian ethnicity. It was one that rested on translations and figurative or non-literal lexical uses whose validity rested, in turn, on inevitably temporary scholarly consent. It was only as such that it authorized innovations (*taṣarrufāt*) of comparable temporal locality by the Indian-born poets whom Ḥazīn had scorned.

Having made these observations on Ārzū's historicism, let us turn to the question of its importance in the more general context of Persian literary history. Among the impediments to a persuasive periodization of classical Persian literature is the very temporality of this literature. From roughly 900–1900 CE its poets variously responded to each other in a densely intertextual tradition of shared aesthetic resources whose origins they believed were recounted in obscure and disputed legends relating New Persian to Arabic and, thence, to Syriac.[8] They cultivated this shared and cumulative heritage of aesthetic resources to inhabit what often appears to us to be a temporality of contemporaneousness with each other across time and space. A way of shattering this image of timeless splendor has been to adopt a genealogical method that would look to traditional critical discourses on poetry – to be found in poetry itself as much as in non-poetic genres – for signs of an indigenous periodicity. This is arguably why the Persian *ghazal* stylistics called 'Speaking Anew' (*tāzah-gūyī*) that originated across the Indo-Persian world in the 1500s has come to be studied intensively in recent years.[9] As the very phrase suggests, the newness in question was a renewal rather than newness *ab initio*. Among the most copious authors of critical discourses related to Speaking Anew and among the most useful to help us better understand the recursive temporality of this kind of literary newness was Sirāj al-Dīn 'Alī Khān Ārzū. The scholarship addressed directly to Ārzū broadly employs two distinct methodologies. The first methodology that characterizes the majority of studies is a historico-biographical one that has neglected to ask what conceptual resources Ārzū drew on in the diverse oeuvre he authored over roughly fifty years. The second focuses on his use of concepts and categories that he shared with his contemporaries and has been motivated explicitly by the genealogical considerations mentioned above.[10] The adumbrations and gains of this second methodology form the basis of this chapter.

I will attempt in this chapter, after limning the complex of political and institutional causes for Ārzū's projects, to infer the conceptual coherence of his diverse oeuvre, characterizing it as a response to and inflection of the problematization of the speaking subject in a range of related disciplines and practices in Islamicate India of the early to mid-eighteenth century. In thus explicating the conceptual matrix that traverses Ārzū's oeuvre and the social circumstances under which this oeuvre was produced, I hope to retrieve for scholarship an understanding of Ārzū's analytical and rhetorical labor by which, for the first time in Persian literary history, he gave the practices surrounding literary authorship an explicitly *conceptual and historicist formulation*, an achievement eclipsed not long afterwards by the fading of Persian in India as a prestigious literary medium and, still later, by the consolidation of a nationalist literary canon in early twentieth-century Iran and an essentialist politics of "the mother-tongue" in both countries. The "universality" of this chapter's title thus refers to the framework of Aristotelian-Islamicate ethical and aesthetic concepts that Ārzū elaborated in Persian on the basis of his Arabic sources while the "locality" in question pertains to the literary and linguistic phenomena submitted to these concepts. What follows will be an explication and explanation of this articulation of locality with universality.

Before colonialism, the systematic study of language in Persian and Arabic was underwritten by two co-related premises: the meaning of any linguistic utterance originates by convention in *waḍ'* (Arabic) or *vaz̤'* (Persian), the act – divine or human – of positing or coining a meaning for a vocable; and poetry is the most prestigious instance of such utterance humans are capable of.[11] The former premise arose from the near unanimous acceptance among learned Muslims throughout Arabic literary history of one of the two ancient Greek theories of the origin of language, namely that it originated, not in "nature" (the Greek *physis*, the Arabic *ṭab'*), but in a *supra*-natural "act" (the Greek *thesis*, the Arabic *waḍ'*) of positing or laying down meaning for a vocable.[12] This is not to suggest that pre-colonial Perso-Arabic discourses on language were stable across all periods before colonialism. Rather, it is to imply that this premise of Arabic philology, dating in its earliest extant formulation to the tenth century and elaborated into a disciplinary axiom in the first half of the fourteenth century, constituted the stable foundation of one particular Arabic-language discipline of long institutional duration since at least around the sixteenth century, namely *'ilm al-waḍ'* or "the science of linguistic coining," that was taught and studied in *madrasa*s or Islamic seminaries in Mughal India as elsewhere in the Perso-Arabic world. For reasons I will presently relate, Ārzū reformulated these already familiar Arabic-language premises in his Persian writings when the requirements for the ideal speaking subject became a topic of controversy.

The historically local reasons for this new problematization of the subject of speech in Persian are the same as the ones explicated in Chapter 1. However, a new account of these reasons, attuned to Ārzū's career and oeuvre, is necessary here. The eighteenth century dispersal of formerly centered courtly power and patronage dissolved the main institutional basis for the determination of literary canonicity. Not only was this an issue of diminished possibilities for patronage, it was also one of a loss of authoritative courtly centers for the arbitration of literary value.[13] Absent by Ārzū's period was the politically and financially powerful Mughal court of the sixteenth and seventeenth centuries whose institution of the *malik al-shu'arā* (literally "king of poets" and figuratively "court poet") and whose patronage of courtly authors of biographical compendia (*taẕkirah*s) of Persophone poets powerfully if not exclusively determined the Persian literary canonicity of the period. The dispersal of political power across provincial fiefdoms from the early 1700s onward, even if under the nominal authority of the Mughal imperium, was paralleled by the dissolution of Safavid power in Iran with the ascension of Nādir Shāh Afshār in 1737. Shaykh 'Alī Ḥazīn, a famous Iranian émigré intellectual and poet with familial and personal ties to the deposed Safavid regime left Iran for India as Nādir Shāh rose to power, eventually settling in India though he was loath to do so. Ḥazīn's disparagements of India's Persian philology and poetry were crucial provocations to Ārzū in the composition of some of his major texts, as will be noted ahead.[14] Also contemporary with these developments was the pervasive rise throughout North India and the Deccan of Braj Bhāshā to the status of a language worthy of courtly presentation and patronage.[15] This complex of causes resulted in increasing numbers of claimants of increasingly diverse social and religious identities and linguistic competencies to membership in the Persian literary community, a fact attested to by the burgeoning number of biographical compendia composed throughout this century to the early decades of the nineteenth century that valorized disparate ideals of Persian literary community and contained frequent references to the Braj tradition. Ārzū, like some of his contemporaries, responded to the resulting competition by stipulating the qualifications for the ideal speaking subject in Persian. However, he did so by simultaneously universalizing and historicizing these qualifications in modes that distinguished him from his contemporaries, modes that form the main topic of this chapter.

The Aristotelian-Islamicate sense of the universalism in question here will become apparent in the course of the following interpretation of Ārzū's arguments. Here is his opening account of his theory of linguistic representation in his *'Aṭiyah-i kubrā* (The Great Gift):

> Metaphorics [*bayān*]: is the discipline in which is discussed the representation [*ḥikāyat*] in words of a thing by another thing. It is evident that humans are naturally disposed to representations for they delight in them. This is why you see that people delight in seeing and contemplating the forms and images of unpleasant animals although they find seeing the thing itself unpleasant. And it is evident that a complete visual image too is not cause for such pleasure because seeing the visual images of unseen animals does not give much pleasure. Thus the pleasure human natures take in representations is neither in visual images nor in their referents. Therefore linguistic utterances comprising representations are more pleasurable and delightful. Thus it is that representation is the foundation of poetic utterance for it is founded on the imagination, not knowledge that is certain [*muḥākat asās-i kalām-i shi'r'īst, zīrā kih banā-i ān bar takhyīl ast na taḥqīq kih yaqīnī ast*]. Thus linguistic utterances containing representations cast a spell on hearts and are wondrous to them, especially poetry [*shi'r*] because rhythm has much to do with this.[16]

Appealing directly to the factuality of experience as aesthetics allows him to do, Ārzū asserts that humans take pleasure in linguistic representations more than in visual ones and that this pleasure derives from the uncertainty of the knowledge they are based on. Does the "we" here cover all humans or only some? Let us suspend answers to this question until attention to another of his passages lets us answer it, noting for now that certain knowledge, implicitly, would not give us the kind of pleasure – if any at all – that the uncertain knowledge of the imagination does. And of the pleasures we derive from linguistic representations based on imaginary or uncertain knowledge poetry gives us the most intense "because meter has much to do with this."

However, these are not just any representations but "representations in words of a thing by another thing." They entail the verbal formulation of a thing *as* another thing. Ārzū does not tell us explicitly whether this being-as is substitutive or imitative. That is, he does not say whether representing a thing in language by means of another thing is to *picture* the referent in its representation or to present a *proxy* for it.[17] That it is a proxy rather than a picture becomes apparent to us when we read in the same text that:

> Humans have faculties named the imagination [*mutakhayyilah*] and the intellect [*mutafakkirah*] among whose distinctions are the combining of forms and meanings, their elaboration and appropriation and the invention of things that in actuality do not exist. And this either occurs by means of the faculty of fantasy [*quvvat-i vahmiyyah*] – in which case it is called "imaginary" – or by means of the faculty of the intellect [*quvvat-i ʻaqliyyah*], then being called "intellectual" [*mutafakkirah*]. Thus a non-existent [thing] that is composed by the imagination out of matters it has comprehended by the external senses belongs to "the sensibles."... And a thing invented by the intellect out of itself belongs to "the intelligibles."[18]

The pleasure taken in poetry is pleasure, not in what is, but in the invention of sensible or intelligible things – or various combinations thereof – *that could possibly be* inasmuch as they constitute elaborations of what we know to be actual. We take pleasure in such elaborations in language of uncertain knowledge of hypothetical stand-ins or proxies for things certainly known to exist. Such uncertainly existing beings, composed of both the imaginary and intellectual, participate in the nature of those that certainly exist. And we delight in rhythmic or metrical speech of that halo of possibilities surrounding actualities. "Certain knowledge" does not yield the kind of pleasure that the uncertain knowledge of imaginatively or intellectually elaborated possibilities does because it limits itself to the observation of what is, not venturing to imagine or intellectualize in language *what could therefore be*. If it is a trait among the members of a literary community to take pleasure in such reality testing, poetry is the most pleasurable kind of reality testing, entailing an actualization in the second-order reality of metrical language of what is potential in the first-order realities of the sensible and the intelligible. Ārzū does not explain why he thinks such elaboration in metrical language of the hypothetical on the basis of the actual yields a peculiar pleasure. His silence on this point here, however, only left unsaid what did not need explication in a pragmatically oriented text since prosody, as he explicates in his historical and structural study of the Persian language, *Mus̱mir* (The Fruition), had long formed a part of the Persian littérateur's training in virtue. This is where it becomes apparent that Ārzū's universalism belongs to the tradition of Islamicate interpretations of Aristotle – in particular the Aristotelian treatise transmitted under the name *The Nicomachean Ethics* – according to which reason or "the rational part of the soul" was universal in the sense of being a trans-human potential even as only some humans (variously determined by gender, class and ethnicity) were afforded the opportunity to actualize this potential. Training in prosody was one of an ensemble of practices by which the subject cultivated his potentiality of reason. That is, it was integral to the formation of a "sound" or "balanced soul" (*ṭabʻ-i salīm*, *ṭabʻ-i mawzūn*) capable of taking and displaying a balanced pleasure in poetry, capable of a shared self-control in ecstasy that reflected the control exercised over poetic rhythm and was thus a condition for participation in literary community. Thus Ārzū says in his *Mus̱mir*:

> Metrical harmony between the two hemstitches of a distich, in fact the concordance [*tavāfuq*] of every one of the distiches of a ghazal or a *qaṣīdah* [i.e., a genre of panegyric], is necessary. Balance in a matter of ecstasy is necessary because the ear of every person of balanced nature [*mawzūn ṭab'*] recognizes it and does not depend on knowing scansion.... In fact, scansion is intended to instruct an unbalanced soul.[19]

In his account of linguistic representation, its concomitant faculty-psychology and his explication of the value of prosodic training, Ārzū was thus formulating what he considered to be universally applicable truths of cognition and evaluations of linguistic practice. That the passage on "metaphorics" opens with lines that are almost direct translations into Persian of an Arabic passage from a text already widely and long authoritative throughout the Perso-Arab world, Al-Sakkākī's *Miftāḥ al-'ulūm* (Key to the Sciences, 1229), signals the universalism of the human subject intended here.[20] Ārzū historicized this universalism which he inherited by arguing that this universal structure of cognition, linguistic representation and prosody was always and everywhere articulated with conventions that were local to pedagogically trained peoples both during a period and across the different periods. What follows are three illustrations of this localizing historicization.

The first, in evidence in his discussion of the rhetorical category of "comparison," is a passage on comparative poetics that had precedents going back to eleventh-century Ghaznavid Persian topography and similar discourses in thirteenth-century post-Mongol Arabic historiography but which assumed a new significance in late Mughal India when Persian was only one of several other languages invested with literary prestige in courtly settings and when ethnographic and topographic texts in Persian came to be composed in increasing numbers.[21] Here is Ārzū's discussion of the cultural relativism of the category of "comparison" (*tashbīh*):

> Although a comparison is the similarity of two things under a certain description, this is not just any description but that which is conventional among that people. For example, the poets of Iran [*shu'arā-i pārs*] compare the color of gold to a lover's face in contrast to the poets of India. The latter compare the eye to a fish in contrast to Persian speakers [*pārsīyān*] while Arabic speakers [*tāzīyān*] compare a lock of hair to a finger in contrast to Persian ones. These distinctions become apparent after a study of the books of masters.[22]

Although "comparison" and its subcategories had been a standard category of metaphor since the earliest twelfth- and thirteenth-century Persian manuals on rhetoric, it had not been opened thus to geographical and ethno-linguistic variations of content, in this case to an item – the comparison of the eye to a fish – recognizably drawn from the poetic conventions of Braj. Ārzū retains a category familiar to his readers from the Perso-Arabic traditions of rhetoric as a trans-human constant. But having thus confirmed their expectations of a "treatise/epistle on the discipline of metaphorics," he asserts, as his predecessors had never done, the local variability of this category's content. By this double procedure, he authorized himself by consistency with an already accepted category of comparison even as he authorized practices of comparison peculiar to the aesthetics of peoples not covered by the earliest formulations of this category.

The second illustration of Ārzū's localization of a universal topic may be seen in the marginal note he added to his student Bindrāban Dās Khvushgū's entry in his biographical compendium of Persian poets, *Safīnah-i Khvushgū*, on Rūdakī (d. 945), the blind and lute-playing Central Asian poet conventionally considered everywhere in the Persian world to have been the first Persian poet. Noting the improbably large number of poetic compositions attributed to him ("thirty thousand or twenty eight thousand, amounting to a hundred and twenty thousand distiches"), Khvushgū interrupts his entry to quote Ārzū's "subtle point" on the margin of his text:

> The humble Ārzū says: The equivalent of the master Rūdakī in Hindi [i.e., Braj] poetry and compositions is Sūr [Dās] who composed a hundred thousand Bishnū Pads and named it "Sūr Sāgar." Every Bishnū Pad which is a kind of Hindī composition is around six to eight hemistiches long or more. The aforementioned Sūr composed three or four new [*tāzah*] *rāgas* [i.e., musical modes] and his compositions are innumerable, as has been noted, and contain strange and remarkable topoi [*maẕāmīn*]. As Miyān Tān Sen Kalāvant the like of whom they do not find in this last half millennium and who was appointed his [i.e., Sūr's] teacher in fact said: "In whichever direction I go, I find a blind man with cane in hand."[23]

By explaining the hyperbolically inflated numbers of compositions attributed to Rūdakī by analogy with Sūr Dās, one of the sixteenth-century masters of Braj poetry who was also blind and was imagined in Braj literary legend as having authored copious numbers of texts, Ārzū was treating the Persian poetic tradition on par with the Braj as peculiar to a locality in the world. Equally, he was elevating the Braj tradition within Persian literary culture to a status comparable to the Persian, a comparability not restricted to biographical equivalences but also applicable to poetic categories such as *maẕmūn-āfrīnī* or "topos-creation" or "topos-elaboration," a category central to the Persian *ghazal* practice of Speaking Anew that Ārzū championed: Sūr created "strange and remarkable topoi."[24] Furthermore, Ārzū who oversaw Khvushgū's biographical compendium and added a laudatory preface to it evidently validated this text's tripartite distinction between the "old," "middle" and "recent" poets and the further tripartite division of each again into "old," "middle" and "recent," a chronological frame bespeaking a sense of the temporal distance from the literary past and the newness or temporal locality of the present. The memory of Rūdakī had grown distant enough in time to be understood on an analogy with Ur-Braj poet Sūr Dās as an amalgam of history and legend.

We may draw the third instance from the third of the three introductions Ārzū wrote to his *Dād-i sukhan* (Justice to Poetry, composed between 1741–43).[25] Here, he declares "The meaning of a distich may be understood in many manners [*vajh*]" and then distinguishes between seven types of readers corresponding to seven manners or interpretative attitudes. The first method is that of the commoners of a linguistic community whereby simple and composite utterances are construed in the familiar and well-known senses that they have heard from their elders. In this, the learned elite and commoners are no different from each other although if a commoner learns the abstruse points of an utterance from a member of the learned elite, he will be more eloquent than someone who has learnt them from a commoner. So, Ārzū opens his classification at the level of ordinary language where differences in hermeneutic sophistication corresponding to differences in class are only incipient. This level includes all the following kinds of interpreters, being the most general. The second manner is "the understanding of Mullāhs," this class of interpreter focusing exclusively and pedantically on a poem's grammatical niceties. The third – and here Ārzū draws on the tripartite distinction he inherited from Al-Sakkākī's *Miftāḥ al-'ulūm* and its famous systematization by Al-Khaṭīb al-Qazvīnī called *Talkhīs al-miftāḥ* (Resume of the Key, 1338, Damascus) – is that of one of the three types of scholars of the three respective sub-disciplines of "linguistic efficiency." (I will discuss the significance of this term ahead, confining the discussion here to Ārzū's *Dād-i sukhan*). This manner is that of a scholar of the discipline of semantics (*'ilm-i ma'ānī*) who focuses exclusively on the syntactical order of clauses, their conjoining, separation, compression and expansion. He does not know what the next and fourth type of scholar – that of metaphorics (*'ilm-i bayān*) – attends to exclusively, namely metaphors. The fifth manner, expectedly, is that of scholars of figures of speech (*badī'iyān*) who, being defective with respect to the other two methods of "linguistic efficiency," focus only on a poem's figures. The sixth interpretive attitude is that of the school headmaster who, ignorant of "linguistic efficiency," "linguistic purity" and authoritative poetic precedent, insists on a grammatical point without seeing that it would ruin the fluency of a poetic text if employed. The seventh and last manner is the:

> comprehension of poetry in keeping with the taste of poets. And this depends on knowledge of the composition of phrasal compounds of apposite words, in keeping with the spoken idiom [*rūz-marrah*] of one's own language and that of the poet and the observance of the technique [*ṭarīq*] a poet has in mind.

Ārzū then lists the poetic techniques in question and notes that "understanding such observance is extremely difficult" because "some of the recent poets" insist on avoiding certain word formations despite ample evidence that such formations were employed by authoritative poets.

While the first interpretative attitude is too commonplace to grasp the subtler meanings of a poetic text, the following five are each defective by being too specialist and partial in their foci. The seventh, that in keeping with "the taste of poets," is "the most comprehensive" and requires a reader to be to attentive to the differences between the common discourse of his own language and that of the poet. However, this attitude – already historicist in its mindfulness of the linguistic differences resulting from temporal locality – is impeded by poets' own ignorance of literary history. And this is where Ārzū's role as a pedagogue who adduced exempla from the various ages or temporal localities of Persian literary history becomes apparent.

These three illustrations of how Ārzū conceived the locality of universal concepts presuppose his more radical historicization of the poetic speech-act itself. What follows is a reading of selected passages from Ārzū's *Muṣmir*, *Mawhibat-i 'uẓmā*, *Sirāj-i Munīr* and *'Aṭiyah-i kubrā* with an attention to this historicization. We may preface this reading by noting that in the Persian literary tradition, authoritative or exemplary poetic innovations by reference to exemplary precedent had been termed *taṣarruf.*[26] In fighting to champion the stylistics of the Speaking Anew *ghazal*, Ārzū marshaled the conceptual criteria that had previously received explicit formulation only in Arabic in defense of the kinds of *taṣarruf* current in Speaking Anew. The two co-related criteria that any act of *taṣarruf* had to fulfill were *faṣāḥat* or "linguistic purity" and *balāghat* or "linguistic efficiency." Offering an account here of either term that would be satisfactory on its own is beyond the compass of this chapter because both terms form the topics of entire books in the Persian and Arabic traditions of rhetoric. I will therefore explain these terms in ways not unlike the authors of the earliest Persian manuals of *balāghat* – with a pragmatist brevity they put in the service of the pleasures of poetic performance and I put in the service of argumentative specificity. Bearing an evident etymological relation to *bulūgh* or "organic maturity," *balāghat* designated something like a mindfulness of how the social situation in which you were employing linguistic and non-linguistic signs could inflect how you were understood, an ability to take into consideration the social context of what you were saying in order best to achieve your purpose. In line with the Aristotelian understanding of the word *ethos*, it is worth noting, *balāghat* was then an adequation of act and circumstance, of meaning-making and the contingencies of the moment. We might thus gloss it as a communicative tact. However, for the sake of adherence to already current English scholarly translation, I will translate it as "linguistic efficiency." Cognate with *faṣīḥ* or "linguistically pure," *faṣāḥat* or "linguistic purity" referred to a threefold requirement internal to *balāghat*. We could gloss this requirement by reference to Ārzū's own oft-cited medieval Arabic exemplar, al-Khaṭīb al-Qazvīnī (d. 1338) whose *Talkhīs al-miftāḥ* (Resume of the Key) was the most famous textbook of Arabic rhetoric before, during and after Ārzū's lifetime. The first component of the requirement of linguistic purity was that the words of an utterance (*kalām*) be pure or free of "the mutual repellence of letters" (*tanāfur-i ḥurūf)*, a defect that makes it hard to pronounce because "the word/words is/are extreme in heaviness upon the tongue."[27] "The concept of 'heaviness' (*thiql*)," Herbjorn Jenssen observes, "is an old one in Arabic morphology, frequently used to explain forms which were considered to be irregular." The second called for an utterance's freedom from contrariness (*mukhālafat al-qiyās*) to the rules of word formation or a word's morphological pattern. A conflict with such morphological rules resulted in the third kind of defect an utterance was required to avoid, namely "strangeness" (*gharābat*) or the appearance of outlandishness to the listener and a consequent failure to convey the intended meaning. Linguistic purity was thus "a negative rather than a positive requirement. If an utterance contains no faults of a phonological, grammatical or semantic nature, neither on the word level nor on the level of syntax, then it can be described as *faṣīḥ*."[28] The positive requirements of utterances were the ones stipulated by the criterion of linguistic efficiency that demanded a concordance between utterance and social context (*maqām*). As such, all linguistically efficient utterances were necessarily linguistically pure though not all linguistically pure utterances were necessarily efficient.

When Shaykh ʻAlī Ḥazīn and other Iranian detractors unnamed by Ārzū criticized poets in India for an inability to practice *taṣarruf*, then, they were implicitly pointing to the lack of the kind of poetic training in Mughal India that would allow such poets to participate in Persian literary community by an avoidance of outlandish or historically unprecedented linguistic usage, a negative requirement of linguistic purity that was a necessary though not sufficient condition for membership. Poets who were perceived not to have fulfilled the criterion of linguistic purity could not be understood to have fulfilled its dependent one of linguistic efficiency and thus risked exclusion from literary community. In this sense, the criteria for literary membership were conservative in that innovations were acceptable only if they authorized themselves by appearing to conserve the authority of prior exempla. Ārzū responded to Ḥazīn's charges explicitly in his *Tanbīh al-ghāfilīn* (Censure of the Complacent) by criticizing his selection of six hundred of the latter's distiches. It is worthy noting here that while several of his criticisms point to Ḥazīn's unprecedented and thus unacceptably strange formulations, some also appear motivated by no more than malice and envy over his local stature.[29] In one of his entries, Ārzū accuses Ḥazīn of the "literary theft" (*saraqa*) of a topos (*maẓmūn*) from Saʻdī's *Rose Garden* (1258) even when Saʻdī's formulation of this topos is differently worded, thus in fact satisfying Ārzū's own condition that innovation be based on authoritative precedent. In any event, that a debate crystallized around Ārzū's response to Ḥazīn bespeaks the general and heightened sense of poetic innovation at the time as well as the communitarian risks of exclusion which such innovation incurred. Some of Ārzū's criticisms of Ḥazīn were taken up by his polymath contemporary from Bilgrām, Ghulām ʻAli "Āzād" Bilgrāmī (d. 1786), who, in the course of his entry on Ḥazīn in his biographical dictionary *Khazānah-i ʻāmirah* (Bountiful Treasury), defended Ḥazīn's criticized distiches by adducing exemplary precedents from the work of generally accepted masters as well as Speaking Anew poets.[30] Ḥazīn had been anticipated in his criticisms of unacceptable poetic innovations by Munīr Lahorī (d. 1644), a poet from seventeenth-century Lahore. In his *Kārnāmah* (Chronicle), Munīr had selected distiches by four poets of the Speaking Anew style who he argued were being unjustly exalted in his milieu and criticized these distiches mainly, though not exclusively, on grounds of the unprecedented and therefore improbable character of their poetic conventions.[31] For Munīr, the resulting strangeness of poetic formulation put in doubt the worthiness of the claims on behalf of its poet's canonicity. In his *Sirāj-i Munīr* ("Bright Lamp" or "Lamp for Munīr") Ārzū responded to each of Munīr's criticisms, taking up the apparently unprecedented formulations in each distich to defend it by reference to poetic, scientific and historiographical precedents unknown to or overlooked by Munīr.[32] So, for instance, the first of Ārzū's defenses of a distich Munīr criticized led him to expound the astronomical context implicit in its apparently strange formulation and then to a discussion of whether or not this poet had stolen his trope from an earlier poetic iteration of the same astronomical metaphor and thus then to a history of the discussion of literary theft that had praised such theft as improved on what it stole. The implication here was not only that 'Urfī had authoritative precedent but also that he had improved on such precedent and had thus "derived" (*akhz*) his topos "on the basis on competitive response" (*min ḥays̱ al-javāb*) to his model rather than "on the basis of weakness" (*min ḥays̱ al-'ajz*) with respect to it. In such references to authoritative precedent, therefore, Ārzū was hardly novel. However, it is to his less confrontational and more systematic work, *Mus̱mir*, that we must turn to appreciate how his innovation lay in taking his historicization of language to the smallest scale of analysis available to him, that of the "strangeness" ingredient in "linguistic purity."

Looking closely at the threefold requirement for linguistic purity, we notice that mispronunciation and contrariness to the rules of word formation may be construed as effects of historically local and variable conditions. If an educated listener found an utterance unintelligible, this "strangeness" may arguably result from *his* unfamiliarity with the educated usage current in the speaker's milieu or the chronologically distant milieu of a poetic text. However, heaviness on the tongue resulting from "the mutual repellence of letters" seems an ahistorical or timelessly applicable criterion, the tongue being a trans-human physiological constant. And this is indeed what the Arabic philologists cited by Ārzū said. However, let us consider Ārzū's subtle but radical modification of even this apparently unproblematic physiological and thus, surely, timeless criterion. In Chapter 16 of his *Mus̱mir*, titled "On Knowledge of the Linguistically Pure [*faṣīḥ*]," Ārzū cites two scholars of Arabic, saying:

> The basis of the linguistic purity of an utterance lies in its frequency of usage.... The opinion of recent Arabic rhetoricians is that it is not possible for an individual to know the entirety of a language because of its antiquity. Therefore, they said linguistic purity is an utterance's freedom from the mutual repellence of letters, unfamiliarity [*gharābat*] and contrariness to the rules of word formation [*qiyās-i lughavī*].... The mutual repellence [of letters] is because of their heaviness on the tongue and difficulty in pronunciation, *this matter depending on time, not on the proximity to or distance from the organ of pronunciation* [i.e., the tongue and its related articulatory apparatus], as some Arabic scholars have said [my italics].

That is, even difficulties in a word's pronunciation vary with its "frequency of usage" by a language's educated speakers, the human tongue thus accommodating itself to the historical vagaries of cultivation and habit. Thus, in his treatise on semantics, *Mawhibat al-'uẓmā* (The Great Gift), Ārzū reiterated the conclusions he arrived at in his *Musmir* to argue that all the three categories of linguistic purity contained historically local content. The difficulties of pronunciation experienced by a sound or trained nature as a result of "the mutual repellence of letters" depended on experience or "taste" rather than on "proximity to or distance from the organ of pronunciation."[33] As to the morphological rule concerning "contrariness to the rules of word formation," such contrariness was practiced to adjust a word in a poetic line to metrical requirements. And some of these adjustments too, Ārzū notes, had historically local authority. Among his examples is the use of the vowel *ye* for rhyme that, he observes, is "permitted especially among the recent poets."[34] Finally, words that were strange or unfamiliar to educated usage occurred "frequently," implying, on the basis of his explication in Chapter 19 of his *Musmir* that is devoted to "the [linguistically] outlandish and strange,"[35] that such transgressions were not contrary to linguistic purity provided they were poetically necessary. Ārzū's examples of poetically necessary and thus linguistically pure strangeness in Chapter 19 of *Musmir* – Khāqānī's Armenian words unknown to the educated Persian of his time and Mullāh Tughrā's Hindavī words unknown to the educated Persian of his – are also interpretable as cases of the mutual repellence of letters and contrariness to the rules of word formation. What I mean is, although he does not state this explicitly, strangeness could include the other two categories of linguistic impurity.

In this implicit but technically possible sense "strangeness" by itself includes the other two kinds of linguistic impurity and becomes, in Ārzū's thought, an alienation that haunts all literary language – and every one of its parts – as a fate. Thus does Ārzū observe that a word's strangeness:

> means that its meaning is incomprehensible. This accords with *most cases in Persian* since, with the passage of ages, they [i.e., meanings] are transformed. For example, some words that were current in age of Rūdakī [d. 941] and others were not so among [poets] of the middle and recent ages. In this case, a dictionary becomes necessary [my italics].[36]

His dictionaries and commentaries were largely responses to this sense of the increasing and inevitable estrangement over time of the language of the temporally distant authorities. Hence his aforementioned *Khiyābān sharḥ-i Gulistān-i Sa'dī*, a commentary on Sa'dī's *The Rose Garden*, and his *Shigūfah-zār* (Field of Buds) and *Sharḥ-i Sikandarnāmah*, commentaries on the first and second parts of Niẓāmī Ganjavī's *Sikandarnāmah* (Alexander Book, 1202) respectively.[37] However, his fourth commentary, on the panegyrics of the Speaking Anew poet 'Urfī Shirāzī (d. 1590), was addressed to the work of a poet considered a contemporary in the sense of having been a progenitor of Speaking Anew.

The reason for this apparent anomaly becomes apparent when we consider that 'Urfī's panegyrics were the focus of widespread commentarial attention in India during this period either because they were admired for their difficulty or, as we have seen in the case of Munīr, discredited for their lack of precedent.[38] If the language of "the old masters" grew strange over time that of the "recent masters" must logically also have been strange from the viewpoint of literary precedent. 'Urfi's panegyrics were an instance of such ambivalent strangeness in the language of a recent master and Ārzū's commentary largely seeks to defend such strangeness either by adducing authoritative precedents for his innovations or justifying them as exemplary for the new period.

In this connection, his famous dictionary, *Chirāgh-i hidāyat* (Lamp of Guidance), must be read as an attempt to authorize poetic phrases he considered peculiar to poets of his age, particularly to those who practiced the Speaking Anew *ghazal*.[39] In its preface he said his dictionary was mainly addressed to "the Persian speakers of India." The poets he cited in it as exemplary were, or had been, located in Safavid Iran as well as Mughal India and formed, in this sense, a trans-regional canon of exemplars by which the Persian poetic community of Mughal India could authoritatively orient itself in the face of charges of aesthetically unacceptable "strangeness."

He was invested in this defense not only as a philologist but also as a poet. The sense of the linguistic foreignness of the old authorities meant for him that his own poetry was articulated with a sense of contemporaneousness, not with the old poets, but with the linguistically familiar and thus historically recent ones as his community of literary interlocutors. This is why four of his seven *dīvāns* or collections of poems were written as *javābs* or poetic responses, not to the old masters, but to the *dīvāns* of Bābā Fighānī (d. 1519), Muḥammad Qulī Salīm (d. 1657), Sā'ib Tabrīzī (d. 1676) and Shafi'ā Asar (d. 1702), practitioners of Speaking Anew whom he considered to be near contemporaries or "recent masters."[40] The alienating unintelligibility that came to literary language from the outside and that had be resisted, recorded and philologically repaired could also be conceptually authorized, appropriated and prescribed in trans-historically or universally valid terms as a historically local and consciously new poetic practice. This work of conceptually authorizing, appropriating and prescribing in universal terms the historical locality or strangeness of Speaking Anew fell to large portions of his *Musmir*, *'Aṭiyah-i kubrā* and *Mawhibat-i 'uẓmā*. If poetic innovation had to be authorized by reference to exemplary precedent, Speaking Anew spoke anew the heritage of what was understood as the pre-eternal heritage of topoi (*maẓmūn, ma'nī*).[41] In thus speaking such primordial topoi anew, such poetry pleasurably estranged them through techniques local to the age. This is why, in his *'Aṭiyah-i kubrā*, Ārzū aestheticizes the strange historical newness of meaning resulting from the encryption of primordial topoi:

> Some of the recent [poets] do not employ the technique of exemplification [*ṭarz-i tamsīl*] in their poetry and do not like it in that of others. This is because in this way the meaning becomes clear and obvious whereas they

> seek abstruseness and subtlety, going so far as to use improbable and abstruse comparisons so that the mind comprehends the topos [*ma'nī*] after much contemplation and endless thought, the meaning being one unknown to those who know poetry. The recent [poets] call those distiches in which subtle comparisons and difficult meanings occur and which do not employ the technique of exemplification distiches in the technique of the imaginary [*ṭarz-i khiyāl*]. This kind is extremely pleasant to natures provided it is not carried to the point of meaninglessness.[42]

Ārzū follows this passage by quoting a distich by Nāṣir 'Alī Sirhindī (d. 1697), a famous poet of the Speaking Anew mode, that helps us grasp what he understood by the preference he shared with some others for a kind of poetry whose topoi were recognized and meanings comprehended only "after much contemplation and endless thought." The distich: "His dark [*sabz*] cheek-down drove the world mad./Lord, what fairy's shadow is this?"[43]

The distich depends for the intelligibility of the logic relating its two hemistiches on the listener or reader's foreknowledge of the topos of a fairy, conventionally imagined as green, driving a person mad by casting her shadow over her or him. It also assumes the reader's foreknowledge of the topos by which a boy-beloved's cheek-stubble was eroticized. Finally, it requires the reader to recognize the pun on the word *sabz* that means both "dark" and "green" and so applies to the stubble and the fairy at once. Taking the pleasure this distich promises thus demands that the reader explicate both inexplicit topoi to himself, recognize the pun on *sabz* and then the combination of topoi and pun to delight in Nāṣir 'Alī's complex and novel iteration of all three. This "technique of the imaginary" was one of an array of techniques cultivated by Speaking Anew and aimed at such a time-taking and contemplative arrest of hermeneutic attention. In validating such techniques by his taxonomical expositions of them, Ārzū considered himself to be validating against its detractors in universally authoritative terms aesthetic and hermeneutic experiences that were only as peculiar to his age as others had been to earlier ages.

In conclusion, the political fragmentation of Mughal power in the course of the eighteenth century and the consequently dispersed and multiple bids for authority in the determination of literary value and canonicity assigned "strangeness" a new significance. Whereas it had been an unproblematic element of the trans-temporal and trans-spatial Perso-Arabic concept of linguistic purity, it now became a problem. Sirāj al-Dīn 'Alī Khān Ārzū participated in this competitive bid for literary prestige by seeking to demonstrate the lack of authoritative precedent for the poetry of those who, like Shaykh 'Alī Ḥazīn, charged the Persian poetry practiced in late Mughal India with lacking precisely such precedent. Furthermore, he marshaled his commentaries and dictionaries to demonstrate that literary language conformed to concepts of linguistic purity and efficiency even as it was susceptible to shifts from place to place and from period to period. It was therefore not geographical or political affiliation, as Ḥazīn had claimed, but a hard-won pedagogical training in these universal or trans-temporal and trans-spatial criteria and their spatio-temporally local constituents, a training he showed himself to have undergone and himself offered, that qualified a balanced and linguistically pure speaker. If Speaking Anew was practiced by such an aesthetically and ethically cultivated subject, it was as legitimate a literary practice and as worthy of esteem as the older exemplars of the tradition. The pleasurable strangeness by which the traditional heritage of topoi was spoken anew was, he acknowledged, local to his age. However, it was only as local as the poetic conventions of every previous age had been, a temporal locality that necessitated dictionaries and commentaries such as he had authored and that was maintained in its exemplarity and intelligibility by the philological cultivation of the universally rational soul.

Notes

1 Originally published in *Indian Economic and Social History Review*, Vol. 50 No. 1 Copyright 2013 © The Indian Economic and Social History Association. All rights reserved. Reproduced with the permission of the copyright holders and the publishers, Sage Publications India Pvt. Ltd, New Delhi.
2 Sheikh Mushriffudin Sa'di of Shiraz, *The Gulistān (Rose Garden) of Sa'di*, trans. Wheeler M. Thackston (Bethseda, MD: Ibex Publishers, 2008), 98.
3 By citing Sa'dī's other work on ethics, *Būstān* (The Orchard), in his Persian *mas̱navī* addressed to the Mughal emperor Aurangzeb, the last Sikh Guru, Guru Gobind Singh (1666–1708), appropriated an idiom and canon of ethics which he shared with the Mughals he was fighting. Louis. E. Fenech, *The Sikh Zafar-namah of Guru Gobind Singh: a Discursive Blade in the Heart of the Mughal Empire* (New York: Oxford University Press, 2013), 36–69.
4 Lālā Tek Chand Bahār, *Bahār-i 'Ajam* (Lucknow: Munshī Naval Kishor Press, 1916), 56.
5 Ibid., 331.
6 Sirāj al-Dīn 'Alī Khān Ārzū, *Khiyābān-i Gulistān: sharḥ-i Gulistān-i Sa'dī* (Islāmābād: markaz-i taḥqīqāt-i Fārsī-i Irān va Pākistān, shumārah-i radīf 154, 1994), 4.
7 For Ārzū's comments on the same word in his commentary on Niẓāmī Ganjavī's *Sikandarnāmah* but with amplified theological and juridical justifications, see Sirāj al-Dīn 'Alī Khān Ārzū, *Shigūfah-zār: Sharḥī bar Sharaf-nāmah-i Niẓāmī* (Tehrān: Firdaws, 1392/2013), 72.
8 A relatively early account of the disputed legendary origins of New Persian poetry may be found in the author's prefaces to the earliest extant biographical compendium of poets in New Persian, Muḥammad 'Awfī's *Lubāb al-Albāb* (The Piths of Intellects), completed in 1221 at the court of the Ghurid vassal Nāsir al-Dīn Qabāja in Sind and dedicated to his vizier 'Ayn al-Mulk. Muḥammad 'Awfī, *Lubāb al-Albāb* (Tehrān: Chāp-i Ittiḥād, 1333/1955), 1–19. Ārzū recounted 'Awfī's legendary transmissions in a brief chapter of his *Muṣmir*, suggesting the persistence of these legends of origin, however disputed. Sirāj al-Dīn 'Alī Khān Ārzū, *Muṣmir* (Karachi: Institute of Central and West Asian Studies, 1991), 17–21.
9 I translate *tāzah-gūyī* as "Speaking Anew" to capture the recursive temporality of this corpus's relations with its own literary patrimony, a temporality of renewal rather than displacement. The word *tāzah* itself literally means "fresh" and "novel" and does not include such a recursive connotation. Accordingly, Paul Losensky translates *tāzah-gūyī* with "speaking the fresh" and Rajeev Kinra by "fresh-speaking." However, since, in practice, it always referred to a renewal of poetic traditions I translate it as

"Speaking Anew" which has the advantage of signaling the recursive character in question by its very morphology. Paul E. Losensky, *Welcoming Fighani: Imitation and Poetic Individuality in the Safavid-Mughal Ghazal* (Costa Mesa, CA, Mazda Publishers, 1998), 195–207. Rajeev Kinra, "Make it Fresh: Time, Tradition and Indo-Persian Literary Modernity," in Anne C. Murphy (ed.), *Time, History, and the Religious Imaginary in South Asia* (New York: Routledge, 2011).

10 The first of the two methodologies, the historico-biographical one, is already in evidence in the earliest work of modern scholarship on Ārzū, Muḥammad Ḥusayn Āzād's *Āb-i Ḥayāt* (1880). Āzād says that "As long as all logicians will be called the descendants of Aristotle, all Urdu-speakers will continue to be called the descendants of Khān-i Ārzū," not explaining this commendation except by observing that Ārzū was a teacher to many of the foremost Urdu poets of the period. Muḥammad Ḥusayn Āzād, *Āb-i ḥayāt: ya'nī mashāhīr shu'arā-yi Urdu ke savāniḥ umrī aur maẕkūr kī 'ahd ba 'ahd kī taraqqīyoṅ aur islāḥoṅ ka bayān* (Lahore: Naval Kishor, 1907), 115. In the only book-length study in any language to be devoted exclusively to Ārzū, Rehāna Khātūn infers Ārzū's biographical narrative from biographical dictionaries and presents a piecemeal summary of the contents of his individual works without abstracting the network of concepts that accounts for their unity of substance and method. Rehāna Khātūn, *Aḥvāl o āṡār-i Sirāj al-Dīn 'Alī Khān-i Ārzū* (Delhi: Indo-Persian Society, 1987). The other studies of Ārzū that employ variants of this method are: Mohamad Tavakoli-Targhi, *Refashioning Iran: Orientalism, Occidentalism and Historiography* (Basingstoke: Palgrave-Macmillan, 2001); Sīrus Shamisa's introduction to his edition of Sirāj al-Dīn 'Alī Khān Ārzū, *'Aṭiyah-i kubrā va Mawhibat-i 'uzmā* (Tehrān: Firdaws, 1381/2003); three essays by Mehdi Rahimpoor, "Sayrī dar aḥvāl u āṡār-i Sirāj al-Dīn 'Alī Khān Ārzū-i Akbarābādī," *Āyinah-i mirās* 1: 1 (Spring 2008), 289–318; "'Aṭiyah-i kubrā va Mawhibat-i uẓmā," *Āyinah-i mirās* 5: 4 (Winter 2008), 334–50; and "Naẓariyah-i daryāft: az Sirāj al-Dīn 'Alī Khān Ārzū-i Akbarābādī tā Hans Robert Jauss-i Ālmānī," *Āyinah-i mirās* 44 (Spring–Summer 2009), 90–109. (In its attempt to compare and contrast Ārzū's views of "reception" to those of a selection of European hermeneuticians, this last essay leaves unexplained Ārzū's debts to Islamicate hermeneutics). The following texts, however, constitute instances of the second method and form the basis of my own essay as they adumbrate Ārzū's conceptual inheritances rather than only summarize his textual topics and relate his biography: Shamsur Rahman Faruqi, "The Need for a New and Comprehensive Persian Literary Theory," at www.columbia.edu/itc/mealac/pritchett/00fwp/srf/srf_persianlittheory_2009.pdf (accessed March 4, 2012); Sayyid Abdullah, "Dād-i Sukhan," in *Fārsī zabān o adab: majmu'a-i maqālāt* (Lahore: Majlis-i taraqqī-i adab, 1977), 142–47; Sayyid Abdullah, *Mabāḥis: Dākṭar Sayyid Abdullāh ke taḥqīqī va tanqīdi maẓamīn* (Lahore: Majlis-i taraqqī-i Urdu, 1965), 42–95; Rajeev Kinra, "This Noble Science: Indo-Persian Comparative Philology, 1000–1800 C.E.," in Yigal Bronner, Whitney Cox and Lawrence McCrea (eds), *South Asian Texts in History: Critical Engagements with Sheldon Pollock*, (Ann Arbor, MI: Association for Asian Studies, 2011); and Kinra, "Make it Fresh."

11 The earliest Arab Muslim interest in the nature of the relation between signifier (*dall*) and signified (*madlūl*) was already premised on the conventional rather than natural origin of this relation. Debates over signification (*dalālat*) related to whether the agent who first laid down the convention in question was divine or human. Thus see "Al-Farabi, *The Book of Letters*," in Muhammad Ali Khalidi (ed.), *Medieval Islamic Philosophical Writings* (Cambridge: University of Cambridge Press, 2005), 5–7. This premise became an axiom of the Arabic language discipline called *'ilm al-waḍ'*, literally "the science of linguistic positing" but is better understood as being similar to the modern field of philosophy of language, that was taught in seminaries from around the fourteenth century wherever Arabic was studied in Islamic world. On this, see Bernard G. Weiss, "*'Ilm al-waḍ'*: An Introductory Account of a Later Muslim

Philological Science," *Arabica*, T. 34, Fasc. 3 (November 1987), 339–56. That this premise informed analyses of the Persian language and the pedagogy of Persian poetry even as late as the early 1800s is evident in Qatīl's (d. 1817) *Nahr al-faṣāḥat* (Stream of Linguistic Purity), written in North India to instruct a nobleman's son in Persian grammar and poetics and widely printed and published in the nineteenth century. Here is a passage from this text that draws without acknowledgement on Al-Khaṭīb al-Qazvīnī's *Talkhīs al-miftāḥ* and its related corpus of Arabic *balāghat*, attesting to the persistence of "linguistic coining" as a foundational pedagogical premise of Persian literary culture even in this late period: "Metaphorics [*bayān*], according to scholars of *balāghat*, designates the enunciation of a word that refers to a meaning other than the one stipulated by its coiner [*ghayr-i vaẕ'-i vāẕa'*]." In his exposition of the kinds of metaphor, Qatīl paraphrases in Persian passages on *waḍ'* that were current in Arabic language textbooks of the period and earlier such as Al-Khatīb al-Qazvīnī's *Talkhīs al-miftāḥ*. Mirzā Muḥammad Qatīl, *Nahr al-faṣāḥat* (Kānpūr: Munshī Naval Kishor, 1885), 36.

12 Weiss, " *'Ilm al-waḍ'*," 341.

13 For an account of diminishing state resources, the loss of central courtly authority and the formation of factions centered on powerful noblemen in this period, see Satish Chandra, *Parties and Politics at the Mughal Court: 1707–1740* (Delhi: Oxford University Press, 2012), 278–92.

14 Muḥammad 'Alī Ḥazīn, *Taẕkirat al-mu'āṣirīn* (Iṣfahān: kitāb-furūshī-i Ta'yīd, 1955), 92–95. And Muḥammad 'Alī Ḥazīn, "Risālah-i vāqi'āt-i Irān va Hind," in *Rasā'il-i Ḥazīn-i Lāhījī*, (Tehrān: Mirās-Maktūb, 1998), 228–31. For a summary and study of Ḥazīn's travel-account, see Muzaffar Alam and Sanjay Subrahmanyam, *Indo-Persian Travels in the Age of Discovery: 1400–1800*, (Cambridge: University of Cambridge, 2007), 226–42.

15 For an exposition of this rise of Braj to courtly prestige, see Allison Busch, "Hidden in Plain View: Braj Bhasha Poets at the Mughal Court," *Modern Asian Studies* 44: 2 (2010), 267–309.

16 Ārzū, *'Aṭiyah-i kubrā*, 51.

17 I am indebted for the formalization of this distinction to Gayatri Chakraborty Spivak, "Can the Subaltern Speak?," in Carry Nelson and Lawrence Grossberg (eds), *Marxism and the Interpretation of Culture* (London: Macmillan, 1988), 271–313. This essay distinguishes between representation as portrait and as proxy. Gadamer formulates the same distinction differently in his *Truth and Method*, citing Neo-Platonism and then Christian canon law as the *locus classicus* for the idea of representation as proxy. Hans-Georg Gadamer, *Truth and Method*, trans. Joel Weinsheimer and Donald G. Marshall (New York: Bloomsbury Academic, 2013), 135–44.

18 Ārzū, *'Aṭiyah-i kubrā*, 54–55.

19 Ārzū, *Muṯmir*, 68.

20 In his *Miftāḥ al-'ulūm*, completed in 1229, Al-Sakkākī glosses it as "the knowledge of signifying a single concept [*ma'nā*] in a variety of ways [...]." William Smyth, "The Making of a Textbook," *Studia Islamica* LXXVIII (1994), 110.

21 We find the Ghaznavid historian Bayhaqī (d. 1077) employing the kind of comparative topography Tarif Khalidi has discussed in the context of Mongol-period Arabic history-writing in his *Tārīkh-i Bayhaq* where he states that the people of each place are distinguished by excellence at a particular science: the people of India at astronomy, those of Arabia at poetry, those of Persia at kingship and those of China at "strange writing." Abū al-Ḥasan 'Alī ibn Zayd Bayhaqī, *Tārīkh-i Bayhaq* (Tehrān: chap-khānah-i Islāmiyyah, 1339/1960), 4. This association of a place's people with excellence at a discipline of knowledge within a system of disciplines shared by all the world's peoples was part of the pre-history of the kind of comparative topography and ethnography that flourished in Ārzū's milieu. For a discussion of such comparative topography in the context of Mongol-period or thirteenth-century Arabic

history-writing, see Tarif Khalidi, *Arabic Historical Thought in the Classical Period* (Cambridge: Cambridge University Press, 1992), 219–22.

22 Ārzū, *'Aṭiyah-i kubrā*, 65.

23 Bindrāban Dās Khvushgū, *Safīnah-i Khvushgū*, Staatsbibliothek, Berlin, Sprenger MS 330, Fl. 11v.

24 The most famous precedent to Ārzū's forays into Braj here and in his Braj to Persian dictionary, *Navādir al-alfāẓ* (Novel Words) that he created by emending 'Abdul Vāsi' Hānsvī's *Gharāyib al-lug͟hāt* (Strange Words), was Mirzā Khān's *Tuḥfat al-Hind* (Gift from/to India), composed around 1675 for the Emperor Aurangzeb's son, Muḥammad A'ẓam, as an exposition of Braj, its grammar and the related arts. A pervasive feature of this work and others like it in Persian is an analogization, taken to the smallest scale of analysis possible, of Braj-related phenomena and categories with already familiar Perso-Arabic ones. By adopting the fiction operative in the *Tuḥfat* and works like it of a reader who was literate only in Persian and its literary conventions, Ārzū was adopting an imperial and trans-local gaze precisely when such a gaze was in question in the political dispersal of Mughal authority in his time. Mirzā Khān lists the Bishnū Pad as the second of the eight kinds of musical composition he considers current among "the recent" musicians, also mentioning Sūr Dās as its inventor. Whether Ārzū knew the *Tuḥfat* directly or knew of the legends surrounding Sūr independently or both, what is pertinent is the ethnographic and comparative gaze available to Ārzū because of earlier Mughal Persian discourses on the local. Sirāj al-Dīn 'Alī Khān Ārzū, *Navādir al-alfāẓ* (Karachi: ATU, 1951). Mirzā Khān ibn Fakhr al-Dīn, *Tuḥfat al-Hind* (Tehrān: intishārāt-i Bunyād-i Farhang-i Irān, 1975).

25 Sirāj al-Dīn 'Ali Khān Ārzū, *Dād-i sukhan*, (Ravalpindi: markaz-i taḥqīqāt-i Fārsi-i Irān va Pākistan, 1974), 9–13.

26 Kinra, "This Noble Science," 363–64.

27 This is an internal quotation from al-Qazvīnī's *Talkhīs al-miftāḥ* in Herbjorn Jenssen, *The Subtleties and Secrets of the Arabic Language* (Bergen: Center for Middle Eastern and Islamic Studies, 1998), 35. Al-Qazvīnī's exposition of *balāghat* was the first to expound the discipline as a tripartite one composed of the sub-disciplines of metaphorics (*bayān*), syntax (*ma'ānī*) and tropology (*badī'*) and, from the sixteenth century onward, was the principle conduit for the transmission of early Arabic *balāghat* throughout the Islamicate world, including Mughal India. Smyth, "The Making of a Textbook," 99–115. I owe the translations "linguistic efficiency" and "linguistic purity" to this study by Jenssen.

28 Sirāj al-Dīn 'Alī Khān Ārzū, *Tanbīh al-ghāfilīn*, (Lahore: Punjab University, 1981), 139–40 (for an instance of criticism on grounds of outlandishness) and 141 (for Ārzū's charge of the "literary theft" of a topos from Sa'dī).

29 Among the eyewitness accounts of the welcome Delhi's ruling elites accorded Ḥazīn on his arrival and his subsequent prestige in the ruling circles of Delhi are Dargāh Qulī Khān, *Muraqqa'-i Dehlī* (Ḥyderābād: maṭbu'a Tāj press, 1973), 43–44; and Ḥusayn Dūst Sambhalī, *Taẕkirah-i Ḥusaynī*, (Lucknow: Munshī Naval Kishor, 1875), 106–09; and, in Lucknow, Mohan Lāl "Anīs," *Anīs al-aḥibbā: taẕkirah-i shu'arā-i Fārsī* (Patna: Khudā Bakhsh Oriental Public Library, 1996), 5–6.

30 Ghulām 'Alī Āzād Bilgrāmī, *K͟hazānah-i 'āmirah*, (Kānpūr: Munshī Naval Kishor, 1900), 196.

31 A fairly representative instance of Munīr's criticism is his observation of a distich's comparison and predication that "the dust of your fame's skirts" was not a formulation "anyone with an attention for detail had ever seen." 'Abul-Barakāt Munīr, *Kārnāmah* in *Kārnāmah, ta'līf-i 'Abul-Barakāt Munīr-i Lāhūrī va Sirāj-i Munīr, ta'līf-i Sirāj al-Dīn 'Alī Khān-i Ārzū* (Islāmābād: markaz-i taḥqīqāt-i Fārsī-i Irān va Pākistan, 1977), 11.

32 Ārzū, *Sirāj-i Munīr*, 33–36.

33 Ārzū, *Mawhibat-i 'uẓmā*, 96.

34 Ibid., 98.
35 Ārzū, *Musmir*, 80–3.
36 Ibid., 62.
37 Sirāj al-Dīn 'Alī Khān Ārzū, *Khiyāban sharḥ-i Gulistān-i Sa'dī*. And Ārzū, *Shigūfah-zār: Sharḥī bar Sharaf-nāmah-i Niẓāmī*.
38 Sirāj al-Dīn 'Alī Khān Ārzū, *Sharḥ-i qaṣāyid-i 'Urfī*, MS 1765, Salarjung Museum and Library, Hyderabad. Some of the other late seventeenth- and eighteenth-century littérateurs to comment on 'Urfī's panegyrics were the author of *Tuḥfat al-Hind*, Mirzā Khān ibn Fakhr al-Dīn, *Sharḥ-i qaṣāyid-i 'Urfī*, MS 1763, Salarjung Museum and Library, Hyderabad; Shaykh Rājū Sambhalī, *Kārnāmah-i Fayz*, MS 1764, Salarjung Museum and Library, Hyderabad; and Quṭb al-Dīn, *Sharḥ-i qaṣāyid-i Urfī*, MS 1766, Salarjung Museum and Library, Hyderabad.
39 Sirāj al-Dīn 'Alī Khān Ārzū, *Chirāgh-i hidāyat* (Bombay: 'Ali Bhai Ashraf and Company Private Limited, 1965).
40 Only one of Ārzū's seven *dīvān*s, four of which he wrote as *javāb*s or poetic responses to the *dīvān*s of four Speaking Anew poets, has been published. This is Sirāj al-Dīn 'Alī Khān Ārzū, *Dīvān-i Ārzū*, Sayyid Muḥammad Asghar (ed.), (Lucknow: Nu'mānī Printing Press, 2013). Ārzū composed this *Dīvān* around 1720 in competitive response to that of the Speaking Anew poet from Iran, Shafi'ā Asar (d. 1702), who never traveled to India but whose *Dīvān* was reportedly very popular there.
41 The "Pre-Temporally Eternal" (*azalī*) character of *ghazal* topoi may be illustrated by this distich by Ghanī Kashmīrī: "Meaning [*ma'nī*] can't be refractory under Ghanī's inner nature [or: "under a spiritually rich inner nature"]/He [i.e., God] handed him topoi [*mazmūn*] bound at Pre-Eternity [*rūz-i azal*]." Mullāh Tāhir Ghanī Kashmīrī, *Dīvān-i Ghanī* (Srinagar: Jammu and Kashmir Academy of Arts, Culture and Literature, 1984), 82. As such, the primordial or God-given topos was a literary analogue to the Pre-Eternal and therefore recurrent character of patterns or "myths" of spatial organization in Persian miniature painting. See Gregory Minissale, *Images of Thought: Visuality in Islamic India: 1550–1750* (Newcastle: Cambridge Scholars Press, 2006), 130–76.
42 Ārzū, *'Aṭiyah-i kubrā*, 67.
43 Ibid., 68.

Bibliography

Abdullāh, Sayyid. *Mabāḥis: Dākṭar Sayyid Abdullāh ke taḥqīqī va tanqīdi mazamīn*. Lahore: majlis-i taraqqī-i Urdu, 1965.

Abdullāh, Sayyid. "Dād-i sukhan," in *Fārsī zabān o adab: majmu'a-i maqālāt*. Lahore: majlis-i taraqqī-i adab, 1977, 142–47.

Alam, Muzaffar and Subrahmanyam, Sanjay. *Indo-Persian Travels in the Age of Discovery: 1400–1800*. Cambridge: University of Cambridge, 2007.

Anīs, Mohan Lāl. *Anīs al-aḥibbā: tazkirah-i shu'arā-i Fārsī*. Patnā: Khudā Bakhsh Oriental Public Library, 1996.

Ārzū, Sirāj al-Dīn 'Alī Khān. *Sharḥ-i qaṣā'id-i 'Urfī*, MS 1765, Salarjung Museum and Library, Hyderabad.

Ārzū, Sirāj al-Dīn 'Alī Khān. *Navādir al-alfāz*. Karachi: ATU, 1951.

Ārzū, Sirāj al-Dīn 'Alī Khān. *Chirāgh-i hidāyat*. Bombay: 'Ali Bhai Ashraf and Company Private Limited, 1965.

Ārzū, Sirāj al-Dīn 'Alī Khān. *Dād-i sukhan*. Ravalpindi: markaz-i taḥqīqāt-i Fārsi-i Irān va Pākistan, 1974.

Ārzū, Sirāj al-Dīn 'Alī Khān. *Tanbīh al-ghāfilīn*. Lahore: Punjab University, 1981.

Ārzū, Sirāj al-Dīn 'Alī Khān. *Muṣmir*. Karachi: Institute of Central and West Asian Studies, 1991.

Ārzū, Sirāj al-Dīn 'Alī Khān. *Khiyābān-i Gulistān: sharḥ-i Gulistān-i Sa'dī*. Islāmābād: markaz-i taḥqīqāt-i Fārsī-i Irān va Pākistān, shumārah-i radīf 154, 1994.

Ārzū, Sirāj al-Dīn 'Alī Khān. *'Aṭiyah-i kubrā va Mawhibat-i uẓmā*. Tehrān: Firdaws, 1381/2002.

Ārzū, Sirāj al-Dīn 'Alī Khān. *Shigūfah-zār: Sharḥī bar Sharaf-nāmah-i Niẓāmī*. Tehrān: Firdaws, 1392/2013.

Ārzū, Sirāj al-Dīn 'Alī Khān. *Dīvān-i Ārzū*, Sayyid Muḥammad Asghar (ed.). Lucknow: Nu'mānī Printing Press, 2013.

'Awfī, Muḥammad. *Lubāb al-Albāb*. Tehrān: Chāp-i ittiḥād, 1333/1955.

Āzād, Muḥammad Ḥusayn. *Āb-i ḥayāt: ya'nī mashāhīr shu'arā'yi Urdu ke savāniḥ umrī aur maẕkūr kī 'ahd ba 'ahd kī taraqqīyoṅ aur islāḥoṅ ka bayān*. Lahore: Naval Kishor, 1907.

Bahār, Lālā Tek Chand. *Bahār-i 'Ajam*. Lucknow: Munshī Naval Kishor Press, 1916.

Bayhaqī, Abū al-Ḥasan 'Alī ibn Zayd. *Tārīkh-i Bayhaq*. Tehrān: chāp-khānah-i Islāmiyyah, 1339/1960.

Bilgrāmī, Ghulām 'Alī Āzād. *Ḵẖazānah-i 'āmirah*. Kānpūr: Munshī Naval Kishor, 1900.

Busch, Allison. "Hidden in Plain View: Braj Bhasha Poets at the Mughal Court," *Modern Asian Studies* 44: 2 (2010), 267–309.

Chandra, Satish. *Parties and Politics at the Mughal Court: 1707–1740*. Delhi: Oxford University Press, 2002.

Dargāh Qulī Khān. *Muraqqa'-i Dehlī*. Ḥyderābād: Tāj Press, 1973.

Faruqi, Shamsur Rahman. "The Need for a New and Comprehensive Persian Literary Theory," at: www.columbia.edu/itc/mealac/pritchett/00fwp/srf/srf_persianlittheory_2009.pdf (accessed March 4, 2012).

al-Fārābī. *The Book of Letters*. Partial translation in Muhammad Ali Khalidi (ed.), *Medieval Islamic Philosophical Writings*. Cambridge: University of Cambridge Press, 2005.

Fenech, Louis. E. *The Sikh Zafar-namah of Guru Gobind Singh: a Discursive Blade in the Heart of the Mughal Empire*. New York: Oxford University Press, 2013.

Gadamer, Hans-Georg. *Truth and Method*, trans. Joel Weinsheimer and Donald G. Marshall. New York: Bloomsbury Academic, 2013.

Ghanī Kashmīrī, Mullāh Tāhir. *Dīvān-i Ghanī*. Srinagar: Jammu and Kashmir Academy of Arts, Culture and Languages, 1984.

Ḥazīn, Muḥammad 'Alī. *Taẕkirat al-mu'āṣirīn*. Iṣfahān: kitāb-furūshī-i Ta'yīd, 1955.

Ḥazīn, Muḥammad 'Alī "Risālah-i vāqi'āt-i Irān va Hind," in *Rasā'il-i Ḥazīn-i Lāhījī*, Tehrān: Mirās-Maktūb, 1998.

Jenssen, Herbjorn. *The Subtleties and Secrets of the Arabic Language*. Bergen: Center for Middle Eastern and Islamic Studies, 1998.

Khalidi, Tarif. *Arabic Historical Thought in the Classical Period*. Cambridge: Cambridge University Press, 1992.

Khātūn, Rehāna. *Aḥvāl o āsār-i Sirāj al-Dīn 'Alī Ḵẖān-i Ārzū*. Delhi: Indo-Persian Society, 1987.

Khvushgū, Bindrāban Dās. *Safīnah-i Khvushgū*. Staatsbibliothek, Berlin, Sprenger MS 330.

Kinra, Rajeev. "Make it Fresh: Time, Tradition and Indo-Persian Literary Modernity," in Anne C. Murphy (ed.), *Time, History, and the Religious Imaginary in South Asia* (New York: Routledge, 2011)

Kinra, Rajeev. "This Noble Science: Indo-Persian Comparative Philology, 1000–1800 C.E.,"

in Yigal Bronner, Whitney Cox and Lawrence McCrea (eds), *South Asian texts in history: Critical Engagements with Sheldon Pollock*. Ann Arbor, MI: Association for Asian Studies, 2011.
Losensky, Paul E. *Welcoming Fighani: Imitation and Poetic Individuality in the Safavid-Mughal Ghazal.* Costa Mesa, CA: Mazda Publishers, 1998.
Minissale, Gregory. *Images of Thought: Visuality in Islamic India: 1550–1750.* Newcastle: Cambridge Scholars Press, 2006.
Mīrzā Khān ibn Fakhr al-Dīn. *Sharḥ-i qaṣā'id-i 'Urfī,* MS 1763, Salarjung Museum and Library, Hyderabad, India.
Mīrzā Khān ibn Fakhr al-Dīn. *Tuḥfat al-Hind.* Tehrān: intishārāt-i bunyād-i farhang-i Irān, 1975.
Munīr Lāhūrī. 'Abul-Barakāt. *Kārnāmah* in *Kārnāmah, ta'līf-i 'Abul-Barakāt Munīr-i Lāhūrī va Sirāj-i Munīr, ta'līf-i Sirāj al-Dīn 'Alī Khān-i Ārzū.* Islāmābād: markaz-i taḥqīqāt-i Fārsī-i Irān va Pākistan, 1977.
Qatīl, Mīrzā Muḥammad. *Nahr al-faṣāḥat.* Kānpūr: Munshī Naval Kishor, 1885.
Quṭb al-Dīn. *Sharḥ-i qaṣā'id-i Urfī,* MS 1766, Salarjung Museum and Library, Hyderabad.
Rahimpoor, Mehdi. "Sayrī dar aḥvāl u ās̱ār-i Sirāj al-Dīn 'Alī Khān Ārzū-i Akbarābādī," *Āyinah-i mirās* 1: 1 (Spring 2008), 289–318.
Rahimpoor, Mehdi. "'Aṭiyah-i kubrā va Mawhibat-i uẓmā," *Āyinah-i Mirās* 5: 4 (Winter 2008), 334–50.
Rahimpoor, Mehdi. "Naẓariyah-i daryāft: az Sirāj al-Din 'Ali Khān Ārzū-i Akbarābādī tā Hans Robert Jauss-i Ālmānī," *Āyinah-i mirās* 44 (Spring–Summer 2009), 90–109.
Sambhalī, Ḥusayn Dūst. *Taẕkirah-i Ḥusaynī.* Lucknow: Munshī Naval Kishor, 1875.
Sambhalī, Shaykh Rājū. *Kārnāma-i fayz̤,* MS 1764, Salarjung Museum and Library, Hyderabad.
Sheikh Mushriffudin Sa'dī of Shiraz, *The Gulistān (Rose Garden) of Sa'di.* trans. Wheeler M. Thackston. Bethseda, MD: Ibex Publishers, 2008.
Shamisa, Sīrus (ed.). "Introduction," in Sirāj al-Dīn 'Alī Khān Ārzū, *'Aṭiyah-i kubrā va Mawhibat-i 'uẓmā.* Tehrān: Firdaws, 1381/2003).
Smyth, William. "The Making of a Textbook." *Studia Islamica* LXXVIII (1994), 99–116.
Spivak, Gayatri Chakraborty. "Can the Subaltern Speak?," in Carry Nelson and Lawrence Grossberg (eds), *Marxism and the Interpretation of Culture.* London: Macmillan, 1988, 271–313.
Tavakoli-Targhi, Mohamad. *Refashioning Iran: Orientalism, Occidentalism and Historiography.* Basingstoke: Palgrave-Macmillan, 2001.
Weiss, Bernard G. " *'Ilm al-waḍ'*: An Introductory Account of a Later Muslim Philological Science." *Arabica,* T. 34, Fasc. 3, (November 1987), 339–56.

5 Khvushgū's dream of Ḥāfiẓ

Building an ark with Ārzū and Bīdil

ṣayqal-gar-i āyinah-i tajdīd qadīm ast
natavān ba naw'ī ghāfil az īn sāz-i kuhan raft[1]

The burnisher of renewal's mirror is the primordial.
No moving to newness heedless of this ancient lute.
('Abd al-Qādir Khān "Bīdil")

We cannot know his legendary head
with eyes like ripening fruit.
(Rainer Maria Rilke, from "Archaic Torso of Apollo," 1907)[2]

When, sometime during the tumultuous years between 1724 and 1735 in Delhi, the Persian-language littérateur Bindrāban Dās "Khvushgū" composed most of his *tazkirah* or biographical compendium of Persian-language poets, *Safīnah-i Khvushgū* ("Khvushgū's Ark" or "Khvushgū's Notebook of Poems" or, punning on his own pen-name, "The Well-Spoken Notebook/Ark of Poems"), he decided to assign three separate volumes respectively to the old, intermediate and recent poets and further subdivided each volume into the old, intermediate and recent, the recent masters of the last volume being his contemporaries.[3] This was a tripartite chronological schema that was conventional in Persian literary history and that he therefore inherited from certain earlier biographical compendia. Into the first volume which was devoted to the old masters he inserted, unsurprisingly, a notice on Ḥāfiẓ (d. 1390, Shiraz), canonized in Khvushgū's time as in ours as the greatest master of the classical *ghazal*. However, in a digression characteristic of eighteenth-century biographical compendia, he gave a part of this notice to reflections apparently only tangential to a biography of Ḥāfiẓ but bespeaking his own investment in the questions they were responding to. At the center of these digressive reflections was his childhood dream vision of Ḥāfiẓ. This chapter reads Khvushgū's dream of Ḥāfiẓ as a manifold response to three analytically distinct needs that may be formulated in terms of the following questions: what were the social functions of Khvushgū's memory of his vision of the poet when he was twelve years old? What relations did this dream vision bear to his multiply periodized temporality in the *Safīnah* of Persian literary history? And how were both these questions co-implicated in the question of his relations with Sirāj al-Dīn 'Alī Khān "Ārzū" (d. 1756) and 'Abd al-Qādir Khān "Bīdil" (d. 1720), his two most revered teachers and among the greatest Persian littérateurs of the age? Rather than answering these questions by turn, this chapter weaves together its responses to them in reflecting on distinct aspects of Khvushgū's dream.

But first, here is Khvushgū's account of his dream of Ḥāfiẓ:

> My father too reposed great belief [*i'tiqād*] in the Janāb-i Khwājah [his Excellency the Master, i.e., Ḥāfiẓ]. When he was pleasurably attached to the world he distributed alms every Friday night for the Khwājah's soul and since this humble writer Khvushgū, too, had had this belief tested by his father, he reposed spiritual belief in that Master from the age of twelve.[4]

Khvushgū then describes how, when his father was employed as the Inspector of Staff (*mushrif-i aḥshām*) in the imperial fort at Ajmer, he:

> too accompanied him like a shadow. I was copying the Master's Dīvān [i.e., collection of poems] and presenting it in the service of a scholar named Muḥammad Fāẓil and had heard from a Gnostic dervish that if someone wished for something he should, with cleanliness of appearance and purity of inwardness, place his [i.e., Ḥāfiẓ's] *Dīvān* under his pillow and sleep and, that in the morning he should read a few of his *ghazal*s with sound intention [*ba nīyat-i durust*] and, finishing them in forty days, will surely attain his wish. Since, at the time, I ardently desired poetry and to be a poet [*ārzū-yi shi'r u shā'irī dāsht*], I placed the *Dīvān* under my head and slept on the floor. By accident, the thirty-first night was forgotten. I then resumed the practice anew for the second time. This time, during the fortieth night, an image [*khiyāl*] took shape. In a dreaming state I saw that I was passing through a very prosperous and fine city and, seeing a beautiful little garden on the city's edge, entered it and asked the gardener the name of that city and place. He said, 'Shiraz and this little garden is Khāk-i Musallā [i.e., taken by convention to be chronogram for Ḥāfiẓ's death and here the name of his mausoleum]. And this grave is that of the Master of Shīraz.' In complete devotion, I rubbed my head in its pure dust and, with an attentive heart, imagined [*taṣavvur*] his auspicious face. All at once his grave split open. A luminous figure with God-given beauty and natural perfection emerged. It was as if that figure had dipped itself into a pool of the purest wine for wine-drops dripped from its pores like sweat. He picked up his own *Dīvān*. He sat on his own tombstone and, raising my head from the dust, kissed my forehead. He handed me the volume and said these words: "O nephew, read aloud!"[*ai barādar-zādah bar khwān*] and began to teach me from the beginning, commenting [*sharḥ mīdād*] for one pass of the night on the meaning of the first hemistich which is "*Alāyā ayyū-hā al-sāqī adir kā'san wa nāwil-hā*" ["O Cup-bearer, fill the cups and hand them around"].

When he reached its second hemistich, my eyes woke from that dream that was, in truth, a wakefulness of the heart.[5] When I tried, on recovering, to recall all those meanings that I had been instructed in I found them altogether erased from my mind's page. God be praised, if I had remembered them so much might have happened! The flavor of that tasting has overcome this indifferent time. That morning, a Mongol named Mirzā Muḥammad Kāẓim who planned to set out for Shiraz appeared before my father for permission to leave. At once, taking *'Ayshī* [i.e., Voluptuary] for a pen-name, I composed a quatrain [*rubā'ī*] in praise of the Khwājah, wrote it down and entrusted it to that Mongol, saying "Send the Khwājah my greetings and present him with this quatrain":

Khwājah Ḥāfiẓ who is in Shiraz
Is both a spiritual adept and a knower of secrets.
'Ayshī, hoping to become a poet,
Presents his lofty threshold with supplications.[6]

Since I consider this quatrain the founding pillars of my balanced poetic nature I permit my quill to set it down. I hope that generous and just readers will overlook its immaturity and will consider it an outcome of that Master's spiritual bounty. Thenceforth, meaning's doors opened before me and the relation of disciple and nephew with the Khwājah's conquering soul stood verified".[7]

In its broadest aspects this dream of a master poet's bestowal of hermeneutic power and its concomitant of authorial authority on a later one, a bestowal that is then confirmed and thus proves to have been a "veridical dream" (*al-rūyā al-ṣādiqa*), conforms to the vast corpus of Islamic dream discourses that had developed over the preceding millennium. Sara Sviri captures these broad aspects thus:

"The veridical dream is one forty-sixth of prophecy," states an Islamic tradition attributed to the Prophet Muḥammad. The statement implies that while prophecy has ceased, Muḥammad being the Seal of the Prophets, messages of divine origin can still be communicated through dreams, albeit on a smaller scale than prophecy. This possibility opened up important avenues for both mysticism and philosophy in medieval Islam. For Sufism it meant that divine inspiration (*ilhām*) could be granted to the Friends of God (*awliyā' allāh*), the holy men of Islam. For philosophy it meant that in a state of suspension from the outer senses, a state which normally occurs during sleep or in deep contemplation, the human intellect could become united with the Universal (or Active) Intellect and thus have access to transcendental truths. It was universally accepted that those who had cultivated their inner faculties and insights could decipher the encoded messages of their own dreams as well as those of others.[8]

Already, then, by his very citation of the veridical dream Khvushgū invokes prophetic authority in his own favor. This prophetic genealogy also already – or proleptically – authorizes his otherwise scrupulously linear chronology and carefully dated history by reference to non-linear and mystical intimacy with a past source of authority – a source connotatively divine by reference to the Prophet and denotatively human by reference to Ḥāfiẓ. This methodological contrast is worth emphasizing. Throughout the *Safīnah* Khvushgū speaks in what is manifestly the voice of a historian in the tradition of the *taẕkirah* or Persian biographical compendium.[9] He thus lets his archives variously intrude on his narratives, opening his history by listing the roughly fifty biographical compendia he will draw from and consistently evincing empirical care for the chronological probability of claims made in these biographical compendia. And yet, these protocols of scholarly verification that seem almost modern to us today come to be employed only because Khvushgū had ascetically "cultivated his inner faculties" to briefly become contemporary with and attain the blessing of a past master poet. Indeed, he undertakes his history for four stated purposes: to redeem himself on the Day of Judgment by the favor he will have found among poet-scholars; to allow his readers the pleasures of ethical self-formation by poets' "excellent words and subtleties [that] do not tire the soul and that amplify the pleasures of taste"; to give "new kindergarten students" a self-sufficient introduction to what they will need to become writers themselves; and to be useful to everyone – "emperor to beggar" – with "a poetry-comprehending temperament."[10] Underlying his strictly periodized and empirically verified organization of time, then, is an eschatologically motivated concern with the pleasurable ethical formation and transformation of selves. That the *Safīnah* is thus not, despite superficial methodological resemblances, a modern work of history is obvious. What precise articulations, then, of the discourse of history with the subjectivity of the historian are we in the presence of here? What conception of reason and rational procedure joined the rhetoric of history to the historian such that the sensuality of ascetically achieved veridical dreams was continuous with an empirically verified chronology? In what follows I will attempt to frame Khvushgū's dream in a variety of contexts to explicate these articulations between historian and history. But my choice of this dream text will also lead my commentary to a point where the historicism of my own hermeneutics breaks down, exposing the limits of such contextualism.

Khvushgū's dream needs to be read, not only with attention to the particular uses it makes of such general philosophical and prophetological precedents as Sara Sviri summarizes, but also with attention to its location in its narrative frame. And this narrative location must condition our interpretations not only of the dream but equally of the surrounding frame. The dream is immediately preceded by an anecdote of his father's divination with the *Dīvān* of Ḥāfiẓ of the malicious intentions of a man who casts doubt on the proclaimed powers of such divination. It thus opens by setting his knowledge and esteem of Ḥāfiẓ within the filial context in which he came to take this attitude. Khvushgū's father served, as Khvushgū indicates in the anecdote, in the emperor Aurangzeb's army. More specifically, he served Navāb Jahān Zīb Bānū Begam, sister of the prince Dārā Shukūh. Such reverence for Ḥāfiẓ among members of the Mughal service elites was thus of a piece with long familial acculturation in the courtly and Sufi ethos of Persian.[11] Furthermore, this patrilineally transmitted acculturation was in keeping with the importance accorded in traditional Persian literature and literary culture to father–son relations.[12] Hence the succession of male teachers in Khvushgū's anecdote: Khvushgū's father who Khvushgū followed "like a shadow" is succeeded in narrative order by another male teacher, a scholar named Muḥammad Fāẓil who, in turn, is followed by Ḥāfiẓ who calls Khvushgū his "nephew," an appellation that literally translates as "brother's son" (*barādar-zādah*). Ḥāfiẓ thus comes to take his place in a series of father-substitutes.

And yet, the dream encounter with him stops short of a perfect intimacy for Khvushgū fails to remember Ḥāfiẓ's exposition of the famous opening distich of his *Dīvān*. Why, at what is arguably the most intense moment of his narrative of an authorizing encounter with the master poet, would Khvushgū admit to having forgotten what Ḥāfiẓ taught him? Here is my proposed explanation: by admitting to having forgotten what the master poet taught him Khvushgū was remembering a certain vision of the origin of the archive of Persian poetry in the ruin of Islamic sovereignty. But this raises more questions than it answers: what precisely was he remembering in remembering the ruinous origins of the archive of Persian poetry? And what resemblances between the historical contexts in which he wrote and in which the genealogy he invokes was first formulated justify such a cross-historical comparison?

Let me begin by answering the first of these questions. This lapse in memory was an iteration of a *historical fiction* familiar to Khvushgū from the earliest biographical compendium of Persian-language poets, Muḥammad 'Awfī's *Lubāb al-albāb* (The Piths of Intellects), completed in 1221 in a Ghurid vassal court in Sind.[13] In the prefatory chapters of his biographical compendium 'Awfī recounts a report of the earliest poetry ever uttered. In this report Adam exclaims the first "metrical utterance" (*kalām-i mawzūn*) in mourning for the murder of his son Abel by Cain. This murder, "the first blood to have been spilt unjustly upon the earth," rends apart a world that had fused together the good and the beautiful, the ethical and the aesthetic. The earliest poetry is "a metrical utterance" because it simulates a now lost ethico-aesthetic cosmic order in beautifully ordered language and serves as a reminder of the sundering apart of the good and the beautiful. Poetry thus emerges, at least in this historical fiction of long currency in the Persian literary tradition, as an anamnesic linguistic response to the origin of evil.

But to grasp the sense in which this fiction is a historical one – in the sense that it bespeaks a certain historical truth – we need to attend to 'Awfī's historically local motivations for employing this historical fiction when and where he did. This brings me to the second of the questions I posed above. As I have argued elsewhere, 'Awfī, by this historical fiction prefacing the earliest of biographical compendium of Persian-language poets, offered a normative account of an archive as a lack-ridden assemblage of documents marshaled under existential threat to government.[14] That is, he – a courtly intellectual of Islamic Central Asia – assembled his archive of Persian-language poetry because he perceived a threat from invading Mongols to the survival of the Islamic states that had patronized such poetry. In marshalling whatever he could salvage of the Persian poetry patronized by dynasties of the eastern Islamic world he thus projected a textual image of Islamic political power precisely when such sovereign political power was being lost.[15] And by his fiction of poetry's origin in primeval Adamic mourning 'Awfī inscribed such loss into his archive as foundational for all archives. This is the sense in which it was – and came to be interpreted as – normative. An archive, thus conceived at the inauguration of the tradition of the Persian biographical compendium, was a testament to the *loss* of textual memory.

Khvushgū adapts 'Awfī's fiction of Adam's mourning in verse in order to demonstrate the temporal continuity of his present with an Adamic origin as well as to authorize the polylingualism of his literary milieu by saying:

> This pain and sorrow that, in poetry, gives pleasure is an effect of this – that the first poetry was uttered in sorrow and mourning. Thus is it shown that this irreplaceable bounty has remained amidst us from Adam's age to this moment. Each group [*firqah*] composed in its own language and uttered poetry in it and, in keeping with the sacred text "We have never sent a messenger but in the language of his people" [Qur'ān 14:4], the Prophets, too, spoke in their own languages.[16]

Khvushgū's iteration of this fiction of epistemic finitude serves comparable ends for he, too, like 'Awfī, had fled urban upheaval, in this case the invasion of Delhi in 1739 by Nādir Shāh of Iran, an invasion that kept him until around 1742/43 from completing his biographical compendium.[17]

Underscoring this fiction of descent from Adamic mourning is Khvushgū's allusion to another primeval rupture in prophetic history by his pun in his title on the word *safīnah* that also means "ark." This allusion to Noah's Ark metaphorically characterizes his biographical compendium as the precious remains of the Persian poetic archive salvaged from a world-submerging flood. It is a conceit that would be developed into an extended historical fiction in the preface to the second volume (*daftar*) of his *Safīnah.*[18] However, it was not Khvushgū who authored this preface but a littérateur writing around 1831 in Qājār Iran called Ḥaqīr Durrī Shūshtarī. It is worth pausing to reflect on Ḥaqīr Durrī's preface to the second volume as it discloses how Khvushgū's conception of the Persian poetic archive appealed to an early Qājār littérateur.[19]

Ḥaqīr Durrī exploits the resonance of the title's reference to Noah's Ark with a *Ḥadīs̱* especially popular in Shi'i traditions, quoting the *Ḥadīs̱*: "My family is like Noah's ark. Whoever climbs onto it will be saved and whoever abandons it will be drowned." He also quotes Ḥāfiẓ: "Ḥāfiẓ don't let go of the company of Noah's ark/Or else this flood of calamities will destroy your foundations."[20] In what follows he recounts that when, in a certain year, the river in the south-western Iranian city of Shushtar rose in flood "the nomads of the Bakhtiyari mountains" (*khaymah-nishīnān-i jibāl-i bakhtiyārī*) withdrew to the heights of the Salāsil fortress, watching the flood destroy everything in its path. The choice of Shushtar is itself continuous with the story of Noah. The famous Shi'i jurist and scholar Qāẕī Nūrullāh Shūshtarī who, in 1584 or 1586, moved from Safavid Iran to Mughal India and joined the service of the emperor Akbar, quoted a report that said, "The first city that Noah founded after the flood was Shūsh and Shūshtar."[21] This report may well have been familiar to Khvushgū as it probably was to Ḥaqīr Durrī of Shushtar. Ḥaqīr Durrī then recounts how one of the nomads retrieved a book floating on a pile of furniture from the flood. The nomad placed the book, which had lost its binding as well as beginning and end, in the desert sun to dry. Hardly suspecting the worth of his discovery, he put it away in a corner at home where his children and relatives, frequently needing scrap paper, would tear away pages from it. A year later, finding an audience with an eminent visiting scholar who had been appointed to administer the politically refractory region, he took the book along with him by way of a gift. The scholar recognized the value of the manuscript that was titled *Safīnah-i Khvushgū* and appeared to be the second volume of a three-volume work. He then appointed Ḥaqīr Durrī to the task of editing it and preparing a table of contents (*fihrist*) for it. This is the form in which the text has come down to us today.

This historical fiction curiously echoes Khvushgū's own anxious political investment in the archive of Persian poetry. Ārzū and his circle of Delhi-based Mughal literati – Khvushgū among them – were responding both to the fall of Safavid state in 1736 and to the dispersal of Mughal Delhi's political authority discussed earlier. They did so by variously trying to marshal Delhi-centric masculine literary solidarities and by projecting Delhi as the true "testing-ground of [Persian] poetry" (*mi'yār-gāh-i sukhan*).[22] Ārzū's biographical compendium, completed in 1750 and titled *Majma' al-nafāyis* (Assembly of Rarities), thus lists a few women poets only to denigrate them and attempts to marshal a trans-regional Safavid-Mughal poetic solidarity of elite and mostly Muslim male poets. The archive resulting from this larger project to shore up Mughal Delhi's cultural prestige, an archive of which Khvushgū's *Safīnah* was a part, appealed at more than one level to a littérateur like Ḥaqīr Durrī. The little we can make out of Durrī's social location from his preface points to his affiliation with the Qājār state. What is noteworthy in Durrī's historical fiction is that it is when a Qājār nobleman arrives to quell a rebellion in the region of Shushtar that Khvushgū's manuscript, until then ruined both by the flood and nomads presented as culturally illiterate, re-enters worthy hands. The worthiness of this readership rests in its entwined virtues, replicating Ārzū and Khvushgū's own, of pretensions to political power and poetic-scholarly cultivation. The entwinement of Durrī's poetic-philological project with his loyalties to the Qājār state thus replicates Khvushgū's literary service to the Mughal state. At various points in the second volume Durrī takes credit for philological and biographical supplements or qualifications he provides to Khvushgū's text, for the list of contents he prepares for it and for his poetic judgments contrary to or at variance with Khvushgū's. What such literary, political and philological esteem accorded to Khvushgū's manuscript in early Qājār Iran makes clear is that Durrī and his Qājār patrons shared Khvushgū's poetics even if they did not share his Delhi-centric and Ārzū-centric politics. That is, their attention to Khvushgū's text was justified by what they shared with him: a poetic heritage and its courtly conception of the Persian poetic archive as salvaged from the apocalyptic ruin of Islamic sovereignty. They also concurred with one of his aims that was aligned with Ārzū's, namely to marshal a trans-regional Mughal-Safavid poetic solidarity. It was these concurrences that led Ḥaqīr Durrī to work up Khvushgū's metaphor of Noah's Ark into what I have termed a historical fiction.

To return to our discussion of Khvushgū, he was not alone in his late Mughal milieu in his historical analogization of eighteenth-century North India with the Mongol invasions of thirteenth-century Iran that had long been the paradigmatic memory of the destruction of Islamic sovereignty. More generally, explaining what a Persianate ruling elite considered to be a major political event by analogy with earlier such events had, after all, been an established historiographical practice. On conquering Delhi, Babur had compared his conquest of Hindūstān with those of earlier Muslim rulers. In Khvushgū's own milieu Ānand Rām Mukhliṣ (d. 1750), who was also a student of Ārzū's and Bīdil's, had described the sacking of Delhi by Nādir Shāh of Iran by comparing it with Timur's sack of the city in 1382–83.[23] But the most conspicuous instance in Khvushgū's Delhi of such cross-historical analogization was the sheer number of late Mughal commentaries on Sa'dī's *Gulistān* (The Rose Garden), the most exemplary formulation of *akhlāq* or worldly ethics in the Persianate world. Sa'dī completed the *Gulistān* in Shiraz in 1258, the very year of the Mongol sacking of the Abbasid capital of Baghdad, and dedicated it to his Ilkhanid Mongol patron. By its compilations and framings of diverse anecdotes the *Gulistān* prescribed an ethics of cautious moderation and worldly wisdom in the immediate wake of the urban upheaval wrought by the Mongols. Though it came in subsequent centuries to be studied as a model of Persian prose in schools throughout the Persianate world it was mainly from the late seventeenth century onward – as central Mughal courtly authority came to be dispersed – that it came to accrue commentaries.[24] An analytical exposition here of even one of the approximately seventeen commentaries that came to be published by Munshī Naval Kishor, the largest nineteenth-century publisher of Persian, Urdu and Hindī books, would swell into the sort of digression only allowed authors of Mughal biographical compendia.[25] I will therefore confine myself to observing that broad as well as individually specific consideration of the circumstances under which such commentaries were composed discloses various appropriations of Sa'dī's ethico-poetic response to urban strife for a variety of purposes that explicitly or implicitly assume a historical analogy between Sa'dī's milieu and the late Mughal one.[26]

Khvushgū partook in his way of this widespread tendency to cross-historical comparison. His own experience of the Iranian, Maratha and Afghan invasions that disrupted urban life in late Mughal North India and of the attendant dispersion of central Mughal political authority into provincial fiefdoms led him to invoke the memory of the thirteenth-century Mongol invasion of Iran.[27] He did so by citing 'Awfī's historical fiction of poetry's origin in Adam's mourning for a loss of world order. This invocation took the subtle form of declaring that he had forgotten what Ḥāfiẓ had taught him. It also took the more overt form of insisting, against the suggestion of some of his friends that he simply list all the notices on poets alphabetically by their pen-names, that his *Safīnah* "observe periodicity" (*ri'āyat-i dawr*) by distributing poets into the ramified tripartite schema in which it has come down to us today. By his admission of a lapse of memory linking him to past authority and by this tripartition of his biographical compendium Khvushgū signaled his concurrence with one of the central theses that his teacher Ārzū had sought to demonstrate: namely that time, as it passed, made the poets of the past seem stranger to a reader by degrees and correspondingly increased the reader's need for lexicographic and commentarial supplements. Indeed Ārzū himself had inserted such philological supplements – notes called "subtle points" (*laṭīfah*) by Khvushgū – into various parts of Khvushgū's *Safīnah* in addition to having authored various other dictionaries and commentaries.

The experience of social upheaval among Delhi's Persianate elite, then, was encoded in the temporality of estrangement in which they read the old masters and with their philological efforts to cope with such estrangement. Even the most intimately read old masters grew hermeneutically alien. And Khvushgū's dream was an instance of such simultaneously intimate and alienated reading. He writes wistfully of Ḥāfiẓ's teachings: "God be praised, if I had remembered them so much might have happened!" Perfect recall would permit a perfect intimacy or contemporaneity with the old masters. But such fathers and forefathers inhabit a time of plenitude not available to their sons except in such short-lived and ascetically achieved dreaming transports that are, "in truth, a wakefulness of the heart." Such hard-won and meager habitation of their superior time allows Khvushgū to become a poet who ventriloquizes, however defectively, for Ḥāfiẓ's "spiritual bounty." In this sense this dream-vision also sets into the midst of the first volume (*daftar*) of Khvushgū's three-volume history of Persian poetry a figural and anticipatory formulation of the poetic novelty of his own time as one in which littérateurs fashioned a fresh poetry by their asymptotic struggle to recover a lost intimacy with old masters, a time when, as Ārzū says in his preface to the *Safīnah-i Khvushgū*, "the days of Speaking Anew [*tāzah-gūyī*] began to put out feathers."[28] This time that is the focus of the third part of the third volume of the *Safīnah* – typically singled out by scholars today for its first-hand social-biographical information on Khvushgū's contemporaries – thus proleptically appears first in a fleeting dream.

If Khvushgū was adapting long established literary precedents in his valorization of his poetic paternity and invocation of the violence and forgetting that inaugurates poetic archives he was also in line with precedents in his very encounter with Ḥāfiẓ. Already by 1436 when Āẕarī Ṭūsī called Ḥāfiẓ "the tongue of the Invisible" (*lisān al-ghayb*), a titular recognition of the poet's esoteric powers that would be more influentially repeated by the Sufi poet 'Abd al-Raḥmān Jāmī in 1478, Persian littérateurs throughout Iran and India had begun to claim such visionary encounters with the master.[29] Such claims had generated a corpus of historical fictions that came to be marshaled for purposes of literary-spiritual authorization and authority. Among the earliest of such authorizing historical fictions, for example, was one that Khvushgū cites – that of the North Indian Chishti Sufi Ashraf Jahāngir Simnānī (d. 1405) who was a contemporary of Ḥāfiẓ and who, his sixteenth-century hagiographers claimed, had traveled to Shiraz and met Ḥāfiẓ. This fiction formed an element in the fund of fictions relating such early Persian masters of undisputed canonicity as Ḥāfiẓ, Sa'dī and Firdawsī to India and that Persian littérateurs located in India had variously invoked to authorize themselves and the geographical locations of their circles.[30] I will later say more on why they would have wanted to authorize their locations.

Let us note for now that the visionary encounter with Ḥāfiẓ was distinguished from encounters with other old masters by its hermeneutic mode. Ḥāfiẓ was encountered in or through *readings* of his *Dīvān*. The tradition of *fāl-i ḥāfiẓ* or "divination by (the *Dīvān* of) Ḥāfiẓ," apparently current by at least 1465 though most widespread in the sixteenth and seventeenth centuries, had established the power of Ḥāfiẓ's verses throughout the Persophone world to predict an event or disclose a hidden state of affairs.[31] This had led, in a development with parallels across Sufi traditions, to his textualization. That is, Ḥāfiẓ had *become* his very words. This is why Khvushgū's description of him – an apparition that "had dipped itself into a pool of the purest wine for wine-drops dripped from its pores like sweat" – conforms to Ḥāfiẓ's own descriptions of the *rind*, an antinomian character type in his *ghazal*s who might be glossed as a voluptuary who breaks rules of social propriety and ritual purity to indulge himself in the symbolic wine of Gnostic intimacy with the divine Real. This is also why Khvushgū recognizes the poet's city and mausoleum not by visual cues but by verbal ones – by the gardener's phrase *khāk-i musallā* that is both a place in one of his famous *ghazal*s and interpreted as a chronogram commemorating the poet's death.[32]

If Ḥāfiẓ was the paradigmatic antinomian and was also his own poetry, it followed that his poetry was itself antinomian. This is one of the reasons why it was characterized by a hermeneutic exceptionalism whereby Ḥāfiẓ ecstatically exceeded periodization or temporal locality as well as all canonizing hierarchizations. Hence Khvushgū's remark on the correlation between Ḥāfiẓ's unique style and the unique pleasure it yields, a remark that overturns even the stylistic novelty for which the poet Ṣā'ib Tabrīzī (d. 1676) was celebrated and imitated among practitioners of Speaking Anew:

> His [i.e., Ḥāfiẓ's] poems have the flavor of greatness so that after studying a few of his ghazals reading another's poems never yields as much pleasure and seems colorless. Till now, nobody has managed to attain to the

> Khwājah's distinct style [*ṭarz-i khāṣ*] to the point that even a master like Mirzā Ṣā'ib has not managed to achieve a familiarity with it as is clear and manifest from the ghazals he wrote in competitive imitation [*javāb*] of the Khwājah.[33]

Khvushgū periodizes literary history on the basis of the distinctiveness of the pleasure each poet affords the reader and even Ṣā'ib, who was exalted by Speaking Anew littérateurs for having afforded them a historically novel poetic pleasure, fails to equal the singular pleasure of Ḥāfiẓ.[34]

This is the point at which to elucidate Khvushgū's other debts to his two major teachers, Ārzū and Bīdil. To Ārzū he owed not only the historicist hermeneutics of estrangement discussed previously but also a vision of Delhi as the true bearer of symbolic capital. To Bīdil and the tradition of Sufi hagiography, he owed his immediate and most authoritative model for the ascetically achieved mystical reversal of the linearity of literary history.[35] I will address his debts to Ārzū first. In the late Mughal milieu that was no longer centered on the Mughal court and its prestigiously authorized *taẕkirah* canons, Persian literary canonicity was renegotiable and came to be widely and diversely disputed. Each respected master poet made his distinct bid for a canon that authorized him in his circle of student-disciples.[36] It was in the context of such literary politics that the Iranian émigré intellectual and poet, Shaykh Muḥammad 'Alī Ḥazīn (d. 1766), had vented his resentment at his exile in India from privilege in Safavid ruling circles in Iran – a court formally deposed by Nādir Shāh in 1736 – by scorning India's Persian literary culture and the ethical dispositions of its people in his conversations, his chronicle and in his widely read biographical compendium that almost exclusively valorized poetry by Shi'i individuals of the Twelver sect from his home city of Isfahan, *Taẕkirat al-mu'āṣirīn* (*Taẕkirah* of Contemporaries).[37] Ḥazīn's politico-ethnically motivated attack had provoked Ārzū among others to defend India – and Delhi in particular – as a location as worthy as any other in the literary geography of Persian. The aforementioned fund of historical fictions that anecdotally related early Persian master poets to India were marshaled anew in the context of this key eighteenth-century Indo-Persian literary dispute. Throughout the first volume of his *Safīnah*, therefore, Khvushgū exploits the rhetorical practice of digression to invoke such fictions to put master poets who spent all their lives in lands to the west of Mughal India into relation with its territory. This is also why Ārzū pervades all three volumes of Khvushgū's *Safīnah* in the form of his aforementioned preface and the notes he inserted into it as well as the leitmotif-like frequency with which Khvushgū remarks in various entries that the selection of verses in question was Ārzū's own. Most of the poets whose entries make up the third volume of the *Safīnah* were individuals who were long acquainted with Ārzū, Bīdil or Muḥammad Afẓal "Sarkhvush" – all three of whom were in Delhi – and tutored in their poetry by them face to face or in correspondence. In this sense, by his descriptions of the many public and private spaces of Mughal Delhi or Shāhjahānābād in which particular poetic soirees (*mushā'irah*) took place, descriptions that vivify the *Safīnah* like almost no other

Persian biographical compendium from India, Khvushgū extended Ārzū's project of restoring and exalting Delhi's symbolic capital.[38]

Ārzū's own particular response took the form of a multi-generic poetic and historico-philological project aimed at consolidating a trans-regional Indo-Iranian solidarity between seventeenth- and eighteenth-century Speaking Anew littérateurs.[39] In his biographical compendium, *Majma' al-nafāyis* (Collection of Rarities), completed in 1750–51 when he around seventy-two years old and mainly given to a defense of such a trans-regional poetic solidarity, Ārzū observed that verses by Ḥāfiẓ continued in his old age to cast him into the ecstatic transport he had experienced on first reading them in his boyhood.[40] This was not only an instance of a trans-regional poetic affinity but also a formulation that would have furnished Khvushgū with a model of Ḥāfiẓ's power to reverse and rejuvenate the temporality of a declining life.

But from such literary disputations – mostly scholarly and sometimes pettily personal – that form the texts, contexts and subtexts of much of the North Indian Persian literature of this period Khvushgū's other great teacher, Bīdil, stayed aloof, commanding his distinct circle of disciples that briefly also included Ārzū.[41] I will now address Khvushgū's debts to Bīdil with an attention to the effects of Bīdil's ascetic example on his disciple's experience of the time of Persian poetry and on his authorial power. But to do so will require us to pause to ask how Bīdil himself accrued his authority. Among the familiar Sufi strategies by which Bīdil fashioned his authorial authority was to claim that all comparisons of his poetry with that of old masters was provisional at best since he excelled them all by circling around their backs, as it were, to achieve a Neo-Platonic intimacy with the Beginningless (*azalī*) Real.[42] In this he was similar to such Sufi littérateurs of eighteenth-century Delhi as Shāh Valī Allāh, Khwājah Mīr Dard and Mirzā Maẓhar Jān-i Jānān, all of whom claimed exceptional spiritual status.[43] However, what distinguished him was his particular appropriation of a temporality consequent on Ibn 'Arabī's (d. 1240) theistic monism. It was an ascetically achieved temporality by which he claimed to be ecstatically contemporary with the primordial origin of world and words in the One out of which the Many had issued.

He found in Ibn 'Arabī's ontological conception of "the renewal of similars" (*tajaddud-i amṣāl*) a widely authoritative metaphysical justification for this attitude. This idea, central to Ibn 'Arabī's theistic monism, entailed the moment-by-moment substitution by God of every body with another like itself. Each such body and its similitudes taken together issued from the "essence" (*jawhar*) in the divine One. Jāmī, who was probably among Bīdil's conduits for this idea, maintained that unperceptive individuals failed to glimpse this perpetual renewal in beings and took them for self-identical.[44] However, Akbarian Sufis such as himself perceived that "there was no repetition in the divine self-manifestation" (*lā tikrār fil-tajallī*) and sought, like Bīdil, to teach disciples to recognize this. A remarkable entailment of this doctrine was the thesis of the greater reality of the present (*ḥāl*) in comparison to the past and future. The past and future were no more than names for the present and, with it, formed "a single event" (*vāqi'a-i vāḥidah*).[45] The value of such a doctrine for a Sufi seeking to fashion his authorial persona and authority in a Mughal Delhi beset with a crisis of courtly authority is not hard to appreciate.

Bīdil maintained that if he had a poetic lineage it was at best a provisional one that likened him "in power to Anvarī [d. 1189], in theoretical gnosticism [*'irfān*] to 'Aṭṭār [d. 1221]," one that he reluctantly conceded only because others demanded it of him. As we have observed in Chapter 1, this is most probably why, despite his versatility across verse and prose genres, he composed in no genre of historical writing, neither composing a biographical compendium (*taẕkirah*) nor a history (*tārīkh*). Such genres would have required him to commit himself to a historical sequence. But he was reluctant to grant his poetic descent from old masters because his innovative command of the technicalities of poetry – dotless and dotted verse among other techniques, for example – derived from his kenotically achieved contemporaneousness with the divine Real and thus – on the implicit model of the Qu'rān – never yielded the same meanings in their ever-shifting disclosure of God: "If the singing of past masters alone is acceptable/I, too, have surpassed myself, O heedless one – beware!"

That Khvushgū discovered paradigms for his own ascetic will-to-power in the practices that enabled such claims is evident from his reverential entry on his teacher, the longest of all entries in the *Safīnah*. The following passage from that entry merits close attention:

> His asceticism often led to forty-day retreats and he would content himself with one glass of milk a week. The wonder [*ṭurfah*] of it was that clock needles in his shadow had no power to move. Often, by way of a test, he kept [a watch] in his shadow for a moment and it [i.e., its needle] crawled to nothing. Also: his locks of the hardest iron had no choice at a gesture of his forefinger but to open. When they queried him on both the matters he said: the first is from the eternity without beginning [*azalī*] and the second from practice [*'amalī*] for it came to [my] lot from the assiduous use of the name "Fattāḥ" [i.e., "The Opener/The Victorious," one of Allah's names].[46]

The first miracle literalizes Bīdil's ascetic claim to be contemporary with the primordial Real and thus immeasurable by clock time, a miracle he claims is an effect of "the eternity without beginning." The second literalizes his pedagogical power to resolve predicaments on the Sufi path of kenotic self-transformation by his internalization, modeled on a paradigm from Ibn 'Arabī (d. 1240), of the "names and attributes" (*asmā wa ṣifāt*) of God. Bīdil's most frequent term in his poetry and prose for such empowering incapacity or kenosis was *'ajz*, a term and practice that Khvushgū, too, therefore predicates of himself in his quatrain.

But if Khvushgū, like Bīdil, comes to be a poet by ceasing to be who he was before his kenotic empowerment, then how are we to historically contextualize the self that is transformed? What does it mean to predicate historiographically verified authorship of persons who evacuate themselves of a false self in order to be inhabited by a transpersonal true One? What, indeed, is the self that Khvushgū fashions and refashions by reading – that is, copying, hearing, tasting, touching and smelling – the master's poetry? Is this not the point at which our historicism meets its limit in a conception of transpersonal selfhood?

In the following discussion I aim to explicate Khvushgū's models for such a transpersonal self, revealing a blurring of boundaries between him and his teachers. We may begin by considering the functions of the practice of copying by which Khvushgū reads Ḥāfiẓ. He copies the master's *Dīvān* not by way of mere scribal reproduction but as an act of pious repetition with parallels in many faith traditions. Such homage through repetition results in a quatrain (*rubā'ī*). This is significant because it places him within a tradition of Sufi appropriations of this genre, a genre favored by Sufis arguably because of the microcosmic correspondences between its four lines and the macrocosmic four elements. Among the oldest hypotexts implicitly cited and transformed by Khvushgū's account is the hagiographical report of how Abū Ṣa'īd Abul-khayr (d. 1049), whose legacy established the quatrain as a genre of Sufi thought, came to first compose poetry by following a teacher's instruction to repeat to himself in solitude a quatrain expressing utter indebtedness to God.[47] Repetition here evacuates the repeater of his ego to let him ventriloquize for a divine or human master, thus paradoxically inaugurating his creativity by negating it.

But Khvushgū's most proximate model for such kenotic repetition – one that he quotes and paraphrases himself in his entry on Bīdil – lay in the latter's autobiographical account of the circumstances in which he came to compose his earliest poem, also significantly a quatrain. I will conclude this chapter with a consideration of this and related hypotexts for Khvushgū's logic of self-presentation. In his autobiography *Chahār 'unṣur* (The Four Elements) that he completed in 1704 Bīdil describes how, when he was ten, his friend in school always spoke with a clove (*qaranfal*) in his mouth, thus perfuming his breath.

> In truth, that fragrance, inciting ardor, was "the Breath of the All-Merciful" [*nafas-i raḥmānī*] in the creation of Bīdil's metered perfumes and, in nurturing ardor in the nose for poetry, that spring-scented freshness was redolent of the Joseph of poetic topoi [*yūsuf-i ma'ānī*]. So that, one day, scenting its balanced message disclosed its face from the soul's veil in this color, blooming from thought's screen in the form of this quatrain:
>
> Whenever my friend begins to speak
> A strange smell arises from his mouth.
> Is this clove-scent or a flower's perfume
> Or the rising fragrance of Chinese musk?[48]

Throughout Khvushgū's *Safīnah* as with the historical self-representations of Sufis in general, bodily contact transmits spiritual authority through initiatic lineages and firms intergenerational solidarities.[49] Khvushgū rubs his head in the pure dust of Shiraz and Ḥāfiẓ raises his head from the dust to kiss his forehead. Here, Bīdil touches his friend by smelling him, finding his friend's breath strangely ambivalent in that it could have been quotidian "clove-scent or a flower's perfume" or the incipiently fabulous "rising fragrance of Chinese musk" (*mushk-i khutan*). China had long been a signifier of the exotic in Persian literature and thus of the far-flung character of the object of Sufi desire and journeying. Moreover, clove was known in the pharmacopoeia of Bīdil's milieu as "the fruit of the Chinese orange," so its metonymic reference to China may here be medical and mystical at once.[50] Its specific medical application was to cure "opacity of the eye." This use may have added medical authority to Bīdil's description of his smelling of "the Joseph of poetic topoi" in metaphors of visual disclosure: his sharpened perception of a source of poetic topoi "disclosed its face from the soul's veil in this color, blooming from thought's screen in the form of this quatrain." "The Joseph of poetic topoi" was an equally canonical characterization of the object of poetic striving, an allusion to the luminous Joseph of the Qur'ān who was rescued from a well and was thus allegorized by Sufi poets to signify the primordial *ghazal* topoi (*maẕmūn*, pl. *maẕāmīn*; *ma'nī*, pl. *ma'ānī*) that were to be ascetically discovered. Bīdil captures this ambivalently mundane and trans-mundane identity of his friend by declaring that his breath proved to be "the Breath of the Merciful" to him. This use of a key term from the aforementioned Andalusian Sufi Ibn 'Arabī, whose monorealist ontology pervaded North India at this time,[51] invests Bīdil's classmate with a symbolic identity. He may have been an empirical individual but was also allegorically the divine One that spoke through Bīdil's loving mimesis of him. As in Ibn 'Arabī's ontology so in Bīdil's creation of poetry, the One bestows actuality upon the many potentialities of creatures by breathing on them, causing them to swell into quotidian actuality. By such an imitation of God at the inauguration of his poetic career Bīdil inaugurates his own asymptotic theosis with a quatrain, calling it "the founding pillars of my balanced poetic nature." But this, we must recall, is the very phrase with which Khvushgū describes his own first quatrain too, disclosing a near identity between him, Bīdil, Bīdil's school friend and the divine Real.

That Khvushgū comes to compose his first poem with "cleanliness of appearance and purity of inwardness" and "sound intention" not only underscores his model in the *namāz* or Islamic prayer, it also locates him in the trajectory of Sufi reading practices which he was instructed in by Bīdil. Such embodied reading is not easy because it breaks with psychophysical habits. Khvushgū forgets to keep the *Dīvān* under his pillow on the thirty-first night and so must resume the forty-day cycle again, the number forty signaling his model in the *chilla* or such forty-day retreats and vigils kept by Sufis like his teacher. Bīdil on philosophy as the practice of ascetic self-control aimed at self-annihilation in the Real: "Perfectly sealed is diving in this ocean by holding your breath/Bubble-shaped here are wine-barrels and Platos."[52]

Though he did not say it – and could not have said it without detracting from the authority of his own claim – this posture of Neo-Platonic priority as a poet over all other poets was one that Bīdil had appropriated from the hagiographical tradition of Ḥāfiẓ. And it was one that he employed to rise above the disputations around him. Bīdil: "Everywhere – is the assembly-adornment of the Shiraz of the heart./Not from Kashmiri or Lahori states does a topos arise."[53] Not mentioning Ḥāfiẓ by name because it was disrespectful to address elders except by titles, Bīdil calls Ḥāfiẓ the "assembly-adornment of the Shiraz of the heart," characterizing Ḥāfiẓ's city as being "of the heart," Persian poetry's inner theater of appearances. This interiorization and generalization of Ḥāfiẓ of Shiraz negates the specificity of the two other poets identified in the second hemistich by their home cities in Mughal India, Ghanī Kashmīrī (d. 1669) and Maṣ'ūd Sa'd Salmān Lahūrī (d. 1121–22). Votaries and critics of Speaking Anew had invoked both in connection with their ethnic and geographical origins. In Bīdil's couplet Ḥāfiẓ overrides such ethno-geographic particularism by his mystical omnipresence as "the Shiraz of the heart," an inner Shiraz of Pre-Eternal topoi invoked in turn by Khvushgū in his first quatrain, "the founding pillars" of his "balanced poetic nature."

Let us step back for a moment to recognize the contrasting hermeneutic attitudes and correspondingly contrasting modes of reading pleasure Khvushgū inherited from his two main teachers. From Ārzū he inherited the awareness that the Persian poetic heritage was estranged by time and thus needed the sort of historicizing philological supplements – called "subtle points" (*laṭīfah*) in the *Safīnah* – which Ārzū provided and Khvushgū occasionally provides in turn.[54] This attitude thus corresponded to an intellectual reading pleasure, mediated by a historicist philology, in past poets. Such philological bridges to the past thus mostly pervade only the first volume of his *Safīnah* that is given to "the old masters."[55] They do not appear in the third volume that is given to his contemporaries except when an authoritative poetic precedent is cited. This is also why he concurs in the third volume with Ārzū's conception of an Indo-Iranian poetic solidarity based on temporal rather than spatial proximity, a concurrence evident in the opening sentences of the third volume of his *Safīnah* that:

> comprises discussion of contemporaries [*mu'āṣirīn*] to some of whom he [i.e., Khvushgū] was related as a contemporary [*nisbat-i ham-'aṣrī dāshtah*]. From the conversation of most of them the humble author benefited. In this final part most are poets of Hindūstān. On account of proximity the distance of those distant is not apparent.

Tested for their sense against the text that follows, the two final sentences in the foregoing passage disclose precisely what Khvushgū means: although most of the poets spoken of in this third and final volume of the *Safīnah* were resident in Mughal India and personally acquainted with Khvushgū, some of them lived outside it in Iran and Central Asia. However, because of their temporal proximity to him he did not experience their spatial distance from him as significant enough to exclude them from his vision of literary community. This is why he includes an entry on a poet called Mīr Hādī "Sharar" who was an elder contemporary in Safavid Iran and never came to India, accounting for the brevity of the entry by saying: "Because of proximity in period [*'aṣr*] and distance in space [*bu'd-i masāfat*] not as much as should be is known".[56]

From Bīdil, by contrast, Khvushgū inherited a simultaneously hermeneutic and ascetic ability to become *almost* contemporary with the oldest masters and, in comprehending their poetry, even compose poetic responses (*javāb*) to them after Bīdil's own model. Here, Bīdil's asceticism negates Ārzū's historicism and corresponds to a tactile reading pleasure, mediated by ascetic self-cultivation, in a somatic proximity to the old masters. So, he proudly notes in his entry on Bīdil that his teacher had composed a poetic response to a famous quatrain by "the father of poets, the Master Rūdakī [d. 941], that had been impossible to poetically imitate [*mumtana' al-javāb*] thus far."[57] He then adds that he, Khvushgū, had composed a poetic response in turn even if it fell short of the two previously quoted ones by the two masters through its failure to rhyme like their quatrains even in the third hemistich. Such a falling short of his living teachers characterizes the whole third volume of Khvushgū's *Safīnah* and signals the ultimately irreducible temporal distance from the old masters. Bīdil's ascetically achieved contemporaneousness with Rūdakī, 'Irāqī, Ḥāfiẓ and other old masters allowed Khvushgū to approximate a fragrant intimacy with them only to fall short, as in his dream encounter with the "Master of Shiraz," of its plenitude.

This literary history authorizes the protocols of empirical verification it shares with modern historicism by reference to its littérateur-author's ascetically achieved and interrupted intimacy with a past master-poet. And such ascetic authorization voids its author of the phenomenal uniqueness of his ego to let him ventriloquize for a more real transpersonal self. If modern historicism has let me contextualize the author's historiographical and ascetic practices by reference to his two main teachers, it has also brought me to its own limit by disclosing the context-resistant primordiality of this authorial self.

Notes

1 'Abd al-Qādir Khān Bīdil, *Kulliyāt-i Bīdil: jild-i avval* (Tehrān: intishārāt-i Ilhām, 1386/2007), 686.
2 Rainer Maria Rilke, *Ahead of All Parting: Selected Poetry and Prose of Rainer Maria Rilke*, trans. Stephen Mitchell (New York: Modern Library, 1995), 67.
3 Bindrāban Dās Khvushgū, *Safīnah-i Khvushgū: jild-i avval* (MS Sprenger 330, Staatsbibliothek, Berlin), 1742/43. All my quotations from the first volume of Khvushgū's *Safīnah* are from this manuscript which, on the basis of the following note inscribed behind the first page of the preface, seems to be an autograph copy: "This text, the first volume [*daftar*] of *Tazkirah-i Khvushgū*, was bought in 1202 Hijri [i.e., 1787 CE] in the city of Banaras from Ram Datt Brahmi and is in the author's own handwriting." Since this also appears to be a fair copy of a draft that Khvushgū mentions it would have been completed, as Sprenger notes in his catalogue, in 1742/43. This volume has not been edited and printed yet. For an encyclopedia entry on *Safīnah-i Khvushgū* mainly focused on the contents of the third volume, see: www.iranicaonline.org/articles/safina-ye-kosgu
4 Ibid.
5 The ample anagogical interpretability of this famous opening distich of Ḥāfiẓ's *Dīvān* may be judged from the four-and-a-half-page long commentary on it in what is the culminating synthesis of anagogical commentaries on the *Dīvān-i Ḥāfiż*, 'Abul Ḥasan 'Abd al-Raḥmān "Khatmī" Lāhorī, *Sharḥ-i 'irfānī-i ghazal'hā-i Ḥāfiẓ* (Tehrān:

nashr-i Qaṭrah, 1378/1999), 2–4. This four-volume commentary, completed in around 1617 in North India, originally bears no known title and was assigned its present title by its modern editors. Khvushgū shows no sign of direct familiarity with this work. But inasmuch as Khatmī builds on a corpus of anagogical interpretations of the *Dīvān-i Ḥāfiẓ* widespread across North India we may reasonably assert that it exemplifies an interpretative community and culture that Khvushgū inherited as scholarship and habitus.

5 *khwājah Ḥāfiẓ kih hast andar Shīrāz*
ham sāḥib-i kāmil ast u ham sāḥib-i rāz
'Ayshī ba umīd-i ān kih shā'ir gardad
dārad ba janāb-i 'ālīsh 'ajz u niyāz

Khvushgū, *Safīnah-i Khvushgū: jild-i avval*, fl. 175r

7 Ibid., fls. 174v–75r.

8 Sara Sviri, "Dreaming Analyzed and Recorded: Dreams in the World of Medieval Islam," in David Shulman *et al.* (ed.), *Dream Cultures: Explorations in the Comparative History of Dreaming* (New York: Oxford University Press, 1999), 252. For an exposition of how Aristotle's originally non-theological explanation of veridical dreams in his *De Divinatione per Somnum* (On Divination by Dreams) came to be transformed by translation in the Late Ancient world into a theory of "God-sent" dreams, see Rotraud E. Hansberger, "How Aristotle Came to Believe in God-given Dreams: the Arabic Version of the *Divinatione per somnum*," in Louise Marlow (ed.), *Dreaming Across Boundaries: the Interpretation of Dreams in Islamic Lands* (Cambridge, MA: Harvard University Press, 2008).

9 The *tazkirah*, originally modeled on the Arabic *ṭabaqāt*, was the principle genre in the Persianate world with which an ideal of community among those engaged in a practice was articulated. Such practices ranged from poetry, calligraphy, music and scholarship to statesmanship. Not everyone who engaged in such a practice did so professionally. Most of the individual poets commemorated by Khvushgū, for example, were major and minor bureaucrats and statesmen by occupation. The individuals making up a community commemorated by a *tazkirah* are therefore best thought of as *practitioners* of the practice in question rather than always as professionally identified individuals.

10 Khvushgū, *Safīnah-i Khvushgū: jild-i avval*, fls. 3v–5r. For a paradigmatic earlier Mughal iteration of the uses of a syllabus of poetry for soul-craft or ethical formation – one that Khvushgū would have known and perhaps even studied, see the letter of advice addressed to his son in *Chahār chaman* (Four Meadows) by "Brāhman" (d. 1662–63), a nobleman littérateur in the emperor Shāh Jahān's court. Chandrabhān Brāhman, *Chahār chaman*, (New Delhi: markaz-i taḥqīqāt-i Fārsi, rāyzani-i farhangi-i jumhūri-i Islāmi-i Irān, 2007), 175–76.

11 For a biographical entry on Khvushgū and a contemporaneous evaluation of his poetry and *Safīnah*, see Lacchmī Nārāyan "Shafīq", *Gul-i ra'nā* (Ḥyderābād: 'Ahd-āfrin Barqī Press, 1967), 63–74.

12 From the scores of possible examples of this value attached to filiality I will cite only two paradigmatic ones: the patrilineally transmitted powers – symbolized by a halo (*farr*) – of Iranian kingship as well as the duties of king-serving heroism in Firdawsī's *Shāhnāmah* (The Book of Kings, 1010); and Niẓāmī Ganjavī's advice to his son in the ninth chapter of his *Laylī u Majnūn* (1188), that he undertake great deeds to win himself a worldly immortality rather depend for this on his famous paternity.

13 Muḥammad 'Awfī, *Lubāb al-albāb* (Tehrān: chāp-i Ittihād, 1914). Khvushgū's teacher Ārzū gave this episode in 'Awfī's text a brief chapter in his largest prose work, *Musmir*, authorizing Khvushgū's use of it as well as attesting to the circulation of 'Awfī's narrative of the origin of poetry in late Mughal India. Sirāj al-Dīn 'Alī Khān Ārzū, *Musmir* (Karachi: Institute for Central Asian Research, 1991), 17–21.

14 Prashant Keshavmurthy, "Finitude and the Authorship of Fiction: Muḥammad 'Awfī's Preface to his *Lubāb al-Albāb* (The Piths of Intellects, 1221 C.E.)", *The Arab Studies Journal*, Vol. XIX No. 1 (2011): 94–120.

15 For an extended discussion of this body of Indo-Persian historiography composed in response to the Mongol threat, see Sunil Kumar, "The Ignored Elite: Turks, Mongols and an Early Secretarial Class in the Early Delhi Sultanate," *Modern Asian Studies* 43: 1 (2009): 45–77. 'Awfī had antecedents for this conception of an archive in Firdawsī's remembering of pre-Islamic Iranian lore in his *Shāhnāmah* and, further back, in its ninth century Pahlavi sources such as the *Kārnāmag-i Ardashīr-i Pābagān*.

16 Khvushgū, *Safīnah-i Khvushgū: jild-i avval*, fl. 7v.

17 Khvushgū says he composed his biographical compendium during the reign of the Mughal emperor Muḥammad Shāh but, because of Nādir Shāh of Iran's invasion in 1739 when Khvushgū happened to be in "the pleasing mountain-country of Kangra, Chamba [...] and other regions of Punjab," could not prepare a fresh copy for seven to eight years, so that "it did not have the good fortune to be published" [*shuhrat yāftan naṣīb-i ān nagardīd*]." After that, in around 1742–43, he managed to reach Shāhjahānābād and present it for corrections (*iṣlāḥ*) to "the master of proofs" Sirāj al-Dīn 'Alī Ārzū who, he notes, graciously agreed because of his generosity towards Khvushgū to add marginal notes and a preface (*khuṭbah*) to it. Khvushgū, fl. 4b. He also notes in his entry on Ārzū that the estate Ārzū had received near his home city of Gwalior had been despoiled by raiding Marathas who he refers to by the appellation, standard in the chronicles of the Mughal state, of "plunderers" (*ghanīm*). Bindrāban Dās Khvushgū, *Safīnah-i Khvushgū: daftar-i thālith* (Patna: idārah-i taḥqīqāt-i 'Arabī va Fārsī, 1959), 319.

18 Bindrāban Dās Khvushgū, *Safīnah-i Khvushgū: daftar-i duvvum*, (Tehrān: Kitāb-khānah, mūzah va markaz-i asnād-i majlis-i shūrā-i Islāmī, 1389/2010).

19 We have little knowledge yet of how this volume of Khvushgū's *Safīnah* came to circulate in Iran. Nothing suggests that Khvushgū ever left Mughal India but it is possible that his westward flight during Nādir Shāh's invasion of Delhi led to this manuscript changing hands. The manuscript may thus have passed into literary circles located in Shushtar that, not being far from the Persian Gulf, is known to have had maritime connections with Mughal India. MS 2655 in the University of Tehran's library is the most complete manuscript of the four known copies of the second volume and forms the basis of the critical edition I have cited here. Asghar, the editor of this critical edition, observes of this manuscript: "Some *taẕkirah* writers refer to it by the name of 'the one fetched from the water' [*āb-āvardah*] and did not consider it worthy of attention." Syed Kalim Asghar, "Āshnāyī bā daftar-i duvvum-i Safīnah-i Khvushgū," *Āyinah-i mirās*, Vol. 15 (1380/2001): 102–08. On 103–04 Asghar notes that this Tehran manuscript contains three kinds of calligraphy. This appears to corroborate Ḥaqīr Durrī's prefatory account of the many hands through which it passed before he edited it into a form presentable to a courtly reader. Since this copy bears the date 1247/1831 in a margin it suggests Ḥaqīr Durrī was alive then.

20 Khvushgū, *Safīnah-i Khvushgū: daftar-i duvvum*, 3.

21 Qāẕī Nūrullāh Shūshtarī, *Majālis al-mu'minīn: jild-i avval* (Tehrān: instishārāt-i kitāb-furūshi-i Islāmiyah, 1365/1986), 69. According to some reports Shūsh was a Middle Persian word for "beautiful" and was the earlier of the two ancient cities that, after falling into ruin, was replaced at a short distance by Shūshtar whose name, by the addition of the Persian suffix of comparison, means "more beautiful."

22 Khvushgū, *Safīnah-i Khvushgū: daftar-i thālith*, 346.

23 George McLeod James, *Ānand Rām Mukhliṣ: his Life and Works, 1695–1758* (New Delhi: Dilli Kitabghar, 2007–11), 242. Mukhliṣ makes this comparison in the course of the eighty pages he gives to the description of Nādir Shāh's sacking in his *Badā'ī-i vaqā'ī* (Novel Events) whose manuscript, MS 2611 in Patna's Khuda Bakhsh Oriental Library, has not yet been edited and published.

24 In his letter to his son containing a syllabus of poetry to be applied in ethical self-fashioning Brāhman gives Sa'dī's *Gulistān* and *Būstān* a prominent place both in his poetic canon as well as in his list of classics of philosophical ethics. Brāhman, *Chahār chaman*, 175–76.

25 Sayyid Musṭafā Ḥusayn Āsif Jāyasī, *Munshī Naval Kishor: ḥayāt o khidmāt* (New Delhi: Center for Persian Research, 2010), 148–49.

26 Take for example the motivations of two of the most prominent of these commentaries: Sirāj al-Dīn 'Alī Khān Ārzū, *Khiyābān sharḥ-i Gulistān-i Sa'dī* (Islāmābād: markaz-i taḥqīqāt-i Fārsī-i Irān va Pakistān, 1996); and Valī Muḥammad Akbarābādi, *Sharḥ-i Gulistān* (Lucknow: Munshī Naval Kishor, 1890). Ārzū's commentary on the *Gulistān* offered him, as I have argued in Chapter 4 as well as my entry on him for *Encyclopedia Iranica* (online at www.iranicaonline.org/articles/kan-e-arezu), a context in which to demonstrate his thesis of the historical locality of literary competence and thus authorize himself in a non-courtly and politically dispersed milieu where Persian literary authority was in question. Akbarābādī completed his commentary in Agra on 15 July 1753 in response to a friend's complaint that no philologically stable copy of *Gulistān* was available, and that if Valī Muḥammad established a definitive manuscript copy in keeping with Sa'dī's most probable intentions, it would ease the task of studying it. Distinct to Ārzū's commentary, this one was apparently motivated by solely pedagogical intentions rather than literary politics. However, attention to its elucidations of particular didactic topics, friendship in particular, disclose a concern with everyday sociality in keeping with the period's strained Persianate urban culture. Khvushgū himself intended his *Safīnah* to be a student's introduction to the most superior Persian poets that would so self-sufficient as to render Sa'dī's *Gulistān* and *Būstān* unnecessary. Khvushgū, *Safīnah-i Khvushgū: jild-i avval*, fl. 5r.

27 For an account of diminishing state resources, the loss of central courtly authority and the formation of factions centered on powerful noblemen, see Satish Chandra, *Parties and Politics at the Mughal Court: 1707–1740* (New Delhi: Oxford University Press, 2002), 278–92.

28 Khvushgū, *Safīnah-i Khvushgū: jild-i avval*, fl. 1v.

29 Maḥmūd Futūhī and Muḥammad Afshin-Vafā'i, "*Mukhāṭib-shināsī-i Ḥāfiẓ dar sadah-i hashtum va nuhum-i hijrī bar asās-i ruyīkard-i tārīkh-i adabī-i heremeneutic*", *Faṣl-nāmah-i naqd-i adabī* 6: 4 (2009), 86–87.

30 Khvushgū quotes from one of his sources, Amīn Aḥmad Rāzī, who completed his biographical compendium *Haft iqlīm* (Seven Climes) between 1595–1610 in the emperor Akbar's court. Rāzī narrated a report of the poet Sa'dī's visit to Delhi when Amīr Khusraw, revered in Timurid and Indo-Persian literary history, was eighteen. Immensely pleased with Khusraw's poetry, he blessed him and set down two of his couplets in his private notebook (*bayāẓ*). This was an iteration of the trope of an already exalted and canonical poet's visit to a place and the honor he shows a local poet by recording some of his verses in his private notebook. It is one that, repeating itself with respect to Mirzā Ṣā'ib's (d. 1676) historically verified rather than apocryphal visit to Kashmir and his recording of twelve of Ghanī Kashmīrī's (d. 1669) couplets, allowed eighteenth-century Indo-Persian literary communities to claim older pedagogical pedigree and courtly authority. Khvushgū, witness to the dispersal of Mughal political authority in his own milieu, was thus transmitting a vision of India's place in Persian literary history that was explicitly authorized and canonized by Akbar's court.

31 Futuhi and Afshin-Vafa'i, "*Mukhāṭib-shināsī*," 111.

32 The immediacy of the perlocutionary effect on Khvushgū of these verbal cues aligns in subtler ways with a prophteological model for the aural rather than visual mode of receiving God's word. We must recall here that the Prophet Muḥammad first heard Gabriel rather than seeing Him. The predominantly aural mode of the Prophet's reception of the divine word would come to be invoked by 'Alī Hujvirī, the author of the

earliest Persian-language exposition of Sufi topics, in seeking ethico-legal legitimacy for the practice of music and its ecstatic audition (*samā'*), a phenomenological invocation in which all the other external senses nestled synesthetically within hearing that took primacy. 'Alī Hujvirī, *Kashf al-maḥjūb* (composed between 1073–77 in Lahore), trans. R.A. Nicholson (London: Luzac & Co., 1911), 393–94.

33 Khvushgū, *Safīnah-i Khvushgū: jild-i avval*, f1. 73v.

34 This exaltation Ṣā'ib enjoyed among Speaking Anew littérateurs may be inferred from the frequency with which his name and verses are cited in exemplary ways throughout the third volume of Khvushgū's *Safīnah* that is mostly given to his Speaking Anew contemporaries. Indeed Khvushgū's very use of the word *Safīnah* would have invoked the most authoritative text by that title in his milieu, namely the *Safīnah* or personal notebook of Ṣā'ib (which is also named *Bayāẓ-i Ṣā'ib* and *Taẕkirah-i Ṣā'ib* in some sources) which he lists as one of his sources. For an anecdote entailing the invocation of an "authoritative poetic precedent" (*sanad*) from Ṣā'ib in defense of Khvushgū's poetic competence, see the entry on Shaykh Sa'dullāh "Akhtar" in Bindrāban Dās Khvushgū, *Safīnah-i Khvushgū: daftar-i thālith* (Patna: idārah-i tahqīqāt-i 'Arabī va Fārsī, 1959), 229–30. Most of the *ghazal* sequences composed in the same *zamīn* (meter and end-refrain) in Bīdil's own two-volume personal notebook or *bayāẓ* begin with Ṣā'ib's *ghazal* that set a series of poets a model for poetic imitations or *javābs*. *Bayaẓ-i Bīdil*, MS 16802, British Library, London. On the authority, manuscript dispersal and varying titles of Ṣā'ib's aforementioned notebook, see 'Alī Riẓā Naqavī, *Taẕkirah-navīsī-i Fārsī dar Hind va Pākistān* (Tehrān: mu'assasah-i maṭbū'āt-i 'Ilmī, 1343/2013), 785.

35 Khvushgū would have known a canonical example of how didactic considerations of spiritual effectivity override those of chronological sequence in 'Aṭṭār's (d. *c.*1230) choice to make an exception to his own commitment to chronology by placing his hagiography of Ja'far al-Ṣādiq before the chronologically earlier Uvays Qaranī. For an interpretation of this, see Paul Losensky's preface to Farīd al-Dīn 'Aṭṭār, *Memorial of God's Friends: Lives and Sayings of Sufis* (New York: Paulist Press, 2009), 20–22.

36 In addition to the overlapping circles centered on Ārzū and Bīdil, there were the those of Muḥammad 'Alī "Ḥazīn" (d. 1766), Fākhir "Makīn" (d. 1806–07), S'adullāh "Gulshan" (d. 1727–28), Muḥammad Afẓal "Sarkhvush" (d. 1715) who gave Khvushgū his pen-name and, extending to the Deccan, Ghulām 'Alī "Āzād" Bilgrāmī (d. 1786).

37 Muḥammad 'Alī Ḥazīn, *Taẕkirat al-mu'āṣirīn* (Iṣfahān: kitāb-furūshī-i Ta'yīd, 1955), 92–95; and "Risālah-i vāqi'āt-i Iran va Hind," in *Rasāyil-i Ḥazīn-i Lāhījī* (Tehrān: Mirās-i Maktūb, 1998), 228–31. The authority of Ḥazīn's *Taẕkirat* may be judged from the example it set for Mohal Lāl Anīs's biographical compendium, completed in 1783, of the Hindu and Muslim poets tutored by Fākhir Makīn in Lucknow, *Anīs al-aḥibbā* (The Intimate of Friends), (Patna: Khudā-bakhsh Oriental Public Library, 1996), 55. The paradigmatic authority of Ḥazīn's *Taẕkirat* in Lucknow must be partly accounted for by reference to Shi'i Avadh's self-conception as a spiritual successor state to the recently deposed Safavids and Anīs's employment in service of that state. Further evidence of how Ḥazīn's literary attitudes aroused a variety of responses may be found in a contemporaneous biographical compendium completed in 1748, Mīr Ḥusayn Dūst Sambhalī, *Taẕkirah-i Ḥusaynī* (MS 334 Sprenger, Staatsbibliothek, Berlin), fl. 68v.

38 A telling entry in this regard is the one on Bābu Bāl Mukund that, in a significant exception, begins without his pen-name. Khvushgū recalls meeting Bāl Mukund in Banaras where Bāl Mukund expressed his "keenest desire to go to Shāhjahānābād that is the testing place of poetry [*mi'yār-gāh-i sukhan*] and benefit by serving the poets of the capital." Khvushgū recounts furnishing him with a letter recommending him to Ārzū and notes that he had lately heard that Bāl Mukund had visited Ārzū, benefited from his teaching and received from him the pen-name of "Shahūd." The entry thus

proves to have been concerned with Bāl Mukund's person and poetry only to the extent that it was indebted to the cultural authority of Ārzū and Delhi. Khvushgū, *Safīnah-i Khvushgū: daftar-i thālith*, 346. For an analogous attempt among late eighteenth-century Delhi's elite practitioners of art music to "shore up the authority of the Delhi *kalāwant birāderī* as the legitimate representative of Mughal courtly traditions," see Katherine Butler Schofield, "Chief Musicians to the Mughal Emperors: The Delhi *kalāwant birāderī*, 17th to 19th Centuries," *Journal of the Indian Musicological Society*, 2013.

39 This is why five of his seven *dīvāns* were poetic responses to seventeenth-century poets, who spent all or most of their careers in Safavid Iran. For an interpretive survey of Ārzū's works, see my www.iranicaonline.org/articles/kan-e-arezu

40 Sirāj al-Dīn 'Alī Khān Ārzū, *Majma' al-nafāyis: jild-i avval* (Islāmābād: markaz-i taḥqīqāt-i Fārsi-i Iran va Pakistan, 2004), 356.

41 Ibid., 240.

42 'Abd al-Qādir Khān Bīdil, *Chahār 'unṣur*, in *Avāz'hā-i Bīdil*. (Tehrān: mu'assasah-i Intisharāt-i Nigāh, 2005), 474.

43 Carl W. Ernst, *Ruzbihan Baqli: Mysticism and the Rhetoric of Sainthood in Persian Sufism* (Richmond: Curzon Press, 1996), 146–47.

44 I depend for this gloss on Sayyad Aḥsan al-Ẓafar, *Mirzā 'Abd al-Qādir Bedil: ḥayāt aur kārname: jild-i duvvum* (Rāmpūr: Rāmpūr Raẕā Library, 2009), 642.

45 Ibid., 647.

46 Khvushgū, *Safīnah-i Khvushgu: daftar-i thālith*, 106.

47 Muḥammad b. Nūr al-dīn b. Abī Ṣa'd As'ad Munavvar, *Asrār al-tawḥīd: bakhsh-i avval* (Tehrān: mu'assasah-i intishārāt-i Āgāh, 1987; compiled between 1179–92), 19.

48 Bīdil, *Chahār 'unṣur*, 451–52.

49 Shahzad Bashir, *Sufi Bodies: Religion and Society in Medieval Islam* (New York: Columbia University Press, 2011), 1–25.

50 Al-Birūni, *Al-Birūni's Book on Pharmacy and Materia Medica, Volume 1*, ed. and trans. by Hakim Muhammed Said (Karachi: Hamdard Academy, 1973), 265. Though Al-Birūni composed the text in the eleventh century, his work was culled and adapted by several physicians in Mughal India, among them by the emperor Shāh Jahān's physician, Nūr al-Dīn Muḥammad 'Abdullāh Shirāzī (one of whose other texts I discussed in Chapter 1) in his *materia medica, Alfāẓ -i adviyah*. Nūr al-Dīn Muḥammad 'Abdullāh Shirāzī, *Alfāẓ-i adviyah*, trans. Francis Gladwin (Calcutta: Chronicle Press, 1793).

51 Ibn 'Arabī's thought was mostly mediated to India through 'Abd al-Raḥmān Jāmī's commentarial and poetic interpretations of it as well as by the interpretations of Shaykh Muḥibbullāh Ilāhābādī's (d. 1648) who was called "the second Ibn 'Arabi" in India. For a study of Jāmī's interpretation of Ibn 'Arabī see Sajjad Rizvi, "The Existential Breath of *al-raḥmān* and the Munificent Grace of *al-raḥīm*: The *Tafsir Surat al-Fāṭiḥa* of Jāmi and the School of Ibn 'Arabi," *Journal of Qur'anic Studies* 8: 1 (2006), 58–87. For a study of Muḥibbullāh Ilāhābādī's place in Ibn 'Arabī's Indian reception, see G.A. Lipton, *Muḥibbullāh Ilāhābādi's 'The Equivalence Between Giving and Receiving': Avicennan Neo-Platonism and the School of Ibn 'Arabi in South Asia* (MA. thesis, University of Chapel Hill, 2007).

52 *ghavāṣī-i īn daryā bar ẕabṭ-i nafas khatm ast*
dar shakl-i ḥabāb īnjāst khum'hā u falāṭūn-hā

Bīdil, *Kulliyāt-i Bīdil: jild-i avval*, 507

53 *hamah jā anjuman-ārā-i shīrāz-i dil ast*
ma'nī az 'ālam-i kashmīrī u lāhūrī nīst

Bīdil, *Kulliyat-i Bīdil: jild-i avval*, 526

54 Khvushgū thus explains the grammar of Bīdil's pen-name, the particle of negation *bī* signifying a negation of the "attribute" of the heart or mind that is the source of

distracting contingencies. He contrasts this with *nā*, a particle of negation applied to the object it qualifies rather than to an attribute of the object. Khvushgū, *Safīnah-i Khvushgū: daftar-i thālith*, 107. In other passages in his *Safīnah* Khvushgū cites authoritative poetic precedent for his own poetry (229–30) or precedent contrary to that of others (18), thus displaying his knowledge of literary history in Ārzū's manner.

55 An example is Ārzū's "subtle point," quoted in Chapter 4, explaining the copious amounts of verse attributed to Rūdakī by comparison with Sūr Dās, his Braj Bhāshā equivalent. Khvushgū, *Safīnah-i Khvushgū: jild-i avval*, fl. 11v.

56 Khvushgū, *Safīnah-i Khvushgū: daftar-i thālith*, 15.

57 Ibid., 119.

Bibliography

Aḥsan al-Ẓafar, Sayyad *Mirzā 'Abd al-Qādir Bīdil: ḥayāt aur kārname: jild-i duvvum* (Rāmpūr: Rāmpūr Raẓā Library, 2009).

Akbarābādi, Valī Muḥammad. *Sharḥ-i Gulistān*. Lucknow: Munshī Naval Kishor, 1890.

Anīs, Mohal Lāl. *Anīs al-aḥibbā: taẕkirah-i shu'arā-yi Fārsī*. Patna: Khudā-bakhsh Oriental Public Library, 1996.

Ārzū, Sirājuddīn 'Alī Khān. *Muṣmir*. Karachi: Institute for Central Asian Research, 1991.

Ārzū, Sirājuddīn *Khiyābān sharḥ-i Gulistān-i Sa'dī*. Islāmābād: Markaz-i taḥqīqāt-i Fārsī-i Irān va Pākistān, 1996.

Ārzū, Sirājuddīn *Majma'al-nafā'is: jild-i avval*. Islāmābād: markaz-i taḥqiqāt-i Fārsi-i Irān va Pākistān, 2004.

Asghar, Syed Kalim. "Āshnāyī bā daftar-i duvvum-i Safīnah-i Khvushgū," *Āyinah-i mirās*, Vol. 15 (1380/2001): 102–08.

'Aṭṭār, Farīd al-Dīn. *Memorial of God's Friends: Lives and Sayings of Sufis*. New York: Paulist Press, 2009.

'Awfī, Muḥammad. *Lubāb al-albāb*. Tehrān: chāp-i Ittiḥād, 1914.

Bashir, Shahzad. *Sufi Bodies: Religion and Society in Medieval Islam*. New York: Columbia University Press, 2011.

Bīdil, 'Abd al-Qādir Khān. *Bayaẓ-i Bīdil*, MS 16802, British Library, London.

Bīdil, 'Abd al-Qādir Khān. *Kulliyāt-i Bīdil: jild-i avval va duvvum*. Tehrān: Intishārāt-i Ilhām, 1995.

Bīdil, 'Abd al-Qādir Khān. "*Chahār 'unṣur*," in *Avāz'hā-i Bīdil*. Tehrān: mu'assasah-i intishārāt-i Nigāh, 2005.

Al-Birūnī. *Al-Birūni's Book on Pharmacy and Materia Medica, Volume 1*, ed. and trans. Hakim Muhammed Said. Karachi: Hamdard Academy, 1973.

Brāhman, Chandrabhān. *Chahār chaman*, New Delhi: Markaz-i taḥqīqāt-i Fārsī, rāyzanī-i farhangī-i jumhurī-i Islāmī-i Irān, 2007.

Chandra, Satish. *Parties and Politics at the Mughal Court: 1707–1740*. New Delhi: Oxford University Press, 2002.

Ernst, Carl W. *Ruzbihan Baqli: Mysticism and the Rhetoric of Sainthood in Persian Sufism*. Richmond: Curzon Press, 1996.

Futuhi, Mahmud and Afshin-Vafa'I, Muhammad. "*Mukhātib-shināsī-i Ḥāfiż dar sadah-i hashtum va nuhum-i hijrī bar asās-i ruīkard-i tārīkh-i adabī-i heremeneutic*," *Faṣl-nāma-yi naqd-i adabī* 6: 4 (2009), 86–87.

Hansberger, Rotraud E. "How Aristotle Came to Believe in God-given Dreams: The Arabic Version of the *Divinatione per somnum*," in Louise Marlow (ed), *Dreaming*

Across Boundaries: The Interpretation of Dreams in Islamic Lands, Cambridge, MA: Harvard University Press, 2008.

Ḥazīn, Muḥammad ʿAlī. *Taẕkirat al-muʿāṣirīn*. Iṣfahān: Kitāb-furūshī-i Taʾyīd, 1955.

Ḥazīn, Muḥammad "Risālah-i vāqaʿāt-i Iran va Hind," in *Rasāʾil-i Ḥazīn-i Lāhījī*. Tehrān: Mirās Maktūb, 1998.

Hujviri, ʿAli. *Kashf al-mahjūb*, trans. Reynold Nicholson. London: Luzac & Co., 1911.

Jāyasī, Sayyid Muṣṭafā Ḥusayn Āsif. *Munshī Naval Kishor: ḥayāt o khidmāt*. New Delhi: Center for Persian Research, 2010.

James, George McLeod. *Ānand Rām Mukhliṣ: his Life and Works, 1695–1758*. New Delhi: Dilli Kitabghar, 2007–11.

Keshavmurthy, Prashant. "Finitude and the Authorship of Fiction: Muhammad ʿAwfi's Preface to his *Lubāb al-albāb* (The Piths of Intellects, 1221 C.E.)," *The Arab Studies Journal* Vol. XIX, No. 1 (2011): 94–120.

"Khatmī," ʿAbul Ḥasan ʿAbd al-Raḥmān Lāhorī. *Sharḥ-i ʿirfānī-i ghazalʾhā-i Ḥāfiẓ*. Tehrān: nashr-i Qaṭrah, 1378/1999.

Khvushgū, Bindrāban Dās. *Safīnah-i Khvushgū*. MS Sprenger 330, Staatsbibliothek, Berlin, 1742/43.

Khvushgū, Bindrāban Dās. *Safīnah-i Khvushgū: daftar-i thālith*. Patna: Idārah-i taḥqīqāt-i ʿArabi va Fārsi, 1959.

Khvushgū, Bindrāban Dās. *Safīnah-i Khvushgū: daftar-i duvvum*. Tehrān: Kitāb-khānah, mūzah va markaz-i asnād-i majlis-i shūrā-yi Islāmī, 1389/2010.

Kumar, Sunil. "The Ignored Elite: Turks, Mongols and an Early Secretarial Class in the Early Delhi Sultanate," *Modern Asian Studies* 43: 1 (2009): 45–77.

Lipton, G.A. *Muḥibbullāh Ilāhābādī's "The Equivalence Between Giving and Receiving": Avicennan Neo-Platonism and the School of Ibn ʿArabi in South Asia*, MA thesis, University of Chapel Hill, 2007.

Munavvar, Muḥammad b. Nūr al-dīn b. Abī Ṣaʿd Asʿad. *Asrār al-tawḥīd: bakhsh-i avval*. Tehrān: muʾassasah-i intishārāt-i Āgāh, 1987.

Naqavi, ʿAlī Riẓā. *Taẕkirah-navīsī-i Fārsī dar Hind va Pākistān*. Tehrān: muʾassasa-yi matbūʿāṭ-i ʿIlmi, 1343/2013.

Rilke, Rainer Maria. *Ahead of All Parting: Selected Poetry and Prose of Rainer Maria Rilke*, trans. Stephen Mitchell. New York: Modern Library, 1995.

Rizvi, Sajjad. "The Existential Breath of *al-raḥmān* and the Munificent Grace of *al-raḥīm*: The *Tafsir Surat al-Fātiḥa* of Jāmi and the School of Ibn ʿArabi," *Journal of Qurʾanic Studies* 8: 1 (2006), 58–87.

Sambhalī, Mīr Ḥusayn. *Taẕkirah-i Ḥusaynī*. MS 334 Sprenger, Staatsbibliothek, Berlin, 1748.

Schofield, Katherine Butler. "Chief Musicians to the Mughal Emperors: The Delhi *kalāwant birāderī*, 17th to 19th Centuries," *Journal of the Indian Musicological Society*, 2013.

"Shafīq", Lacchmī Nārāyan. *Gul-i raʿnā*. Ḥyderābād: ʿAhd-āfrīn Barqī Press, 1967.

Shirāzī, Nūr al-Dīn Muḥammad ʿAbdullāh. *Alfāẓ-i adviyah*, trans. Francis Gladwin. Calcutta: Chronicle Press, 1793.

Shūshtarī, Qāẓī Nūrullāh. *Majālis al-muʾminīn: jild-i avval*. Tehrān: instishārāt-i kitāb-furūshi-i Islāmiyah, 1365/1986.

Sviri, Sara. "Dreaming Analyzed and Recorded: Dreams in the World of Medieval Islam," in David Shulman *et al.* (eds), *Dream Cultures: Explorations in the Comparative History of Dreaming*. New York: Oxford University Press, 1999.

Index

'Abd al-Qādir Khān *see* Bīdil
Alam and Subrahmanyam: focus on Persian history-writing 3–4
'Ālam's hypertext for Bīdil's tale: circulation of 95–7
'Ālam's hypotext for Bīdil's tale: interpretation of 98–101
Ārzū: Braj tradition, and 136; comparative poetics 135; distich, meaning of; foreknowledge of listener or reader 143; God, on 129–30; historicizing canons of Persian-language literary scholarship 10–12; historicist philology 129–30; *Lamp of Guidance* 142; linguistic purity, and 139–41; locality of universal concepts 138–9; localization of universal topic 136; poetic responses 142; political and institutional causes for projects 131; speaking subject, and 127–50; strangeness 143; strangeness of word, on 141–2, *sukhan,* conception of 128; technique of the imaginary 127; *The Rose Garden* 128; theory of linguistic representation 133
Asadullāh Khān *see* Ghālib
author and speaker 68–86

Bahār: *ghazal* styles 5–6
Bīdil: autobiography 15–16, 17; Beloved's self-disclosure 45; blurring of identity 32; characteristics of text 17; colorless tracing 35; critique of rational investigation of causality 34–5; dervishes and the zealously abstinent 22; disciple at imaginary Sufi hospice 28; disciples 26–7; djinns, and 20; entirety of *ghazals* 24; erotic aesthetic mood 117; excursus on two related stylistic features 111–12; father of meanings 48–9; gaze of the Perfect Man 44; *ghazal* oeuvre 26; hypertext: interpretation 101–3; iconoclasm-as-anti-illusionism 37; illness 38–40;immediate readership 27; kenotic chorus 61–89; *masnavī 'Irfān* 90–126; medically motivated pragmatism 43; myths for speech and action 33; *naqsh* 47; necessity of bodies as signs 40; optics 42–3; participation in Sufi rhetoric and practice 30; patterns, conformity to 33; poetic enactment of theistic monism 19; poetic lineage 163; political crisis, response to 92–3; politically effective literary persona 9–10; polyphony of poetry 27; portrait 31, 33–6; readership 26; recovery 38–40; rhetorical antecedents for prose 18–19; ringlet of hair 25; science of letters, and 31–2; self-effacement 39; semantic level of sentence 30; sense-perceptible reality, on 43–4; spiritual-pedagogical aims 30; students 27–8; *Subtle Points* 22; Sufi metaphysics, and 42; *tārji'-band* 61–89; taste and hearing, on 18; *The Four Elements* 10, 15–16, 17, 18; things as they are 42; voice 69; with, interpretation of word 22–3;
Bindrāban Dās *see* Khvushgū
Bukhārī: *tarjī'-band* 71

Chittick, William C: barzakh, on 41
compound simile 83–4

dialectic of author and speaker 68–86

ekphrasis as ascetic self-transformation 15–60

excursus on imaginal world of the body 41–6

Foucault, Michel: subject, on 4

Ghālib: Bīdil, and 2–3
Ghanī Kashmīrī 68
ghazal styles 5

Ḥāfiẓ: *ghazal* couplet 71–2
heretical suggestion of metempsychosis 40
Hindu allegory of Islamic philosopher-king 90–126
human's career in the world 90

iconoclastic hypotext beneath Bīdil's ekphratic hypertext 46–8
'Irāqī: *tarjī'-band* 70
Islamic cosmologies 29
Islamic optical tradition 36
Islamic philosopher-king: Hindu allegory of 90–126

kenosis 61–89
Khiyāl, *ghazal* poetics of 12–17
Khvushgū: Adam's mourning 156; ascetic will-to-power 163; biographical compendium of Persian-language poets 151; biographical dictionary 69–70; cleanliness of appearance 165; debts to Bīdil 162; dream of Ḥāfiẓ 151–74; iteration of historical fiction 155–6; kenotic repetition 164; literary historian, as 12; literary history, and 161; location of dream in narrative time 154–5; models for transpersonal self 164; modes of reading pleasures 166; Mongol invasions of Iran 158–9; Noah's Ark 156–7; poetic responses to oldest masters 167; political investment in archive of Persian poetry 157–8; purity of inwardness 165; social upheaval among Delhi's Persianate elite 159; sound intention 165; taẕkirah 3; theistic monism 162; veridical dream 153–4
kuhhān 19

lamentation: imagery 78
light as a metaphor for truth 73
light imagery: use of 72–3
literary canonicity: institutional basis for determination 132
literary studies 5–6
local universality of poetic pleasure 127–50
love: personification 76

Madan and Kāmdī 90–126; allegorical frame of reference 108; interpretation of circulation 93; metempsychosis, and 107; narrative prefiguration 106–11
metempsychosis 103–6
Minissale, Gregory: Mughal Indian art, on 35
Mīr: Bīdil, and 2–3
Mīr Taqī *see* Mīr
mise en abyme 36–7
models of visuality 36–8
Mughal historiography 3–4
Mughal India: dispersal into provincial fiefdoms 26
Mughal painting technique 45
Mughal state: political crisis 92–3
myths for the Sufi reader 32–3

oneness of being 73

Persian: two kinds 7–8
Persian before and under the Mughals 7–9
Persian poetic culture: aesthetic significance 8–9
Persian poetry: Mughal polity, and 8–9; politics, and 6
physis 132
poetry: reality testing, and 134
political frailty and poetic power in late Mughal Delhi 1–14

Reynolds, Dwight F.: medieval Arabic autobiographies, on 16

self as breath 108
semantic encryption 46
Shaykh Ahmad Sirhindī 23
Shirāzī: medical encyclopedia 43
Sirāj al-Dīn Alī Khān *see* Ārzū
Solomon and the ant 82–3
Som Prakash Verma: Anūp Chhatr, on 30–1
structuralism 69
Sufi reading practices 28–9
Sufi self-governance 91–2
Sufi way 63–4
Sufism: political power, and 4–5
Sufism: tradition of ethical reflection 21
sukhan 20–1

tarjī': meaning 65
tarjī'-band 61–89; core thesis 64–5; distinction between most real and transpersonal 62–3; inner contradictoriness 67; sparse grid of concepts or terms 62; spiralling structure 65–6; theses 62
tāzah-gūyī 2
technique of the imaginary 79
the Breath of the All-Merciful 19–20
thesis 132
Thirty-Two Tales of the Throne: synopsis and interpretation 94–5
Timurids 2

ultra-monorhyme 72
Urdu: elevation into literary language 2

yearning 80–1
Yoga Vāsistha 109